Webb Society
Deep-Sky Observer's Handbook

Volume 1
Double Stars
Second Edition

Compiled by the Webb Society
Kenneth Glyn Jones, editor

WEBB SOCIETY DEEP-SKY OBSERVER'S HANDBOOK

VOLUME 1
DOUBLE STARS, Second Edition

WEBB SOCIETY DEEP-SKY OBSERVER'S HANDBOOK

VOLUME 1
DOUBLE STARS, Second Edition

Compiled by the Webb Society
Edited by Kenneth Glyn Jones, F.R.A.S.
Written by Robert W. Argyle, M.Sc., F.R.A.S.
Illustrated by John Lewis, F.R.A.S.

With a foreword by Dr. Paul Couteau
(Observatoire de Nice, France)

ENSLOW PUBLISHERS, INC.

Bloy St. & Ramsey Ave.	P.O. Box 38
Box 777	Aldershot
Hillside, N.J. 07205	Hants GU12 6BP
U.S.A.	U.K.

Library of Congress Cataloging in Publication Data

Webb Society deep-sky observer's handbook.

  Bibliography: v. 1, p.
  Contents: v. 1. Double stars.
  1. Astronomy—Observers' manuals.   I. Jones, Kenneth
Glyn. II. Webb Society.
QB64.W36 1986 522 85-20553
ISBN 0-89490-122-2 (v.1)

Printed in the United States of America

10 9 8 7 6 5 4 3 2 1

To the memory of Maurice Duruy
Double-Star Observer *par excellence*

Author's Acknowledgements

Robert Argyle wishes to express his gratitude to Sir Richard Woolley and Dr E.M.Burbidge for permission to use the two refractors at Herstmonceux for double star observations, and to Dr A.Hunter, formerly Director of the Royal Greenwich Observatory, for permission to publish the results. He is also grateful to the late Mr.L.S.T.Symms who gave up his spare time to demonstrate the operation of the 28-inch refractor. The benefit of Mr. Symms' great experience with this telescope was much appreciated.

It is clear to all who look at the list of measures at the end of the book that there are a number of keen observers who have contributed much to the success of the Webb Society Double Star Section and further evidence of their commitment can be found in the Double Star Section Circulars which are available from the address in Appendix 2. I would therefore like to thank most warmly Domenico Gellera, Colin Pither, Reg Waterworth, Keith Sturdy and Roberto Frangetto for their continuing support. I'm also grateful to John Lewis, Director of the B.A.A. Deep-Sky Section for supplying the excellent drawings for the figures.

The greatest debt which I have is that to the late Maurice Duruy whose recent death (Sept. 1984) robbed me of a friend whom I had come to know through a mutual exchange of letters for 12 years and I will always regret that I never had the opportunity to meet him personally. His warmth and generosity were clear to all who knew him and there can be no better tribute, I venture to think, than by re-dedicating this volume, to which he contributed so much, to his memory.

Maurice Duruy was indebted to M. M.Dufay, late Director of the Observatory of Lyons for permitting the use the 32.5-cm Coudé refractor for his measures.

Figures 2 and 5 are reproduced by permission of D.Reidel (Dordrecht).

CONTENTS

FOREWORD

The contributions of amateur astronomers to the observing of double stars have been important. We can cite the example of S.W.Burnham (1838 - 1921) who used the largest instruments of his time, the Reverend T.H.E.C.Espin(1858 - 1934) in England, R.Jonckheere (1889 - 1974), Dr P.Baize and M.V.Duruy (1894 - 1984) in France. The abundance and quality of these observers' measures are sufficient evidence of this.

Nowadays, astronomy has made fantastic progress with large ground-based telescopes so we may wonder if an amateur astronomer with his limited resources is still able to contribute efficiently to the observation of the Universe. The answer is YES, for two reasons: To begin with, astronomical research does not belong exclusively to the professional astronomer because the amateur astronomer can gain access to large telescopes. In addition, amateurs can buy powerful instruments from firms specialising in telescope making and with a 50-cm aperture most of the binary stars can be observed.

There remains a lack of information on binary stars since the publications in which measures appear are not easily available to amateurs. Aitken's Double Star Catalogue was printed in 1932 and no similar publications have appeared since that time.

One of the merits of the Webb Society has been to establish a link between binary star astronomers all over the world. Accurate observations of orbital pairs are far more useful than accumulating measurements of many nearly motionless binaries.

Paul Couteau
Astronome Titulaire
Observatoire de NICE,
FRANCE

LIST OF FIGURES

LIST OF TABLES

General Preface to the Handbook

Named after the Reverend T.W.Webb (1807 - 1885), an eminent amateur astronomer and author of the classic <u>Celestial</u> <u>Objects</u> <u>for</u> <u>Common</u> <u>Telescopes</u>, the Webb Society exists to encourage the study of double stars and deep-sky objects. It has members in many countries where amateur astronomy flourishes. It has a number of sections, each with a director with wide experience in the particular field, the main ones being double stars, nebulae and clusters and galaxies. Publications include a Quarterly Journal containing articles and special features, book reviews and section reports that cover the Society's activities. Membership is open to anyone whose interests are compatible. Applications forms and answers to queries are available from S.J. Hynes, 8 Cormorant Close, Sydney, Crewe, Cheshire, CW1 1LN, England.

Webb's <u>Celestial</u> <u>Objects</u> <u>for</u> <u>Common</u> <u>Telescopes</u>, first published in 1859, must have been amongst the most popular books of its kind ever written. Running through six editions by 1917, it is still in print although the text is of more historical than practical interest to the amateur of today. Not only has knowledge of the Universe been transformed totally by modern developments, but the present generation of amateur astronomers has telescopes and other equipment that even the professional of Webb's day would have envied.

The aim of the new <u>Webb</u> <u>Society</u> <u>Deep-Sky</u> <u>Observer's</u> <u>Handbook</u> is to provide a series of observer's manuals that do justice to the equipment that is available today and to cover fields that have not been adequately covered by other organisations of amateurs. We have endeavoured to make these guides the best of their kind: they are written by experts, some of them professional astronomers, who have had considerable practical experience with the problems and pleasures of the amateur astronomer. The manuals can be used profitably by the beginner who will find much to stimulate his enthusiasm and imagination. However, they are designed primarily for the more experienced amateur who seeks greater scope for the exercise of his skills.

Each Handbook volume is complete with respect to its subject. The reader is given an adequate historical and theoretical basis for a modern understanding of the physical role of the objects covered in the wider context of the universe. He is provided with a thorough exposition of observing methods, including the construction and operation of ancillary equipment such as micrometers and simple spectroscopes. Each volume contains a detailed and comprehensive catalogue of objects for the amateur to locate - and to observe with an eye made more perceptive by the knowledge he has gained.

We hope that these volumes will enable the reader to extend his abilities, to exploit his telescope to its limit, and to tackle the challenging difficulties of new fields of observation with confidence of success.

Editor's Preface

Volume 1:   Double Stars   (2nd Edition).

When the first edition of this volume was published in 1979, serious double star observing by amateur astronomers was only just beginning to revive from a long period of neglect. That revival was largely initiated by the Webb Society and since then, under the energetic and able directorship of Robert Argyle, our double star section has flourished, enrolling many keen and dedicated newcomers to this rewarding field of observation.

By hard work and careful application, this team has produced a satisfying total of micrometric measures to professional standards, together with a soundly based series of photographic colour determinations of some 200 double stars. Some results of this excellent work have appeared from time to time in the Webb Society Quarterly Journal and the advent of this new edition of the first volume of our Deep-Sky Observer's Handbook gives us the opportunity not only to disseminate the material more widely but also to incorporate the text a more thorough survey of the whole subject under review, including new, up-to-date information concerning technical equipment and observational techniques.

With these and other improvements we are confident that this second edition of "Double Stars" provides the serious double star observer with a comprehensive guide to successful enterprise in this particular branch of astronomy, and it may well be that the work will establish itself as the standard work for amateurs in the field for many years to come.

The author, Robert Argyle, has been a member of the Webb Society since 1968 and Director of the Double Star Section since 1970. After graduating he joined the staff of the Royal Greenwich Observatory in 1972 as night assistant on the 98-inch Isaac Newton Telescope at Herstmonceux. He gained his M.Sc. degree in 1977 and then moved to the Galactic Astronomy department at R.G.O. More recently he has acted as project manager for the plate and CCD cameras on the one-metre telescope in the Isaac Newton Group of telescopes on La Palma, Canary Islands, where , in October 1984, he is about to begin a two-year tour of duty as Support Astronomer. His chief astronomical interests lie in the determination of accurate optical positions, stellar photometry and, of course, visual binary stars.

He has observed at Izana, La Palma, Sutherland, Johannesburg and Cape Town and his published papers include double star measures and the proper motion of radio stars. In Bob Argyle's case the separation between his professional work and his amateur interests is almost non-existent, and for this amateur astronomy in general and the Webb Society in particular, have every reason to be grateful.

The Webb Society also owes a considerable debt to Ridley Enslow Jr., President of Enslow Publishers, whose expert advice and keen enterprise have paid so large a part in presenting the results of our work before what has turned out to be an appreciative public. The entire Deep-Sky Observer's Handbook series has indeed been a profitable venture to all concerned - especially, we hope, to its readers.

Dr. Paul Couteau is one of the world's foremost practitioners in the field of Double Star Astronomy and we greatly appreciate his generous contribution of a Foreword to this volume. With him we stress the value of amateur participation in this branch of astronomy, and we, too, hope that many more enthusiastic observers will continue to add impetus to the rewarding study of visual double stars.

PART ONE

1. A BRIEF HISTORY OF DOUBLE STAR OBSERVING

The systematic observation of double stars began in earnest in the
year 1779 when William Herschel began the famous series of observations
which finally led to his paper in Philosophical Transactions in 1803
when the existence of binary stars was proved beyond doubt.

Previous to this, very little work had been done and it is
interesting to note that Huyghens found theta Orionis to be triple in
1656 (the fourth component being found in 1684) and yet it was 1755
before the two components of beta Cygni (Albireo) were discovered.
Considering that the Trapezium is the more difficult of the two, this
illustrates the neglect which double star observing suffered during the
first century and a half of the telescopic era. The first pair to be
discovered with a telescope was zeta Ursa Majoris (more accurately,
Mizar, the brighter of the naked eye pair) by Riccioli in Bologna in
1650.   It was followed by the Trapezium and on Feb 8, 1665 Robert Hooke
dicovered gamma Arietis whilst following Comet Hevelius.   In the
southern hemisphere alpha Crucis was found in 1685 and alpha Centauri in
1689. Two important binaries gamma Virginis and Castor, were found in
the years 1718 and 1719 respectively, the latter being found by Bradley
who made an estimate of the position angle which helped to fix the
period of revolution.   The first real list of double stars appears to
have been made by Christian Meyer of Mannheim using an eight foot mural
quadrant with a power of between 60 and 80. His catalogue, published in
1781, included gamma Andromedae, zeta Cancri, alpha Herculis and beta
Cygni.

In 1779 Herschel set out to investigate stellar parallax using
accurate measurements of close, very unequal double stars. He assumed
that the apparent brightness of a star was directly related to its
distance.   Thus, if in a pair of stars one component appeared much
fainter than the other, it was reasonable to suppose that the fainter
star was, in reality, much more distant. Hence Herschel intended to
measure these pairs from different points in the Earth's orbit in order
to ascertain the change in position of one with respect to the other,
the motion being due to the parallax of the brighter star. In order to
find suitable pairs, he began searching with his 7-foot telescope and
soon published a list of 269 pairs, 42 of which were already known.
(Apparently Meyer had already tried to ascertain the motion between
unequal pairs but Herschel considered that his (Meyer's) instruments
were inadequate to show the close pairs required). Herschel continued
to measure numerous pairs and after a while he found that some stars had
indeed changed position with respect to their neighbours. However the
cause of the change was not due to parallax, which should have shown
itself over a period of six months. Herschel found that in some cases
the motion of one star with respect to the other was not linear and in a
beautiful analysis came to the conclusion that orbital motion was the

cause. On June 9th 1803, his paper entitled 'Account of the Changes that have happened during the last Twenty-Five Years in the Relative Situation of Double Stars; with an Investigation of the Cause to which they are owing', appeared in Philosophical Transactions. This was the first great step forward in double star astronomy.

In addition to showing that binary stars existed, Herschel introduced systematic methods of observation and discovery which were sadly lacking in his time. His telescopes were by far the largest that had been used on double stars, and his home-made micrometers were good enough to give reliable results on fairly close pairs. Only an observer with Herschel's skill, however, could operate the altitude and azimuth motions of his reflector whilst making micrometric measures and taking notes. His last list of discoveries (145 pairs) was made before 1802 but not published until 1822.

In 1816, Herschel's son John, together with Sir James South, began to review his double stars (Hh). They remeasured virtually all of the H stars as well as producing a large list of new, if somewhat wide, pairs (Sh).

Two years previously, in 1814, Friedrich Georg Wilhelm Struve, in the poorly-equipped observatory at Dorpat in Estonia decided to compile a general catalogue of all known double stars. Although he had only an eight-foot transit circle and a five-foot telescope by Troughton (power 126), he began to observe the positions and occasionally the position angles and separations of double stars. In 1820 he published the catalogue of double star positions and in 1822 his "Catalogus 795 Stellarum duplicium" appeared. In 1824, a refractor with an object glass some 9.6 inches in diameter, made by Fraunhofer, was delivered to Dorpat. It was mounted equatorially, and the driving clock was of such good quality that an object would remain in the centre of the field at a power of 700. The focal length of the objective was 14 feet and a battery of 10 eyepieces supplied Struve with powers ranging from 86 to 1500. He set to work immediately on his great survey of the heavens from the North Pole to -15 declination for the purpose of discovering new double stars and of the formation of a general catalogue. Between 1825 February 11th and 1827 February 11th he examined 120,000 stars and found 3,112 double stars whose distance apart did not exceed 32 arc seconds. Measurements continued until 1835 and in 1837 the great "Mensurae Micrometricae stellarum duplicium et multiplicium" was published. Struve himself accounted for 2,343 of the discoveries in the catalogue and each pair was measured three times. His skill and the quality of the 9.6-inch refractor resulted in this Catalogue representing a great step forward both in the total number of pairs listed and the accuracy of the measures obtained. Struve himself paid tribute to the excellence of his telescope, declaring:- "We may perhaps rank this enormous instrument with the most celebrated of all reflectors, viz. Herschel's".

In 1839 the observatory at Poulkova was established and Struve became its first Director. A 15-inch refractor, then the largest of its kind in the world, was delivered and the first programme of work was to re-survey all of the stars in the northern hemisphere down to magnitude 7.0 - some 17,000 in all. This was completed by December 7, 1842, and in that time 514 new pairs had been found by Otto Struve who had taken over the survey from his father a month after it had commenced. Otto Struve added another 33 discoveries, and the catalogue of 547 stars , known as the Poulkova stars was published in 1850, 106 of the original 514 being omitted for various reasons.

With the completion of this work there was a lull in discovery for about 20 years. At this time several celebrated amateur observers were making their name in England and on the mainland of Europe.

Admiral William Smyth began observing in 1830 with a 5.9-inch refractor on a mounting by Dolland. The object glass by Tulley was considered by Smyth "the finest specimen of that eminent optician's skill". Between 1830 and 1843 he made measures of 680 pairs. His "Cycle of Celestial Objects", which also included extensive notes on other deep-sky objects was published in 1844. In 1860, the "Speculum Hartwellianum" containing later measures was published.

The Reverend W.R.Dawes began observing in 1831 at Ormskirk in Lancashire with a 3.8-inch achromat by Dollond. He later obtained a 6-inch Merz refractor followed by a 7.5-inch Alvan Clark and an 8.25-inch Alvan Clark which was set up at Haddenham in Buckinghamshire in 1859. Finally in 1865 an 8-inch Cooke refractor was obtained, with which he continued to make measures of double stars. His work, which extended from 1830 to 1868 was of a high standard, and, indeed, he was referred to as "the eagle-eyed" by the Astronomer Royal, Sir George Airy. His catalogue, published in 1867, is enriched by the addition of valuable introductions, notes and lists of measures made by other observers.

The most valuable work in the field of double stars was done by Baron Ercole Dembowski who was one of the most celebrated observers. He began his observations in Naples in 1852, using a 5-inch refractor without a driving clock or a position-angle circle on his micrometer.By the year 1859, some 2,000 sets of measures of high quality had been secured. Only an observer of consummate skill and the highest dedication could have produced such accurate results with such limited equipment. In the same year, he obtained a 7-inch Merz refractor with circles, micrometer and a good driving clock, and between 1862 and 1878 made a further 21,000 measurements. These included all of the F.G.W.Struve stars with the exception of 64 which were too difficult for his telescope. Some 3,000 sets were made of the Pulkovo stars and a further 1,700 refer to the catalogues of Burnham and others. After his death in 1881, Dembowski's measures were published in two fine volumes in 1883-1884 and today they are regarded as being as valuable as the "Mensurae Micrometricae" itself.

It can be said that the second great period of discovery was initiated on April 27, 1870 when an unknown American amateur, Sherburne Wesley Burnham found his first double star. He was a stenographer in the U.S. Court in Chicago during the day and had become interested in astronomy, obtaining his first telescope, a 3-inch refractor in 1861. This was followed by a 3.75-inch equatorial and finally in 1870 he obtained the 6-inch Alvan Clark refractor which he mounted in a home-made observatory in the backyard of his home in Chicago. Armed with a copy of Webb's "Celestial Objects for Common Telescopes" he commenced his observations. By 1873 his first list of 81 new pairs was published in the Monthly Notices of the Royal Astronomical Society. His article began with the words "It is believed that the stars enumerated in the following list have been hitherto unknown as double stars, as they are not found noted in the numerous catalogues and publications relating to this subject". Burnham was possessed of remarkably keen eyesight and some of his discoveries are difficult objects in much bigger telescopes. His great ability and skill earned him the key to virtually all of the major American observatories. He made discoveries with a large number of telescopes including the 36-inch refractor at Lick, the 40-inch at Yerkes and the 26-inch at Washington. In a career spanning 42 years he discovered 1,340 pairs, many of which are in rapid orbital motion. Whilst at Lick Observatory, Burnham often used to help and encourage younger observers. One of the most notable to benefit from his advice was Robert Grant Aitken who arrived at Lick in June 1895.

In 1899 Aitken and Professor W.J.Hussey initiated at Lick a survey of all the stars in the Bonner Durchmusterung (B.D.) down to magnitude 9.0 and as far south as -22 declination, not known to be double. Hussey left Lick in 1905 but Aitken persisted until 1915 when the survey was complete apart from the area of sky between declination -14° and -22°, and right ascensions 1 hour to 13 hours respectively. By agreement with the observers at the Union Observatory in South Africa, Aitken was able to extend this survey down to -18° in the 12 hours mentioned. The result was the discovery of 1,329 pairs by Hussey and 3,105 pairs by Aitken, the great majority being separated by less than 5 arc seconds.

At this time, the most modern General Catalogue was that of Burnham (1906) which contained details of 13,665 pairs. The great number of new double stars discovered at the Lick and Union Observatories made it necessary for a thorough revision of Burnham's Catalogue. Aitken imposed stricter limits on the magnitudes and separations involved, with the result that some pairs were rejected. Aitken's Catalogue was finally published in 1932 and is known as the A.D.S. It contains 17,180 pairs, many of which are binary in nature.

In England at the beginning of this century, interest in double stars was still strong. There was a Double Star Section in the B.A.A. but unfortunately this petered out in 1914 through lack of support. The Reverend T.H.E.C.Espin had initially been interested in cataloguing red stars, but from 1901 onwards he began to publish lists of new double stars which were discovered using a 17.25-inch Calver reflector mounted in an observatory in Tow Law, County Durham. The first few pairs were casual discoveries, but he later set out to examine all the stars in the Bonner Durchmusterung north of +30° declination for uncatalogued double stars of 10 arc second separation or less.

He added a 24-inch reflector later and ably assisted by W. Milburn continued his observations for over 30 years. He published all his discoveries in the Monthly Notices of the R.A.S. and his last pair bears the number 2,575. Milburn carried on working and eventually reached a total of 1,051 pairs. It is interesting to note that Espin and Milburn were the only major observers since the Herschels to use reflectors.

The delivery of the new 28-inch refractor to Greenwich in 1893 allowed the observers there to make numerous and valuable measures of pairs in the Burnham, Hussey, Hough and Aitken catalogues as well as the closer Dorpat and Pulkovo stars. The lists of measures can be found in "Greenwich Observations" which extend from 1893 onwards. The chief observers were T.Lewis,H.Furner,W.Bryant,W.Bowyer and F.Dyson (later to become Astronomer Royal) — names not unfamiliar to those acquainted with Volume II of "Celestial Objects for Common Telescopes". Lewis, in particular, was noted for his great summary of all the measures of the Dorpat Catalogue pairs in his book "Measures of the Struve Double Stars". When the 28-inch refractor was moved to Herstmonceux in 1956, work on double stars was continued by Sir Richard Woolley, L.S.T.Symms, M.P.Candy and other observers until September 1970. Early in 1972, however, the telescope was taken back to Greenwich where it is now housed in a replica of the famous 'Onion' dome in which it once resided. In 1975, on the 300th anniversary of the founding of the Royal Observatory at Greenwich, the telescope was inaugurated by Her Majesty the Queen.

In the Southern Hemisphere, the serious task of discovering and cataloguing double stars did not really start until the arrival of John Herschel at the Cape of Good Hope in 1834. Using his father's 20-foot reflector (with several 18.25-inch mirrors) and a 5-inch refractor, he catalogued 2,102 pairs in four years, publishing the results of these observations in 1847. Herschel continued to contribute double star measures regularly to the R.A.S. and was working on a General Catalogue of double stars when he died in 1871 aged 79.

It was not until 1896 that serious double star work in southerly latitudes was resumed when Dr R.T.A.Innes joined the staff of the Royal Observatory at the Cape of Good Hope. Using 7-inch and 18-inch refractors, he brought his total of discoveries to 432. In 1899 he produced a First General Catalogue of Double Stars containing 2,140 entries. In 1903 he became Director of the Meteorological Observatory which was set up at Johannesburg at the recommendation of Sir David Gill, then H.M. Astronomer at the Cape. In 1912, the Transvaal Observatory as it had come to be known became a purely astronomical institution and in 1925 a 26.5-inch refractor was set up on the site. When Dr Willem van den Bos joined the staff from Leiden in the same year, a survey for new double stars, similar to that conducted by Aitken and Hussey in the north, was set in motion. Dr van den Bos carried out the major part of this survey helped by W.S.Finsen and Dr Innes (until his retirement in 1927). By the end of 1931, Innes had found 1,613 pairs, Finsen 300 and van den Bos more than 2,000. At the nearby Lamont-Hussey Observatory at Bloemfontein where a 27-inch refractor had been erected, a co-operative programme with the Union Observatory astronomers produced another 4,712 dicoveries. The Director, Professor R.A.Rossiter, found 1,961 pairs whilst his two assistants M.K.Jessup and H.F.Donner found respectively 1,424 and 1,327 new double stars. Rossiter carried on alone after 1933 and continued his discoveries until his retirement in 1952. In his final year in office he produced a "Catalogue of Southern Double Stars" which contains 8,065 pairs.

Mention must be made also of the work done by Robert Jonckheere over a period of more than 56 years, ending in 1962 using telescopes in Belgium and France mainly. Between 1909 and 1914, Jonckheere discovered 1,319 pairs at the University of Lille Observatory and during the first World War continued his observations at Greenwich where he added a further 252 pairs using the 28-inch refractor. He later continued his work with the 80-cm refractor at Marseilles and by 1962 had discovered 3,350 pairs. Other prolific observers during this period were Paul Baize who used the instruments of the Observatory at Meudon and Wilhelm Rabe who worked at Berlin for 43 years.

At the time of writing Worley, Heintz and Couteau are the principal observers with the micrometer but the important new technique of speckle interferometry which has McAlister as its leading proponent, is allowing observations of many close visual pairs near periastron and has also contributed substantially to our knowledge of spectroscopic pairs, some of which can now be directly resolved using large reflectors.

For many years the Lick Double Star Index (or I.D.S.) was the main source on information on visual double stars. It has now been updated by Charles Worley and the new version is known as the W.D.S. or Washington Double Star Catalogue. A version on tape was released in April 1984 and contains 400,000 observations of 73,000 pairs.

Double star work is currently being carried out at several professional observatories throughout the world. Brief details of some of the work done at the more important stations are given below:-

Observatory of Nice

Since 1951, the main observer has been Couteau. He has carried out an extensive examination of B.D. stars from +17° to +53° and to date has made a total of 2,200 discoveries. The 50-cm refractor has been used for nearly all these new pairs but the 76-cm refractor, which was put back into service in 1969 is also being used by Morel. Muller has continued his examination of BD stars between +52° and +90° which he started in 1969 at the Observatory of Paris-Meudon.

United States Naval Observatory

The telescopes available here include the 12-inch and 26-inch refractors and the 24-inch reflector at Washington and the 40-inch and 61-inch reflectors at Flagstaff Station in Arizona. Since 1962, the main observers have been Worley and R.L.Walker who has taken a special interest in visual pairs containing variable stars. A photographic programme started in 1962 has now terminated.

Sproul Observatory

The 61-cm refractor is used for both photographic and micrometric work. Over the last few years astrometric plates have been taken at the rate of nearly 5,000 per year. Drs J.L.Hershey and S.L.Lippincott have carried out investigations which involve the orbit determination for both visual doubles and stars with unseen companions, primarily to calculate parallax and mass-ratio.

The micrometer work has been done by Dr W.D.Heintz who is also active at Cerro Tololo using the 91-cm and 100-cm reflectors. His measures add up to 2,000 per year over the last few years.

Observatory of Belgrade.

Observations started in 1951 under the direction of P.M.Djurkovic. In 1974, a complete list of all observations to date was published by Popovic. It contains 6,527 measures of 1,641 pairs. To date more than 100 discoveries have been made principally by re-examination of BD stars in the zone +34 to +44 by Popovic. The principal observers with the 65-cm Zeiss refractor are Popovic and Zulevic. A photographic programme is planned.

Observatory of Pulkovo

The photographic programme of wide double stars is continuing with the 26-inch refractor and Carte du Ciel Astrograph. Future work will concentrate on neglected binaries especially those in the north circumpolar area, determination of trigonometric parallaxes of double stars with appreciable orbital motion, and determination of orbits.

Georgia State University

Dr H.A.McAlister has continued to carry out observations of close visual pairs, spectroscopic pairs and stars with composite spectra, using the 2.1 metre and 4 metre telescopes on Kitt Peak. The results of these observations have appeared in a series of papers which have appeared in the Astrophysical Journal and its supplements since Jan 1977. To date some 360,000 exposures on 35mm film have been made resulting in 7,175 measures requiring 50 exposures per observation on average to give the required signal-to-noise ratio in the combined fringe pattern. The smallest resolution which has been achieved on the 4 metre telescope is 0".026 in the case of an observation of 31 Cygni.

Dr McAlister has also contributed papers on individual systems such as 51 Tau, phi Cyg, gamma Per and 12 Per, where the combination of interferometric and spectroscopic data can yield extra information.

University Observatory, Torino

A program of photographic observations of wide binaries was started in April 1976 using the 1.05 metre astrometric reflector. To date some 1,100 measures have been reported, principally by Dr R.Pannunzio. A programme of visual double star measurement has also been initiated by Dr Ferreri.

Observatory of Brere-Merate

The 23-cm refractor is being used for a series of micrometric measures by M.Scardia who is also active in the field of orbital computation.

2. TYPES OF DOUBLE STARS

Although this Handbook deals specifically with the observation of visual double stars, it is worth summarising the several different categories of stellar pairs which are to be found in the heavens.

(a) Those which can be detected as double at the eyepiece of the telescope. These are divided into two main types:

(i) Visual binaries

The components of these systems are physically related, rotating around their common centre of gravity in periods ranging from less than 2 years to many centuries. Orbital motion results in the change of relative position between the two stars. Astronomers measure this change by using a filar micrometer and regarding the brighter star as fixed measuring the distance (ρ) and position angle (θ) of the fainter star or comes (Fig 1). By plotting ρ and θ the comes is seen to describe an elliptical path with the primary situated in one focus.

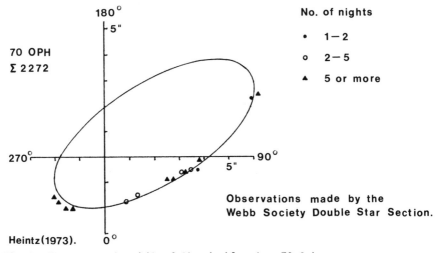

Fig 1. The apparent orbit of the double star 70 Oph.

The ellipse is known as the apparent ellipse because it is only a projection on the true ellipse onto the plane of the sky, but by observing the size and shape of the apparent ellipse, the characteristics, or elements of the true ellipse can be found. The size, shape and orientation in space of the true orbit and the period of revolution can be described by seven elements. (see Figure 2.)

(a) The period of revolution in years is P, or sometimes the mean motion or n = 360/P is quoted.

(b) The time at which periastron passage (closest approach) occurs is denoted by T. This is also the point at which the motion of the comes in the true orbit is a maximum.

(c) The semi major-axis of the true ellipse in seconds of arc is a.

(d) The eccentricity of the true ellipse is denoted by e where, of course, 0 < e < 1.

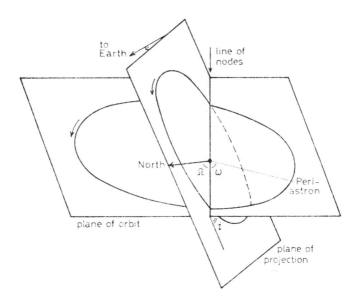

Fig. 2. The real and apparent orbits of a visual binary (after Heintz)

There are three elements which determine the projection of the true orbit onto the plane of the sky.

(e) The nodes are the two points where the true and apparent orbits intersect. The position angle of the line between them is denoted by ω. It lies between 0 and 180 degrees and the acsending node is that point where the comes is moving away from the Sun.

(f) In the true orbit, the angle between the node and the point of periastron, reckoned in the direction of motion, is called Ω. In cases of circular orbits, i.e. e = 0, ω = 0^c so that T then becomes the point of nodal passage.

(g) The parameter i is the inclination of the true orbit to the plane of the sky and ranges between 0 and 180 degrees. If i equals 90 degrees for instance, the orbit will be edge on to us and the comes will appear to oscillate in a straight line along the line of nodes. In the case where the position angle appears to be increasing and i is less than 90 degrees, then the motion is said to be direct, and if i is greater than 90 degrees then it is retrograde.

The orbital elements for a pair can lead to the determination of the sum of the masses of the individual stars, $m_1 + m_2$ provided that the parallax is known. The absolute orbit of each star about the centre of gravity is required before the mass ratio can be found, enabling m_1 and m_2 to be calculated. This is done by measuring each star relative to fixed background stars and correcting for parallax and proper motion.

The best example of a binary star in the northern hemisphere is gamma Virginis (Struve 1670). Its two components, of magnitudes 3.6 and 3.7 rotate about each other in 172 years. At the moment they are closing up and by the year 2008 they will only be 0".39 apart and hence visible in large telescopes only. In the southern sky, alpha Centauri is the finest binary of all with the stars orbiting once every 79.95 years and the separation varying from 22 arc seconds to about 2 arc seconds. At the time of writing (1984), the pair is just beginning to close in again.

(ii) Optical doubles

In these systems, the two stars appear to be close together but they are in no way linked. This is a line-of-sight effect with one star being much further away than the other. The motion of both stars will be rectilinear and uniform if they are not gravitationally connected. Some doubt remains in cases where there are faint, wide pairs with little motion. The proper motion and parallax of such a pair, if measurable, will decide if they are optical or binary in nature. A good example of an optical pair is delta Herculis (STF 3127) which has two components of magnitude 3.2 and 8.3. In 1821 F.G.W.Struve measured the position angle at $171^c.6$ and the separation at 27".8, whilst the IDS (for 1958) quotes figures of 236° and 8".9 respectively. A measure made in 1981 by R.S.Waterworth shows that the position was $265^o.2$ and 9".07.

(b) The second main category of double stars consists of those which are so close that they cannot be detected either visually or with the interferometer.

(i) Spectroscopic binaries

In 1889, Pickering discovered that the spectrum of Zeta Ursa Majoris (Mizar) showed doubling at regular intervals. By comparing the spectrum of the star with a laboratory spectrum, it was found that each component of a doubled line varied in step with the other component. This indicated that there were in fact two stars in orbital motion about each other. The magnitude of the shift was found to be directly proportional to the component of the orbital velocity in the direction of the Earth, also known as the radial velocity.

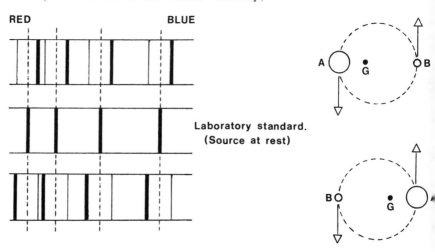

Fig.3. The spectral shift of a spectroscopic binary.

When one component is approaching the Earth, the spectral lines are shifted towards the shorter wavelengths as a direct result of Doppler's law. In other words the light gets bluer, and similarly when the star is moving away from the Earth the light reddens and the spectral lines are shifted towards longer wavelengths. The point at which the greatest separation of spectral lines occurs corresponds to the stars moving exactly towards and away from us respectively, as illustrated in Fig. 3. When the stars are moving at right angles to the line of sight there is no radial component of velocity and the spectral lines appear single. These star systems are known as double-lined spectroscopic binaries, and represent pairs of stars in which the components have a similar brightness. If the difference in magnitude is greater than about 2 then the spectrum of the fainter star will not show up, and the pair becomes a single-lined system. Instead of plotting position angle and separation, orbit computers plot radial velocity (usually in kilometres per second) against time (which can be minutes, hours or days). All the

normal elements can be obtained from the resulting velocity curve except
the orbital inclination i .

    Figure 4 shows the observed velocities of the lines in the double-
lined system alpha Equ in which stars of spectral type A5 and G2 and
revolve around the common centre of gravity in 98.8 days (Stickland,
1976).

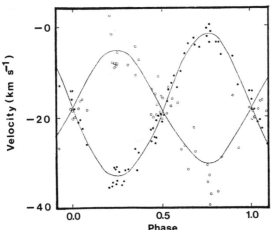

Fig. 4. The radial velocity of the double-lined binary alpha Equ.

The symmetrical nature of both velocity curves indicates that the orbit
of each star is a circle or nearly so, and in fact the eccentricity here
is only 0.03. The amplitude of the velocity variation, 12.5 km/sec for
the A star and 15.7 km/sec for the G star, show that the masses of the
two stars are in the ratio of 1.25:1.

    A special case occurs when i = 90 and the orbit plane is edge-on to
the plane of sight. Mutual occultations then occur and the pair is
known as an eclipsing binary. The consequent light variations serve to
give extensive information about the size and shape of the stars and
their atmospheres. It must be noted, however, that the pulsating
variables such as delta Cephei and RR Lyrae also show these
characteristics, i.e. variable light output and variable radial
velocity (due to expansion and contraction processes). In general, the
eclipsing binaries show very distinctive radial velocity   curves
indicative of orbital motion, although some cases of doubt remain.

    (ii) Astrometric binaries

    These are apparently single stars which are deduced to be double by
virtue of variable proper motion. The classic case is that of Sirius,
whose companion was found because it has a large mass and relatively

short orbital period (50 years). This results in a well –defined periodic wobbling in the motion of Sirius A with respect to background stars. The comes was confirmed visually by Alvan G. Clark in 1862, after being predicted by the great German astronomer F.W.Bessel in 1844.

Strictly, however, astrometric binaries are not visual. A good example is the slow moving binary Mlb 377 (also known as Vys 2). This pair has a separation of about 3 arc seconds and the position angle is increasing at the rate of about 1 degree per year. In 1947, Alden,in attempting to measure the mass ratio of the two stars, found a perturbation in the motion of A. Hershey (1973) found that the mass of the invisible star was about 0.13 M and that the period was nearly 16 years. Fig. 5 shows the apparent motion of B about A and the 'wobbling' of A due to the companion a. Attempts to see a by Charles Worley with the USNO 155-cm reflector have failed, indicating that the difference of magnitude between A and a is at least 3.5.

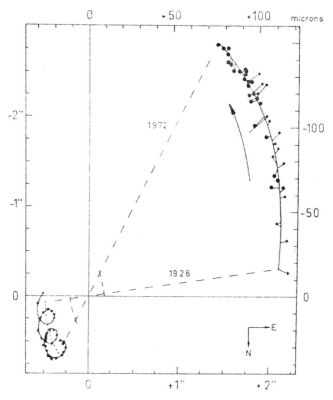

Fig. 5 The astrometric binary BD +66° 34 A,B. (After van de Kamp)

3. OBSERVING METHOD

The observation that a star is double in a telescope depends on the following factors:

(a) The separation of the components and the aperture and quality of the telescope.

(b) The brightness of the components.

(c) The state of the atmosphere.

(d) The keenness of the observer's vision.

(a) The separation of a double star is usually defined by the angular separation (in seconds of arc) between the centres of the respective Airy disks (this will be explained later).

All stars, with the exception of the Sun, are so distant that it is impossible to see their real disks through any existing telescope. Special techniques, using instruments such as the Michelson Stellar Interferometer, have enabled measurements to be made of the diameters of some of the giant stars such as Betelgeuse, Antares and Mira. In 1976, Code et al, using a stellar intensity interferometer at Narrabri in Australia reported on the diameters of 32 stars brighter than magnitude 2.5.

In a good telescope on a night when the atmosphere is steady the appearance of a bright star is that of a small disk. This is not the true disk of the star but the so-called Airy disk formed by diffraction of the incident starlight in the telescope. The diffraction is produced by the aperture through which the starlight is passing and is modified by any additional obstruction in the light path. Thus in a reflector, the secondary mirror and its supports will introduce additional diffraction, the spider arms producing "spikes" which extend radially from the central disk. Fig 6(a) shows the idealised image of a star in a "perfect" refracting telescope. In 1834, Sir George Airy found a mathematical relationship which explained the distribution of the light into a central disk surrounded by a system of concentric rings. Airy found that the radius of the first dark ring, r, was given by:

$$r = 1.22 \, \lambda/D \qquad \text{(Fig 6(a))}$$

where λ is the wavelength of the starlight and D is the aperture of the telescope in inches. Hence it is apparent that the Airy disk becomes smaller as the diameter of the telescope objective increases.

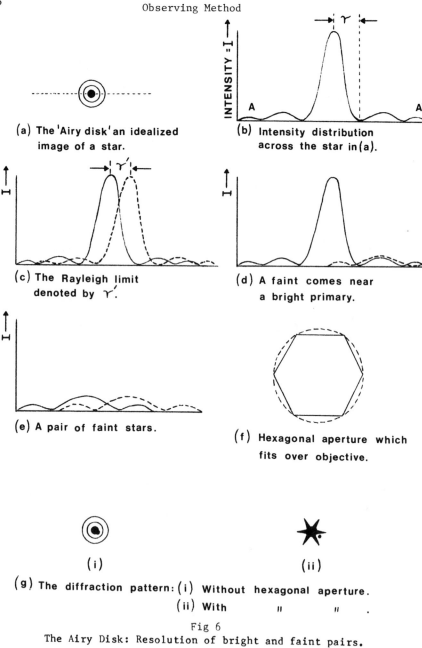

(a) The 'Airy disk' an idealized
    image of a star.

(b) Intensity distribution
    across the star in (a).

(c) The Rayleigh limit
    denoted by γ'.

(d) A faint comes near
    a bright primary.

(e) A pair of faint stars.

(f) Hexagonal aperture which
    fits over objective.

(i)   (ii)

(g) The diffraction pattern: (i) Without hexagonal aperture.
                            (ii) With   "   "   .

Fig 6
The Airy Disk: Resolution of bright and faint pairs.

The Airy formula is sometimes used as a measure of the resolution of a telescope. The Rayleigh criterion states that for a double star to be just resolved, the separation of the two peaks (Fig 6(c)) should be equal to the radius of the first dark ring. It can also be expressed by:

$$r' = 5.15 \text{ arc secs}/D(\text{inches}) = 13.1 \text{ arc secs}/D(\text{cm})$$

The value of λ is in fact that of the mean wavelength, since it is not monochromatic but contains the light of many elements, each emitting at different wavelengths. The value of mean wavelength depends on the spectral class of the star involved and ranges from 5650 A for a star of spectral class A0 to 5765 A for one of spectral class K5. The large majority of visual double star components lie in this region.

Thus the Rayleigh limit depends almost exclusively on telescope aperture and only slightly on the wavelength of the incident starlight. It should be noted that magnification has no effect on resolving power. If a star is double when seen with a low power, then the components will appear further apart when higher magnifications are used. If the image of a close double star is single in the focal plane of the objective then the eyepiece which magnifies this image will always produce a single image irrespective of focal length. The resolution of a double star will depend only on the aperture of the objective.

(b) In the above notes, the double star was assumed to consist of two equally bright components. Although many double stars have fairly equally bright components, some of the more interesting systems such as Zeta Her, 85 Peg and Sirius, for instance, are very unequal. Since the Airy disk diameter does not depend on the brightness of a star, it follows that the distribution of light in a faint star must be much less marked than in the case of bright stars. Fig 6(d) shows the situation where a faint star is close to a bright primary. For certain separations the comes would be coincident with the first diffraction ring of the primary star, if it is bright. This would reduce the visiblity of the comes. A good example of this is the pair delta Cygni (magnitudes 3.0 and 7.5, separation 2".38 - 1985). Sirius presents a slightly different problem since the separation of the two stars can reach 11 arc secs. (At present, 1985, the pair is closing in again and the separation is 8.2 arc seconds). The magnitude of Sirius B is 8.4 and it is thus 10 magnitudes or 10,000 times fainter than the brilliant primary and difficult to see in the glare of the great star. In order to see it the aperture should be at least 15-cm although it was seen by D.Gellera in 1983 using a 11-cm Zeiss refractor. From Britain and the northern United States, the star is always low in the sky and hence always a difficult object. It is sometimes useful to use a hexagonal diaphragm which fits over the end of the telescope tube (Fig 6(f)). This modifies the diffraction pattern and produces a six-pointed star effect which "diverts" light forming the central disk into the spikes thus reducing its size and revealing any close, faint stars.(fig 6(h)). If the diaphragm is arranged to rotate, a faint star can be seen between two adjacent spikes where the sky is comparatively dark. A regular hexagon will produce a light loss of only some 17% which corresponds to a fraction of a magnitude.

A pair of equally faint stars does not conform to the Rayleigh limit because there is not enough light available for the eye to detect the small contrast between the stars and the gap between them. (Fig 6(e)). The Rayleigh limit, whilst based on theory, does give a limiting separation, r, which is slightly larger than that found for telescopes in practice. An empirical limit, known as Dawes' limit after the Reverend W.R.Dawes who first determined it , gave the value:

$$r(\text{arc sec}) = 4.56/D(\text{inches}) = 11.58/D(\text{cm})$$

This was based on the observed limit of resolution by a number of observers using a range of apertures. It is approximately valid only for a pair of 6th magnitude stars in a small telescope and does not take into account the cases of unequal or faint pairs. Thomas Lewis and Robert Aitken both determined extensions of the Dawes Limit to cover these situations. To quote some examples: Lewis, using results from 31 observers with 24 different apertures, found for a pair of mean magniudes 5.7 and 6.4 that the limit was 12.3/D(cm) arc secs whilst Aitken obtained 10.9/D(cm) for a pair of 6.9 and 7.1 magnitude stars. For faint pairs, Lewis found 21.6/D(cm) arc secs for a pair of magnitudes 8.5 and 9.1 whilst Aitken got 15.5/D(cm) arc secs for stars of magnitudes 8.8 and 9.0.

(c) The two previous sections consider the rather unlikely situation of the atmosphere being perfectly steady. In reality, the images obtained in a telescope rarely, if ever, resemble those shown in the previous sections.

The primary effect which the atmosphere has on star images is to swell them out into disks several times larger than the size of the Airy disk. This is known as the seeing, and is often quoted as being the apparent diameter of the star image in seconds of arc. Other effects are often observed; the image may appear to vibrate randomly (known as wandering) or may occasionally swell and contract (boiling). In addition, near the horizon atmospheric dispersion distorts the star images into short spectra, and it hardly needs stating that if a close or difficult pair is being examined it should be done when the pair is highest in the sky. It is thus useful to have a list of pairs so that the observer can be prepared to take full advantage of a night when the seeing is particularly good. It can be a source of great satisfaction when a close binary is seen for the first time after periastron has occurred, or a particularly close, elusive comes is seen after many attempts on inferior nights.

(d) Another variable concerned with the practical side of double star observing is the keenness of the observer's vision. It is undoubtedly true that some of the great observers such as Burnham, Aitken, Dawes and Dembowski were possessed of remarkably keen eyesight, and this coupled with a lifetime's experience in examining stellar disks, enabled them to detect very small elongations and faint, close companions to bright stars. The amateur observer should not be put off by this knowledge. The author, who cannot claim to have keen eyesight, has found that Dawes limit can usually be reached on all the telescopes that he has used. The concern here is not with very close and rapid binaries but those double stars comfortably within reach of amateur instruments.

Having discussed some of the observing problems raised in this particular sphere of observation, it remains to decide what type of observation an amateur observer can carry out. The field can be divided into four distinct sections.

(a) Photographic

Photography of double stars is something of an unknown quantity in amateur circles and is rarely done in the U.K. Later in the book, E.G.Moore has devoted a chapter to this particular subject and anyone interested in trying double star photography will find it a great challenge.

(b) Visual

This category is mainly applicable to small telescopes (below about 15-cm aperture). In making estimates of magnitudes and sketching field drawings a large field is a definite advantage. Most double star observers will have done this sort of work at one time or another and it is very useful for giving the observer a general introduction to the subject. The author observed several hundred pairs, making notes of colours, magnitudes and estimated separations and position angles before starting micrometric measures. All of these pairs were found using Norton's Star Atlas and Vol II of "Celestial Objects for Common Telescopes" by Webb, together with an eyepiece a fairly large field - about 1 degree in this case. Several other eyepieces of higher power were available for examining the pair more closely after identification had been made. Eyepieces should cover a range of magnifications from about 3A to 25A where A is the aperture in centimetres. As the telescope aperture increases, the upper magnification which the telescope will stand gradually decreases and for the large refractors the value drops to 20A or less.

It is very useful to determine the diameter of each eyepiece field in minutes of arc. This can be easily done by timing the passage of an equatorial star across the field of view. Knowledge of eyepiece field size helps to find faint pairs by offsetting, and the position of unidentified pairs to be noted for future reference. It is important that the eyepieces be of good quality if the O.G. or mirror is excellent so that the best performance can be extracted from the telescope as a whole. Good eyepieces can last a lifetime and, of course, can be used when larger optics are acquired.

(c) Micrometric

For those observers with apertures greater than about 15-cm the addition of a micrometer to their equipment can be considered. Filar micrometers used to be difficult to acquire but in recent years two commercially made instruments have appeared, one in the U.K. and one in the U.S.A. The addresses can be found in Appendix 2. The cost is likely to be of the order of £200 - 300 depending on the eyepieces required but with care many years of useful service should be obtained. Those who are members of the British Astronomical Association should enquire about the loan of instruments from the Curator of Instruments or the Director of the Deep-Sky Section, the addresses of whom are given in Appendix 2.

Whilst filars are very useful they are not necessary in order to make measures of brighter pairs. The diffraction micrometer (described at length in Chapter 5) is a very simple alternative and is easy to construct. It is not a substitute for the filar but will certainly be very useful in helping an observer to get started with measures, and hopefully will persuade the serious observer that something better is worth getting. In the opinion of the author, the best instrument is the comparison image micrometer (see Chapter 5). It is more accurate than the filar for measuring separations, it doesn't have webs that need replacing and doesn't need field illumination. With a little extra work it can be used to measure differences in magnitude. It does however need to be engineered properly and the biggest snag is the birefringent prism needed to produce the artificial pair. However there is no reason why it should cost more than an average filar to produce since many of the other optical components can be bought cheaply in war surplus stores. (See Fig. 7)

(d) Lunar occultations

One of the most valuable ways in which the amateur observer with a small telescope can help with the observation of double stars is to observe occultations of stars by the Moon. It is not proposed to go into any detail about this here but the interested reader is referred to two organisations which have specialised in lunar occultations. These are the International Occultation Timing Association (IOTA) in the

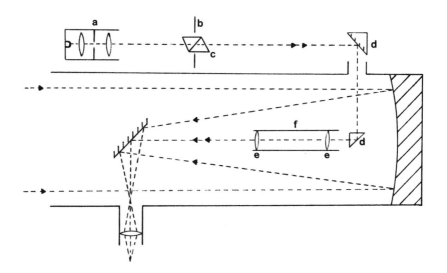

Fig 7. Comparison Image Micrometer for Reflector.

(a) Pinhole to produce initial image.
(b) Position Circle to measure P.A.
(c) Wollaston Prism to produce Double Image.
(d) Prisms or Optical Flats.
(e) Supplementary Lenses.
(f) Tube to hold supplementary lenses

United States of America and the Lunar Section of the British
Astronomical Association.   Again addresses are given in Appendix 2.

(e) Photometry

The vast majority of the double stars listed in the IDS have only
approximate magnitudes.   These are assigned by the discoverer usually
and have probably not been rechecked since.   There is a huge and
practically uncovered field awaiting a serious observer equipped with a
photoelectric photometer and a 30- to 40-cm telescope.   There are
probably many more double stars with variable components waiting to be
discovered and followed.   R.L.Walker has compiled a catalogue of visual
pairs with variable components.

The measurement of binaries is one of the most fascinating and
exacting pursuits in observational astronomy.   There are a number of
bright pairs whose orbital motions are such that changes can be detected
in periods of a year or less and which are available to small
telescopes.   However, there are a great number of wider pairs which have
not been measured for some considerable time.   The acquisition of a
larger telescope provides the observer with a corresponding increase of
observational material and at present even the 30-cm reflector is not an
uncommon size amongst amateurs.   In the U.K. and U.S.A. today there
are many large telescopes which are underutilised or even unused.
Programmes of double star measurement by the committed double star
observer would not only repay all the work put in by the telescope
makers but it would also inject valuable data into visual double star
astronomy at a time when the number of professional observers is
certainly less than ten.   The Webb Society Double Star Section exists to
give all the help it can to those who want to observe double stars.

4. RECORDING OBSERVATIONS

(a) LOCATION

The pairs to be observed may be found (if no setting circles are available) by two main methods.

(i) Differentiation from a Known Star

To employ this method it is necessary to know the diameter in minutes of arc of the field of view of the eyepiece being used. To evaluate this quantity, the telescope should be centred on an equatorial star such as delta Ori, zeta Vir or zeta Aqr. With the telescope stationary, time the passage of the star across the centre of the field from edge to edge in minutes of time and then multiply by 15 to get the diameter of the field in minutes of arc.

(ii) Sweeping for a Pair

This is a less certain method than (i) and should be used if the RA and Declination co-ordinates do not correspond to the equinox of the star atlas available.

(b) POSITION

If a double star is found during observation and cannot be identified its position in terms of RA and Declination can be obtained by differentiating from a known star. After locating it, the position angle, separation, colours and magnitudes of the pair should be estimated. Never neglect a pair because it cannot be identified. By giving as much information as possible it may be possible to find it in the Lick "Index Catalogue of Double Stars".

(c) SEPARATION

The diameter of the eyepiece field is again useful in estimating separation. If a high power is used then the separation of a wide pair becomes an estimable fraction of the total field diameter and it becomes quite easy to make a direct estimate (in arc seconds) of the angular separation. Observers should always make estimates of separation wherever possible. If a micrometer is being used at least three measures of separation should be made and the mean value corrected to the second decimal place if this seems realistic based on the scatter of the individual measurements.

Observers should determine whether the stars in a close pair are single, elongated or divided. If single, the fact should be noted.

(d) <u>BRIGHTNESS</u>

   Estimates of magnitude should always be made where possible to the nearest 0.1 magnitude. If the pair is very close then it may be easier to estimate the difference in magnitude and then with a lower power estimate the magnitude of the single image. From these two values the brightness of each star can be determined.

   If C is the combined magnitude and A and B are the magnitudes of the brighter and fainter components, and d is the estimated difference in magnitude of the two stars, then :

$$A = C + x$$

$$B = A + d$$

   Table 1, below, gives the value of x for a range of values of d and then, since C is known, the values of A and B can be found.

TABLE 1

Parameters allowing calculation of individual magnitudes
knowing the total magnitude and difference in magnitude.

d	x	d	x
0.0	0.75	1.2	0.31
0.1	0.70	1.4	0.26
0.2	0.66	1.6	0.22
0.3	0.60	1.8	0.19
0.4	0.57	2.0	0.15
0.5	0.53	2.5	0.10
0.6	0.49	3.0	0.06
0.7	0.46	3.5	0.04
0.8	0.42	4.0	0.03
0.9	0.39	4.5	0.02
1.0	0.36		

   e.g. The pair STT 174 was observed to have a combined magnitude of 6.2 and a difference in magnitude of 1.5, thus approximately:

$$A = C + x \quad \text{and} \quad B = A + d, \quad \text{where} \quad C = 6.2 \quad \text{and}$$
$$d = 1.5 \text{ (whence } 1 = 0.24 \text{ from Table 1}$$

$$A = 6.2 + 0.24 = 6.44$$
$$B = 6.44 + 1.5 = 7.94$$

and correcting to the first decimal place gives 6.4 and 7.9 as the estimated magnitudes of the pair.

(e) <u>COLOURS</u>

Table 2 (by Hagen) provides for most of the hues which observers are likely to meet during examination of double stars. If a colour which is not in the table, such as purple or green is found, then this should be written out in full in the column when the observer makes out his report. Otherwise the colours can be converted into two numbers which saves space when the results are entered into the card index.

TABLE 2

Colours of Double Stars (after Hagen)

-3	Pure blue	4	Orange yellow
-2	Pale blue	5	Yellow orange
-1	Blue white	6	Pure orange
0	Pure white	7	Reddish orange
1	Yellowish white	8	Orangey red
2	Pale yellow	9	Red, slight orange tint
3	Pure yellow	10	Pure red

(f) <u>POSITION ANGLE</u>

This is estimated by allowing the pair to drift across the field and estimating the angle between a line joining the stars and the direction of drift. The position angle always lies in the direction from the brighter to the fainter star. Fig 8 shows the arrangement in an astronomical (inverting) telescope.

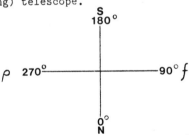

Fig. 8 The measurement of position angle

With practice, estimates of position angle can usually be made to within 10 degrees. If a micrometer is used it will usually suffice to make three independent determinations of position angle unless the pair is particularly difficult. The mean figure should be quoted for the nearest 0.1 degree and should contain any zero-point correction (see Chapter 5).

Micrometric measurements should be reported for each nightly mean on the back of the reporting form shown at the end of this chapter (if used). The date of each night's mean should be reported in terms of 0.001 year. This can easily be found by taking the number of nights from the beginning of the year, multiplying by 0.00274 and rounding up to the nearest 0.001.

(g) DRAWINGS

It is not considered necessary to draw fields of identical diameter and it is left to the observer to include features which he considers interesting - for instance the proximity of a nearby double or galaxy. It is always necessary to show the north-south line and to include the size of the drawing in minutes of arc. Other data noted should include size and type of telescope, magnification(s) employed and brief notes on the sky conditions.

The Antoniadi scale of seeing from I to V can be used to describe the steadiness of the atmosphere, i.e.:

I. Perfect seeing without a quiver.
II. Slight undulations, with moments of calm lasting several seconds
III. Moderate seeing with large tremours.
IV. Poor seeing, with constant troublesome undulations.
V. Very bad seeing.

In order to standardise all field drawings the following symbols are suggested to represent field stars and double star components:

Table 3

Symbols for star magnitudes

✦	Magnitude 5	●	Magnitude 8
▲	" 6	•	" 9
●	" 7	·	" 10 and below

A standard form for recording observations is shown on the next page as an example of how the observations might be laid out.

WEBB SOCIETY DOUBLE STAR SECTION   OBSERVING FORM

PAIR   CATALOGUE: (if any)   ADS:

RA: DECL: EQUINOX:

RA:*   DECL: *   EQUINOX 2000 (Leave * blank)

DATE: OBSERVER:

APERTURE: (state if OG or spec):   MAGNIFICATION(S):

SEEING: MICROMETER (if any)

TRANSPARENCY:

....

FIELD DRAWING   ↓   . NOTES
                       N   .
                              .   MAGS (Est.):
                              .
                              .   COLOURS:
                              .
                              .   P.A. (Est):
                              .
                              .   DIST (Est):
                              .
                              .   P.A. (Meas.):
                              .
                              .   DIST (Meas.):
                              .
Scale: **   .   No Readings:
....
Magnitudes: .   OTHER COMPONENTS: (give details
                              .   as above):
                              .
                              .
    ◆   ▲   ●   ●   ●   ·   .
                              .
    5   6   7   8   9   10 and .
                       below .
                              .
....

** The observer should indicate the scale of the field drawing by
   means of a line, typically thus: |__20'__|

5. MICROMETERS FOR DOUBLE STAR MEASUREMENT

In this chapter it is proposed to describe the various instruments which can be used to measure the position angle and separation of visual double stars. It covers four basic classes of micrometer which will be described as follows:

(a) FILAR MICROMETERS

The filar micrometer, which is probably the most well known and widely used instrument for this purpose, was first described by Auzout in 1667 in a form which has not changed radically to this day.

Basically the instrument consists of a spider thread stretched across a frame which is itself mounted in a box and free to move to and fro within it. A second thread is fixed across the box parallel to the movable thread and will be referred to as the fixed thread. It is displaced slightly along the optical axis of the telescope to allow free movement of the movable thread. The frame containing the movable thread is controlled by a micrometer screw of fine pitch usually graduated in one-hundredths of a revolution. A second screw known as the box screw controls the movement of the whole box, hence both threads may be moved together while remaining equidistant. A third thread, also fixed across the box, is inserted perpendicular to the movable and fixed threads and is used to measure position angle. The micrometer is generally able to rotate through 180 degrees in the plane perpendicular to the optical axis, although some instruments have frames which rotate through 90 degrees. The P.A. can be read off from a circle graduated in intervals of 1 or 0.5 degrees, generally by means of two verniers, and illumination of the threads is obtained by a small bulb in the body of the micrometer which is connected to a low voltage circuit with a potentiometer to allow the level of illumination to be varied.

Before a double star can be measured, it is essential to determine the screw value of the movable screw with great care and accuracy and also the zero reading of the position circle P_0. If a fairly bright equatorial star is allowed to drift across the field of view with the driving clock stopped, then by turning the position angle thread until the star drifts exactly along it, the angle on the circle corresponds to $P_0 + 90$. If the angle on the circle is, for example, $89°.2$, then $0°.8$ must be added to each measure of P.A. made and this value must be checked regularly. Thus, in this case, P_0 corresponds to $359°.2$.

There are two main methods for finding R, the screw value of the micrometer or movable screw.

(i) By measurement of the difference in declination of two stars.

The Pleiades are well suited for this purpose, containing stars of similar magnitude and R.A. and whose declinations are accurately known. Having determined P_0, the micrometer is then arranged so that the fixed and movable threads are both horizontal (i.e. they move in declination only).

Depending on the micrometer the difference in declination between suitable members is about 50 - 100 turns of the screw and this necessitates the use of stepping by means of intermediate stars. The measures should include a reading from the north star to the south star and back again on several separate nights. Precession, proper motion and refraction should all be taken into account.

(ii) Using the transit of circumpolar stars.

With the circle reading P_0 + 90 , the star to be used is observed with a low power just before upper or lower culmination. The movable wire is placed just preceding the star as it enters the field, with the driving clock stopped. Using the sidereal timepiece, the transit time of the star on the thread is noted. The thread is advanced one revolution (or a suitable fraction of a revolution) and the transit time is again noted. This is repeated 30 - 40 times both before and after culmination.

Full details of both these methods can be found in Aitken's book "The Binary Stars" which is essential reading for all observers.

The telescope can now be turned on the double star in question, but before any measures are made it is useful to estimate the m (difference in magnitude) of the two stars and the quadrant in which the fainter lies if they are not equally bright.

The first measurement is that of position angle. The P.A. thread is turned until it appears to bisect the images of both stars simultaneously. The reading is noted on the circle and several more determinations made. (The number of readings taken here will depend on the difficulty of the pair being observed. For wide pairs, three angles will probably suffice if the agreement appears good, whereas close pairs will benefit from six or more determinations. This argument can also be applied to the measurement of separation with equal, if not greater, force since each distance measure is subject to two readings of the movable screw). The correction to the position angle ($0°.8$ in our case) must be added to the mean P.A. at the end.

To measure separation, the micrometer is first of all turned through + 90 degrees where 0 is the mean P.A. without correction.

Fig 9 shows the position of the position angle thread (P) and the movable and fixed threads (M and F respectively) during the measurement of separation.

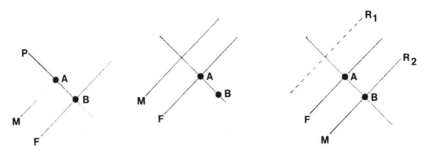

Fig 9. Filar micrometer. Arrangement of threads for measurement of separation.

Firstly the micrometer screw and box screw are adjusted until the movable thread bisects the image of the brighter star and the fixed thread bisects the fainter star. The box screw is then adjusted until the fixed thread now bisects the brighter star A. The reading on the micrometer or movable screw (R) is noted. Keeping the fixed thread bisecting star A, the movable thread is adjusted until it bisects star B, the new reading (R2) being noted. The value (R2 - R1) gives twice the number of revolutions required to move between the two components A and B, and knowing R, this distance can be converted into seconds of arc.

The placing of wires upon the stellar disks becomes more difficult, both as the separation gets very large and very small. In the first case the eye cannot accommodate both wires in the same field of view and has to dart rapidly from one wire to the other when making the separation setting. In the case of very close pairs, the separation of the stars may be comparable with the thickness of the wires. William Herschel used the Airy disk as a means of estimating the separation. Dembowski made some settings using the wires but his final separations also included a series of estimations using the Airy disk.   Herschel also used to set his wires tangential to both the inner and outer edges of each Airy disk and then take the mean values to represent the position of the centres of each image. This cannot be recommended since the Airy disk is not always visible and the seeing disk varies depending on the condition of the atmosphere. John Herschel outlined two methods in the book by Crossley, Gledhill and Wilson (1879).

(a) Set the wires to the same apparent distance that the stars subtend from their image centres. This is repeated 5 or 6 times and then the wires are placed in contact and the difference between the two positions gives the required separation in revolutions of the screw.

(b) Set the wires at a known distance of 1 arc second and estimate the ratio of the distance between the disk centres and the wire centres.

To give some idea of scale, modern fibres with diameters of 5 microns can be obtained. These will subtend 0.7 arc seconds in the focal plane of a 15-cm f/8 reflector and 0.6 arc seconds in a 30-cm f/6 reflector. The introduction of a Barlow lens can increase the effective focal length of a telescope by up to three times. However, the screw value will depend on the position of the Barlow and this must be fixed solidy otherwise measures will not be reliable.

It might also be useful at this point to say something about the materials which can be used to make micrometer threads. The traditional material is spider thread which combines tensile strength, thinness and elasticity. The main drawbacks are that it is difficult to replace, fragile and hard to acquire. Alternatives include nylon filaments obtained by unravelling dental floss for instance. Polystyrene cement can be drawn with care to give reasonably uniform filaments to a diameter of 10 microns or less. Hand-drawn glass or quartz is found to give filaments no thinner than 25 microns and is thus unsuitable for micrometry. Full details combined with an exhaustive bibliography can be found in the article by Darius and Thomas (1981).

The main advantages of the filar are its accuracy and range of application, whilst its drawbacks include:

(a) The illumination of the threads of the field will render very faint comes invisible.

(b) The closeness of the pair may necessitate the use of a magnification which is too high for the state of the atmosphere, resulting in ill-defined and moving images, with reduced accuracy in the measures.

(c) The movable and fixed threads are not parfocal and refocussing is necessary.

Another form of filar micrometer is the bi-filar which has two movable threads and two fixed threads and is used extensively in cometary photography as a guiding eyepiece.

Jonckheere's skew-thread micrometer (1950) consists of two threads on a movable frame which make an acute angle with the axis of the screw and a fixed thread which is oriented so as to bisect the obtuse angle formed at the intersection of the two movable threads.

For pairs which are too wide to measure with the crossed threads, another thread, mounted on the same arrangement of carriage but parallel to the fixed thread can be added. This has a different screw value and this is determined as for the conventional filar micrometer.

The distance actually measured is several times greater than the distance between the two stars which form one side of the triangle and thus the screw constant is correspondingly smaller - Jonckheere's value was 1.078 arc seconds per revolution. Another advantage is that since the movable threads are fixed with respect to each other, they can be stretched in the same plane. The fixed plane is used to measure position angle.

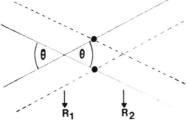

Fig 10. Jonckheere's micrometer. Method for measuring separation.

The separation of the pair (ρ) depends upon R1, R2 and the angle between the fixed threads. This angle can be determined by rotating the micrometer and allowing an equatorial star to drift along each wire in turn. This procedure should be carried out several times with great care. The separation of the pair is then given by:

$$\rho = (R2 - R1)\tan(\theta/2)$$

The advantages of this micrometer are:

(a) Both fixed threads can be placed in the same focal plane.

(b) Only one screw is required for the measurement of separation.

(c) The screw constant can be very small.

Two further varieties of filar micrometer will be mentioned here although the first of these may properly be included with the graticule instruments.

Durand (1981) has described the construction and operation of a micrometer in which a pair of wires at a narrow angle are laid against a dark background with a third wire at right angles to the 'V' thus formed. They are then photographed and reduced to fit into the telescope eyepiece. One of the arms of the 'V' is also graduated with divisions at equal intervals along its length and each of these is numbered.

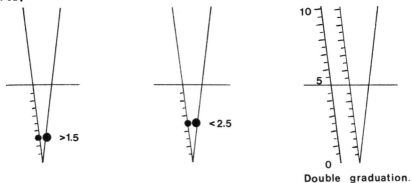

Fig 11. The arrangement of 'wires' in the 'V' micrometer.

Measurement of separation is made by rotating the eyepiece, which is fitted with a position circle, until the two stars are bisected by the wires of the 'V'. The graduations can be calibrated by examining a number of double stars of differing separations (see the list drawn up by Paul Muller (1949) and repeated in Paul Couteau's book (1978)). The exact orientation of the three wires should be determined accurately by trailing an equatorial star along each in turn. This will supply the correction, if any, to be made to the micrometer after position angle has been measured and before the separation is attempted. If the two stars are not exactly at right angles to the vertical axis of the 'V' an error in the estimated separation will result. Durand also experimented with a second graduated 'wire' parallel to the first to give a further range of measurement.

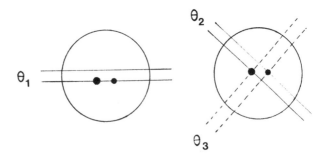

Fig 12. The parallel wire micrometer. Methods of use.

D Godillon has proposed a micrometer which consists simply of two parallel wires in the eyepiece and a position angle circle.(Fig 12).

The settings are shown in fig 12(a) and (b) and the angle at which each occurs is noted. Position (b) can be achieved in two different orientations, separated by p degrees. The separation of the pair is given by :

$$\rho = d/\sin(p)$$

where d is the angular separation of the wires. This instrument cannot be used for close pairs.

An interesting micrometer developed by Bigourdan (1895) has two glass points attached to fixed and movable frames of the micrometer. The two glass needles are used to "point" at the two components of the double star and measurements are made in the same way as with the filar. However, a thread is still needed for P.A. measurement.

One group of micrometers has no moving parts. The movable and fixed threads are replaced with a graticule at the focal plane. The graticule may have a variety of forms - lozenge, circle, two concentric circles (ring micrometer). The relative co-ordinates of the two stars are obtained by noting the instants of contacts as the stars drift over the graticule. The accuracy of such observations is, however, much inferior to those obtained with a filar micrometer. For further details see the article by Phillips (1979a, 1979b) and the chapter on micrometers in Sidgwick (ed. Muirden) (1979).

(b) IMAGE MICROMETERS

The two main instruments in this category are the double image and comparison image micrometers. A third instrument, the diffraction micrometer will be discussed in detail later in this chapter.

The most familiar instrument in this group is the double image micrometer which began life in the form of a divided object glass known as a heliometer. This arrangement, however, produced aberrations which prevented the use of high powers for the measurement of close double stars. As its name suggests, it was used to measure the diameter of the Sun's disk, with each half of the objective producing a separate image of the Sun. A later development consisted of placing a divided lens just in front of the eyepiece and using a normal objective. By displacing one half of the lens with respect to the other along the axis of division, two images of a single star are obtained. By displacing in the opposite direction, the two images appear to merge and then widen again. When viewing a double star, therefore, four images are produced and by moving the half-lens (by means of a micrometer screw with a milled head) so that certain combinations of the four images are obtained, the distance between the pair of stars can be found, knowing the screw constant. To make a measure, the micrometer has to be rotated until all four images form a straight line or a square.

For example, let ① and ① represent one pair of images of the double star to be measured and let ⊖ and ⊖ represent the other pair of images. In the "zero" position of the half-lens, they coincide, and now suppose that the micrometer screw is rotated until the images appear as if in Fig 13. If the distances between all the stars are judged to be equal then the shift of the micrometer is D/2, where D is the separation of the double.

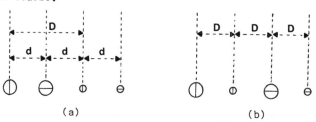

Fig 13. Image micrometer; method of measuring separation.

This combination is now obtained on the other side of "zero" and hence the difference in the two micrometer readings equals D, and the zero reading is eliminated. Similarly in Fig 13(b) the total shift is in fact 4D, this method being preferred for close pairs.

The micrometer is also fitted with a graduated position angle circle and the angle at which co-linearity occurs corresponds to the position angle - remembering to take careful note of the quadrant in which the fainter star lies.

Later instruments such as those used by P. Muller use birefringent or double refracting prisms, in place of the split lens. In these prisms, which actually consist of two prisms of quartz or calcite mounted with their crystal axes perpendicular (see Fig 14), an incident light ray is split up into two rays known as the ordinary (o) ray and the extraordinary (e) ray. Dr Muller developed this prism (which is now named after him) in 1937. When the prism moves perpendicularly to the optical axis of the telescope, a variation in the separation of the o and e rays is produced.

Measures of double stars are made in a similar manner to that of the split lens micrometer. One advantage of the Muller prism is that the light is polarised, and by fitting a thin polarising sheet (which acts as an analyser) the difference in magnitude between the two components can be measured. According to Dr Muller the average mean error for observations made in one night is 0.04 magnitude. Pairs as close as 0".45 have been measured in this way with the 60-cm refractor at Pic-du-Midi Observatory.

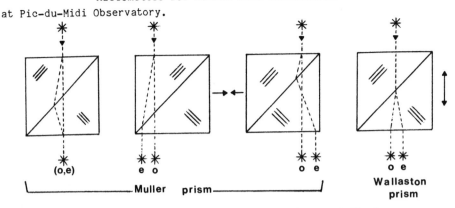

Fig 14. Birefringent Prism Micrometer (after Muller).

The comparison image micrometer (CIM) which was described by F.J.Hargreaves (1931) produced an artificial pair of stars. A modified instrument was then introduced (Hargreaves, 1932) and this was adapted for use on the Greenwich 28-inch refractor by C.R.Davidson and L.S.T. Symms (1938).

In this instrument, an illuminated pinhole is imaged onto a Wollaston prism by means of a system of biconvex lenses. The Wollaston prism (fig 14(c)) then splits the image into two components (the o and e rays) which are polarised. The separation of the two images depends on the motion of the prism towards or away from the image of the pinhole. A centimetre scale is used to measure this movement, which is directly proportional to the separation of the artificial stars which must be now imaged in the eyepiece in sharp focus, alongside the images of the pair to be measured. This is achieved by projecting the images up the outside of the telescope tube to an elliptical flat which reflects them onto a reflecting prism side by side with the lamp housing. They are reflected into the telescope tube and fall upon a small object glass of 11.25 inches focus and via a quarter-silvered cube into the field of the eyepiece in sharp focus. The Wollaston prism is mounted on a graduated P.A. circle and is free to rotate to allow P.A. measurements to be made. A pair of crossed Nicol prisms, also rotatable, can be adjusted to make either of the artificial stars as bright or as faint as required to match the pair being measured. Finally, a blue filter adjusts the colour temperature of the lamp's tungsten filament (2,800 K) to one of 5,500 K which is the colour temperature of an average star as seen in the 28-inch.

A movement of 1 cm in the lamp housing is equivalent to a change of separation of 0.0794 seconds of arc of the artificial stars in the eyepiece. The CIM is capable of measuring pairs whose distances range from about 4.5 arc seconds to less than 0.2 arc seconds and it is extremely easy to use. A filar micrometer which is also fitted to the 28-inch is preferred for P.A. measurement.

In general, image micrometers have three main advantages over the filar micrometer:

(a) No field illumination is necessary.

(b) There is no masking of the star images.

(c) On poor nights, it is easier to compare two pairs of stars than to try and bisect two moving images.

On the debit side, the measurement of position angle tends to be produce rather less accurate results than with the filar.

(c) THE BINOCULAR MICROMETER

This micrometer was devised by M.V.Duruy in the mid-1930's. It consists basically of two eyepieces, one of which forms the image of a double star from the telescope, the other images an artificial double star produced by one of the methods described later in this section. When viewing both pairs of stars simultaneously it is possible to detect very small differences in the observed separations. Knowing the focal length of each eyepiece, the true separation of the artificial pair in seconds of arc can be calculated, knowing the true linear separation.

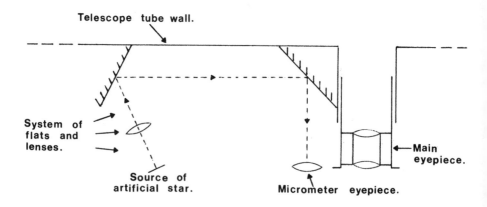

Fig 15. Method of projecting artificial stars into left eyepiece.

Fig 15 shows how the artificial double star images are projected
into the left-hand eyepiece of a pair of "binoculars". there are three
different ways in which the artificial double stars may be produced.

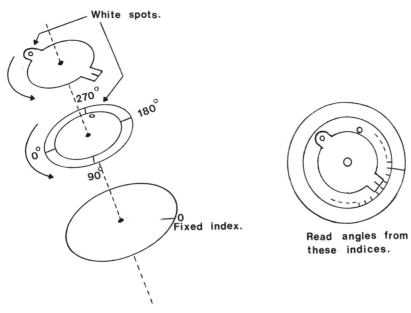

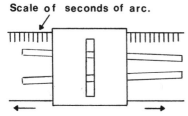

Fig 16 The separate components
       of the micrometer compass.
       The upper two components
       rotate about the axis.

Fig 17 View of components in
       Fig 16 assembled. The white
       spots are projected into the
       micrometer eyepiece.

Fig 18 The image formed by the
       slits with rear illumination
       forms the artificial star.

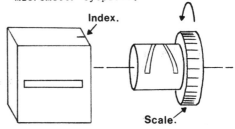

Fig 19 A similar method to Fig 18
       with a rotating scale. A
       lamp is housed inside.

(i) A pair of compasses is used with a white spot representing a star on each branch. This is seen against a dark background, preferably black velvet, and the position of each branch is read off from a 360 degree protractor. If the angle between the branches is β and the distance between the two artificial stars is d, then the position angle is given by $(\beta/2) + 90$ where $\beta = (\theta_2 - \theta_1)$ and θ_2 and θ_1 are the two angles "pointed at" by the branches. The separation d is proportional to $\sin(\beta/2)$ and can be calibrated by measuring several standard pairs and plotting d against $\sin(\beta/2)$. When a new pair is measured a knowledge of $(\theta_2 - \theta_1)$ will yield d directly.

It is useful to have several sets of compasses having a pair of bright stars, a pair of faint stars and an unequal pair to prevent systematic errors. By using an optical system as shown in Fig 15 the scale could be increased so that 1 arc second could·be represented by a distance of several mm between the artificial stars.

(ii) A second method involves cutting two thin lines which are slowly converging in a piece of paper. If these are illuminated from behind and viewed by means of a perpendicular thin line, also cut from paper (Fig 18) then when the paper containing the converging lines is moved, two artificial stars are seen which appear to vary in separation.

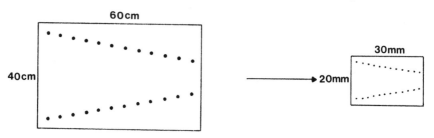

Fig.20 Artificial stars of known separation, drawn as black
stars on a white background and photographed to produce
clear images on a black background.

(iii) If a number of "double stars" of varying separation are drawn on paper (Fig.20) and photographed, this can be reduced and projected into the lefthand eyepiece in a similar manner to the first two methods.

The errors in these methods are close to those inherent in the filar micrometer. The advantages are that the whole aperture of the telescope is available and that no field illumination is required, making fainter pairs accessible to the observer.

(d) THE DIFFRACTION MICROMETER

The appearance of a bright star in a small telescope is that of a small, brilliant point of light. If a coarse diffraction grating is placed over the object glass or mirror, then a succession of fainter images will be seen extending linearly from the star image in a direction perpendicular to that of the grating slits and becoming fainter as they do so. The number of satellite images visible depends on the brightness of the star and the number and width of the slits in the grating.

If two stars are seen close together in the eyepiece then each star will be accompanied by its own system of images. By rotating the grating the images can be arranged into certain patterns which allow the observer to measure the distance between the two stars and to determine their position angle. Fig.21 shows the appearance of a double star with the grating slits (a) horizontal and (b) vertical.

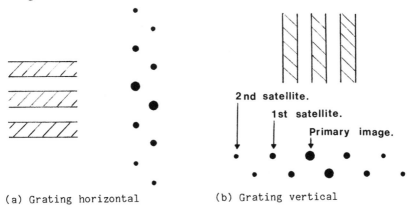

(a) Grating horizontal   (b) Grating vertical

Fig.21 Appearance of a Double Star through a grating.

Each satellite image is equidistant from the other by a distance z arc seconds, where:

$$z = 206265 \lambda / p \qquad \text{--- 1.}$$

p being the total width of the grating bar and slit and λ is the mean wavelength of the incident light. (In a pair of stars where the components are of differing spectral type, the value of z is different for each star but the difference cannot be detected visually). It is sufficiently accurate, to within 1%, to determine one's own value of mean wavelength.

This can be done in two ways:

(i) By measuring a well known pair whose separation and position angle are well defined. Such pairs are eta Cassiopeiae (STF 60) and zeta UMa (STF 1744). Appendix 1 gives the predicted PA and separation for every five years from 1985.0 to 2000.0 and in addition a number of other stars whose positions are well known are included. With an accurately known separation and knowing z, the observer can find λ although many measures should be made before adopting a mean figure to be used in later observations.

Table 4. Values of z for various values of p ($\lambda = 5560\overset{o}{A}$).

z"	p(cm)	z"	p(cm)
11.47	1.0	1.91	6.0
7.65	1.5	1.76	6.5
5.73	2.0	1.64	7.0
4.59	2.5	1.53	7.5
3.82	3.0	1.43	8.0
3.28	3.5	1.35	8.5
2.87	4.0	1.27	9.0
2.55	4.5	1.21	9.5
2.29	5.0	1.15	10.0
2.09	5.5		

(ii) For a second method of determining one's personal mean wavelength λ, it is necessary to observe a star of high declination, preferably Polaris. The procedure is to use a grating whose value of z is fairly large, (M.V.Duruy used 7 arc seconds) and to orient the grating so that the images are aligned E - W in the stationary telescope. An eyepiece with a single wire is rotated so that the wire is N - S and the time, t, between images A' and A" crossing the wire is noted (Fig.22).

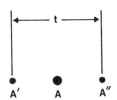

$$t = 2z/15\cos D$$

where t is in seconds of time, z is in seconds of arc and D is the declination of the star.

Fig 22. Eyepiece wire method for determining λ.

In the case of Polaris where D = 89 11' 49" (for 1985.0) the time required for A' - A" to cross the wire is about 66.6 seconds. Using a stop watch, this time can be determined to within about 0.2 seconds and this corresponds to a mean error of about 0.3%. Thus, knowing z and p, equation 1 can be used to determine λ .

Ideally, there should only be two satellite images visible for each component of the double star, making six in all. When bright stars are examined, many satellites are visible and the brighter ones are actually short spectra and rectangular in shape. M.V.Duruy, using a 24-inch reflector found that in that instrument, satellite images of stars fainter than magnitude 3 do not show up as spectra. For a 6-inch reflector this corresponds to magnitude 0 and it is clear that the vast majority of satellite images in double stars will appear circular because they are too faint for the eye to distinguish between a circle and a square.

The number of satellite images can be controlled by means of the grating slit and bar width. Duruy has studied the variation of intensity of successive satellites with the ratio a/p and the results are illustrated in Fig. 23.

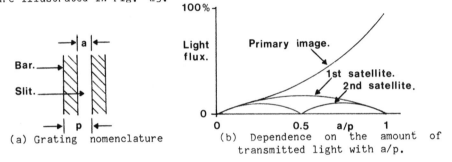

(a) Grating nomenclature

(b) Dependence on the amount of transmitted light with a/p.

Fig 23. The variation of satellite brightness with the bar/slit ratio.

When a/p = 1, the bars disappear and there is no diffraction. When a/p = 0, no light passes through and it was found that when a/p = 0.5 (i.e. slit width equal to bar width) the second satellite disappears whilst the third and higher are usually too faint to be seen. This optimum value of 0.5 for a/p was adopted by Duruy for his micrometer.

The grating and position circles should be so arranged such that when the pointer (parallel to the slits) shows a PA of 90° or 270° the images are horizontally aligned and hence parallel to the direction of drift of an equatorial star with the telescope stationary. The pairs 24 Com (STF 1657) and gamma Ari (STF 180) have position angles of 270° and 180° respectively and they can also be used to check the setting.

Fig 24 shows the arrangement used by John Lewis to mount the diffraction grating onto a reflecting telescope.

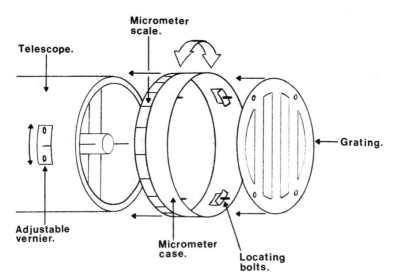

Fig 24. A method of mounting a grating to a reflecting telescope.

To measure the separation of a pair there are two main configurations which can be used.

(i) The method of right angle triangles.

The grating is turned until the angle ABA" (as shown in Fig.25(a)) is adjudged to be a right angle. The reading on the circle,α_1, corresponding to this position is noted. Then the grating is moved in position to give the configuration in Fig 25(b), and the angle α_2 noted.

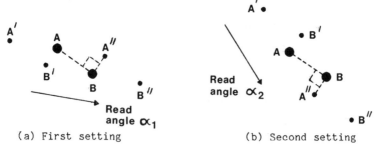

(a) First setting   (b) Second setting

Fig 25. Configuration of images for measurement of separation using the method of right angled triangles. ABA" = $90°$ at each setting.

If $\alpha = \alpha_1 + \alpha_2$ then ρ which is the distance AB is given by:

$$\rho = z(\cos \alpha/2)$$

where z is known and hence ρ, the separation of the pair can be found.

Also, $\theta = (\alpha_1 + \alpha_2)/2$ where θ is the PA of the pair.

(ii) The method of isosceles triangles.

In this method, the grating is successively rotated to give the configurations as in Fig 26 (a) and (b), the criterion of setting being that AA' = BA' and that AB" = BB". α_1 and α_2 are read as in the first method and ρ and θ can be obtained from:

$$\rho = 2z(\cos \alpha/2) \qquad \text{and} \qquad \theta = (\alpha_1 + \alpha_2)/2$$

where $\alpha = \alpha_1 + \alpha_2$ as in the method of right angled triangles.

With the same grating, two different methods can be used to find the position angle and separation of a pair. It is better to make a large number of measures of each pair, preferably using both methods. By constructing several gratings each with a different value of z it is possible to cover a large range in separation.

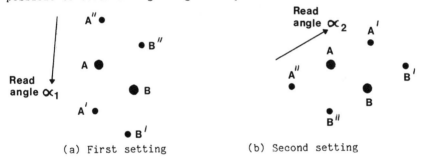

(a) First setting   (b) Second setting

Fig 26. Configuration of images for measurement of separation using the method of isosceles triangles. AA' = A'B' at each setting.

An example of an observation of the pair xi UMa (STF 1523) is given below by kind permission of the observer John Lewis who was using a 20-cm Schmidt-Cassegrain at powers between x222 and x500. The grating z value was 2.86 arc seconds corresponding to p = 4 cm and the method of right angles was used.

α_1	α_2	PA	Sep.	Date
67.75	119.25			
72.00	121.50			
71.75	123.50			
68.75	119.00			
72.50	123.00			
71.00	122.00			
70.63 MEAN	121.38	96.0	2.58	1983.282
67.25	122.75			
70.00	122.00			
70.50	124.00			
68.50	123.50			
71.00	120.00			
67.50	122.00			
69.13	122.38	95.8	2.56	1983.312
Average of two nights		95.9	2.57	1983.297

Another method of using the grating requires a single wire in the
eyepiece and a position angle circle to read the orientation of the
wire. This is shown in Fig 27.

In this method, the value of z is greater than the separation of
the pair. The grating is oriented so that the secondary images lie in
PA 0 , i.e. N - S. The wire is turned so that the angle between A' and
B' and this reading is noted together with the orientation of the
grating. Then the angle A"B is measured and noted and the grating then
turned so that the images lie in a different known angle, say 330 .
Again the angles A'B and A"B are taken and noted, the drawing as in Fig.
27 being reproduced on paper at the desk later. By drawing it to scale,
the position angle and separation can be obtained geometrically.

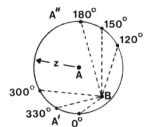

The radius of the circle is z. The
three points A" are at known angles
which are set up on the grating
circle. By measuring three angles
A'B and three further angles A"B,
construction of the diagram shown
to a fixed scale will give the
value of ρ and θ .

Fig 27. Configuration of images, eyepiece wire method. (ρ < z).

A similar method exists for the case when z is less than the separation of the pair. It has been found by Duruy that in this case the position angles are better defined than the separations - when z is greater than the separation, the opposite is true.

The main disadvantage of the diffraction micrometer is the loss of light suffered due to obstruction by the bars of the grating. When a/p = 0.5, only 50% of the incident light from the pair will reach the mirror or object glass. Duruy has calculated that 25% of the incident light goes into the primary image making it 1.48 magnitudes fainter than without the grating. Of the remaining 25%, some 10% goes into each of the first order images which are thus 2.48 magnitudes fainter whilst the remainder is spread amongst the images of higher order.

Two instruments using the same principle as the Duruy micrometer have appeared previously. In 1896, Karl Schwarzchild had used a hinged grating in front of the object glass, both halves being tilted with respect to the lens by means of a rack and pinion. This allowed a variable value of z but involved the measurement of another angle. Lawrence Richardson (1924,1925,1927a,b and 1928) also described a rectangular coarse grating which was tilted on a pivot in front of the object glass. Both of these devices are more elaborate than the Duruy micrometer.

Colin Pither (1980) has described the construction of an 'interrupted' grating in which the bars near the centre of the grating are removed to increase the amount of light transmitted by the grating. This allows fainter pairs to be measured but at the cost of diverting more light into the primary image from the higher orders and consequently increasing the difference in magnitude between them.

It only remains here to acknowledge the debt of the author to Maurice Duruy for making available all the notes which he had acquired during his use of the grating micrometer. The fact that amateurs in England and France are using this device is due entirely to him.

(e) INTERFEROMETERS

The application of interferometers to the measurement of close double stars was primarily due to the work of Albert Michelson (1890). He suggested that interference methods could be used to measure the position angle and separation of close pairs. However, it was not until 1920 that Anderson (1920) using a simple two slit device, measured Capella with the Mount Wilson 100-inch reflector (Fig 28).

When observing a star with two-slit device, the image appears as an enlarged and elongated diffraction disk, crossed by a number of bright and dark fringes. These fringes are a result of the interference of the light from the two slits and their width depends on the wavelength of the incident light.

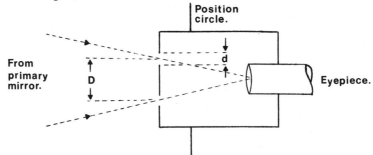

Fig 28. The Two-Slit Interferometer.

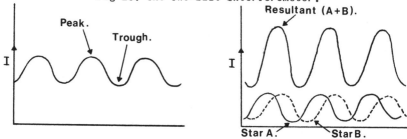

(a) For a single star   (b) For a double star.

Fig 29. Fringes produced by a Two-Slit Interferometer.

If the star is a very close double, each component will produce its own set of fringes in the eyepiece (Fig.29), the separation of the two sets depending on the distance between the slits D. If the value of D is changed, the fringe patterns will move relative to each other and if the peaks in each system co-incide with each other the result will be a brighter set of fringes. If, however, the peaks of one system and the troughs of the other are co-incident, there will be cancelling out of the two fringe systems and the fringes will disappear completely if the components are equally bright. For the smallest value of D at which the fringe visibility is a minimum:

$$\alpha = \lambda/2D$$

where α is the angular separation of the two stars in arc seconds and λ is the effective wavelength of the incident light. This value of α 2.44 times smaller that that for a normal telescope in which Dawes limit applies, but due to practical difficulties the effective gain is about

2.0,i.e. the lower limit of resolution for the 100- inch reflector is about 0.025 arc seconds with the interferometer and 0.050 arc seconds without.

When the slits are rotated about the optical axis in their own plane, the fringes disappear at certain angles. This is because the bright fringes of one component are in exact register with the dark fringes of the other but they are laterally displaced, and instead of the normal minimum being formed, a zig-zag pattern is seen. This pattern occurs four times in one revolution of the slits, forming two sets, 180° apart. Knowledge of these angles allows the position angle of the pair to be found, although one extra reading will be required to find in which quadrant the comes lies.

A modern application of this method was developed by W.S.Finsen at the Republic Observatory at Johannesburg (1951, 1954, 1964). He constructed an eyepiece interfermeter in 1933 and later produced an improved version. Dr Finsen made thousands of observations with this device attached to the 26.5-inch refractor and was familiar with the many fringe patterns that are possible. He also made extensive investigations into the effect of atmospheric dispersion on the fringes. This has the effect of shifting the centre of the fringe pattern away from the centre of the diffraction pattern at certain position angles. Other effects which complicate the fringe pattern include the fact that starlight also contains a spread of wavelengths and any difference in brightness between the components of the double star. Finsen found that measures could not be made effectively if the difference in brightness between the stars was more than one magnitude because the fringe pattern became very indistinct. Many of the measures which Dr Finsen made with the eyepiece interferometer are extremely valuable because they are more reliable than ordinary micrometrical measures for very small separations (0.1 arc seconds and below).

A new application of Michelson's work has proved to be a very powerful tool in the measurement of double stars with separations less than 0.030 arc seconds.The method makes use of the fact that even in stellar images affected by turbulence in the Earth's atmosphere there is diffraction limited information. A highly magnified short exposure of a bright star taken through a narrow band filter will show a large number of small grains in the image. This is known as the speckle pattern and it is due to random interference between the starlight in the Earth's atmosphere. The minimum size of the speckle grains is equal to the size of the Airy disk for the telescope. If the star is a close double then there will be two identical speckle patterns superimposed and shifted relative to each other by an amount smaller than the Airy disk. If the negative of a speckle photograph is illuminated with a laser, interference fringes will be seen, the separation of which is proportional to the separation of the double star. By combining a number of short exposures, a better fringe pattern is obtained. The orientation of the fringes yields the position angle. From photographs taken on the 200-inch reflector by Gezari, Labeyrie and Stachnik (1972) it was found that beta Cep had a hitherto unknown companion some 6 magnitudes fainter at a separation of 0.25 arc seconds. Such a star could not be found by visual means. Other photographs in Sky and Telscope for Apr 1970 show resolution of the binary Capella which has a maximum separation of 0.055 arc seconds.

An excellent review article on speckle interferometry by Harold MacAlister can be found in Sky and Telescope (1977).

f) PHOTOELECTRIC SCANNERS

These consist of a slit or series of slits which can move in the focal plane of a telescope. The light passed by the slit is detected by a photomultiplier tube and the data is collected into 'bins' in the computer memory which may be of the order of 10 millisecs long. In this way a profile of the star image is built up and the shape of the profile will depend on whether the star is single or double. Data about the position angle and separation can be gained if the star image can be scanned at several different slit angles, either by rotating the instrument turntable or by having two slits which are arranged at 90° to each other (Rakos et al, 1982). The observed profile is 'deconvoluted' by either by dividing it by the observed profile of a nearby known single star or by assuming an analytical form for the profile of a single star. The corresponding profile is that of the two components of the double. The position angle is a function of the position of the slits and the separation depends on the distance between the two peaks in the profile and the scale factor of the telescope. The amount of light under each profile is also a direct measure of the brightness of the star and so this apparatus can be used to give apparent magnitudes for each component.

CONCLUSIONS

To sum up, for the benefit of the amateur observer who wishes to try a construct a micrometer for his own use, the instruments described earlier can be divided into two distinct classes.

The simplest devices to make are the diffraction and binocular micrometers. The former can be made from wood or cardboard but aluminium is to be preferred. It is important that the grating is constructed with accurately parallel bars and slits. Since all measurements are made with the position circle it is important that this too is accurate and can be easily read. It should not be too small and a minimum diameter of 30 cm is recommended. This will result in degree marks which are about 2.5 mm apart. This also applies to the binocular micrometer and it should also be noted that with this instrument the scale constant is dependent upon the magnification and should be determined separately for each eyepiece.

The double image, comparison image and filar micrometers and also the eyepiece interferometer all have to be accurately engineered. There are now two filar micrometers which are commercially available and the addresses are given in Appendix 2 at the end of the book. The interferometer is of limited application since it will only operate on pairs where the Δm is less than 1 and the stars are fairly bright. However, Finsen reached magnitude 7 with the 26.5-inch at Johannesburg and there are several amateur telescopes in existence of similar size, so that it would not be beyond the capabilities of a determined amateur to try his hand at this instrument. Both the Muller version of the double image micrometer and the comparison image micrometer require birefringent prisms which are expensive. Again these micrometers would well repay the trouble taken in constructing them since they do not suffer from field illumination or broken wires. The author has found the comparison image micrometer extremely easy to use, but to date he knows only of the instrument on the 28-inch refractor and no-one yet appears to have attempted the reflector version.

For the amateur with little engineering capacity the diffraction micrometer is strongly recommended as a first instrument for the measurement of double stars.

6. PHOTOGRAPHY OF DOUBLE STARS

(a) THE PHOTOGRAPHIC PROCESS

Before discussing the photography of double stars it would be as well to re-capitulate upon the photographic process generally. There are many methods of writing-by-light, and in this respect any change of colour or density by the action of light might be termed photography.

The particular process that we are interested in is that which utilises a suspension of silver halides in gelatin spread onto a transparent base, either glass, (in which case the product is termed a plate), or a flexible material, now usually cellulose acetate, (in which case the product is called a film).

This process has developed from the original work of Fox Talbot, who, more than 100 years ago first successfully produced a 'negative' picture with light and shade reversed, and from which a number of subsequent copies could be taken. His process was complex and somewhat hit-and-miss, and it is a good thing that we have available the emulsions, (as the suspensions of silver halide are termed), that science has developed for us.

The modern emulsion consists of a very carefully prepared suspension of silver halides, together with sensitising agents etc., produced to a quite remarkably consistent quality and available to meet practically every photographic need.

Early emulsions were only sensitive to the blue end of the spectrum, hence the use of the classic red darkroom lamp for their processing. The methods were found to extend the range of sensitivity into the yellow and green, giving 'orthochromatic' emulsions, and later, with the aid of further sensitizing dyes, panchromatic (or 'Pan') materials were produced. These respond to the entire visible spectrum, although, except in the case of some very special films, they are still more sensitive to blue light. In addition, virtually all films respond to some degree to the ultra-violet.

Modern processes also allow us to control the 'speed' of emulsions, that is, whether it will take a lot or a little light to have a given effect in a given time. Many systems of quoting these speeds have been used, those in common use now being the DIN system, which is logarithmic and the ASA system which is arithmetic. It is not proposed to discuss these in detail; they are covered adequately in any book on basic photography. Suffice it to say that the slowest films have a speed of about 6 ASA whilst the fastest that can be attained with special processing is 10,000 ASA or even higher, depending on the method used in measuring the speed. With the comment that faster films generally have coarser grain structure, and cannot therefore resolve such fine detail, the discussion of the nature of emulsions will be left to consider what happens when a photographic emulsion is exposed to light.

As we are considering stellar photography (and stellar images are essentially point images) let us consider a photographic emulsion that had previously been un-exposed to light and upon which a point of light of very small dimension is allowed to fall. The silver halides are in the form of very small crystals, and for reasons still not completely understood, the action of light is to produce in them what is called a 'latent image'. This means that if, subsequent to exposure the emulsion is acted on by a suitable reducing agent, or DEVELOPER, the affected crystals of silver halide will be reduced to metallic silver, which, in the finely divided form it takes, appears black.

If we now use a further chemical, called a FIXER, which is capable of dissolving any undeveloped silver halide, but which does not affect metallic silver, then we may, provided certain precautions are taken, let our emulsion see the light of day and we shall have a permanent record of out point of light as a dark spot on an otherwise clear background. If the point of light had been the image of a star in a telescope, then we would now have a permanent record of that star.

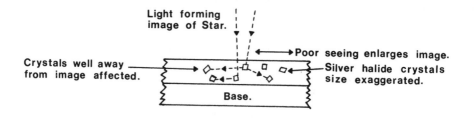

Fig 30. Formation of photographic image of stellar disk. (Simplified)

So far so good. The foregoing has necessarily been simplified and in order to undertake stellar photography, (including double stars), there are a number of other factors that have to be taken into consideration. Those that have a bearing on the matter are as follows:-

(i) Film speed.

The speed of the film, or more correctly, the speed of the film/developer combination, since these are inter-related. Obviously the faster the film, the fainter the star it will record in a given time.

(ii) Image size.

Some light will be reflected from the crystals of silver halide and will illuminate adjacent crystals, which will become developable. The image will then be larger, (many times, perhaps scores of times larger for bright stars), than the original image, even assuming that this was perfect in the first place. Imperfect seeing, either wandering or boiling, will enlarge the image further.

(iii) Failure of the Reciprocal Law or 'Reciprocity Failure'.

Manufacturers usually quote the speed of their emulsions for exposures in the region of 0.1 second. In theory, if a given amount of light gives a certain degree of developability in a given time then half that amount of light should have the same effect in twice the time and so on. This relationship fails for very low levels of illumination, when long exposures must be used, and for extremely short (micro-second) exposures in very intense light. In each case the emulsion seems to be slower than expected.

The micro-second exposures do not concern us, and for the purpose of such double star work as will be discussed, the effect of low level illumination and the resultant exposure times will not have sufficient effect to be appreciable. Fast films generally suffer more from reciprocity failure than slow films. As examples, materials with speeds in the order of 400 ASA or higher will start getting 'tired' by the time an exposure of 30 minutes has been reached, whilst slower films, around 25 to 50 ASA will continue at their rated speed for a couple of hours or more.

(iv) False reciprocity failure.

This occurs with very bright images, and should not be confused with true reciprocity failure, which occurs with all images and is a function of exposure time.

Briefly, what happens is as follows. A bright image will rapidly affect all the crystals of silver halide that it falls upon, and although these affected crystals will continue to reflect light to adjacent crystals so causing the size of the image to expand, there can be no further action on the central crystals. Any light absorbed by them is lost as far as producing an image is concerned. This is of especial importance when the image diameters are used to assess the magnitudes of the stars forming them. It would be safe to say that any star more than about two magnitudes above threshold (i.e. that star brightness which has just produced a fully dark circular image) will start to exhibit false reciprocity failure.

(v) Background darkening.

No sky is completely dark, and the rate at which the general
background will affect the film will depend on the focal ratio of the
system. For this reason, refractors are better than reflectors,
although by adding a 2x Barlow of suitable quality, the situation can be
remedied. Subject to certain minor considerations which do not affect
the matter sufficiently to merit inclusion, the faintest magnitude
reached will be a function of linear aperture, as in visual work, whilst
the degree of darkening will be a function of focal ratio.

Thus a 15-cm reflector of f/8 will record to a given magnitude on a
given film in a given time. A 15-cm refractor of f/16 will reach the
same magnitude in the same time under the same conditions, but can
continue for four times as long before the background has darkened to
the same degree. The linear scale will also be twice as large, but this
will be discussed in greater detail later in this chapter.

The above are the chief factors that affect the behaviour of the
photographic emulsion in the recording of stellar images, it being
assumed that these are being taken at the focal plane of the optical
system. So far as double stars are concerned, photography cannot be
considered the most accurate method of recording and measuring - the eye
and micrometer must take first place here.

Two deficiencies that occur in the photographic process are as
follows. Assuming perfect seeing, perfect guiding and perfect optics,
the developed images of a double star ought to be two circular patches
of silver of a size determined by the optics, film speed, exposure and
magnitude, and of a spacing determined by the separation of the stars
and the geometry of the optics. Unfortunately, this is not so.
Firstly, there are random movements of the order of 10 - 20 microns in
the gelatin of the emulsion during processing that cannot be predicted,
and secondly there is an effect in which the by-products of the
development of the image have a restraining effect in their immediate
vicinity, and this can distort the shape and even the position of
closely adjacent images, possibly partly inhibiting their full
development. Each of these factors detracts from the usefullness of a
photograph of a double star for the purpose of accurate measurement,
although with wider pairs and a long focal length, results are not far
short of those obtainable with a filar micrometer.

(b) CHOICE OF MATERIALS

It might seem that a very fast material would be the best to use,
as exposure would then be short and the accuracy of guiding need not be
of a such a high order. In practice this is not the case. If a stellar
image on a piece of film is examined under a microscope at a
magnification of about x100, it will be seen that the edge of the image
is indeterminate, gradually shading into the clear background. The
faster the film, the coarser the grain and the less determinate the form

of the image. On the other hand, very slow films will give images with beautifully crisp edges but are rarely circular due to difficulties in guiding for the required long exposures.

A good compromise is to use medium speed film, such as Ilford FP4 which has medium fine grain, a good panchromatic response, and if used with Hyfin developer may be taken as having a speed of 200 ASA. This is not spectacularly fast, but Hyfin developer gives crisp, sharp images. This is nothing to be gained in terms of finer grain by using anything slower. If a higher speed is required, then Ilford HP4 can be used, being processed in Acutol-S (for optimum speed/grain characteristics), or Acuspeed, (for maximum effective speed). Use these developers in accordance with the manufacturers directions. Their use at lower concentrations for longer periods of development will not increase the effective speed, although for bright stars there will be less background darkening. In this case, however, such a fast film is not really required. In addition, the effects of reciprocity failure seem to occur earlier when the dilute developer/extended processing time procedure is followed.

It might be as well to mention that it useful to be able to load one's own cassettes with bulk film in short lengths, thus allowing the film and its subsequent processing to be matched to the subject. Beware of some of the very cheap film that is advertised, as this is sometimes cine film, and is very subject to chemical fog, which is the random reduction of silver halide crystals to silver independent of the effect of light on the emulsion.

Always buy fresh material, it is not expensive in lengths of 5 and 17 metres, and also in 100 feet lengths from some supply houses. This will cut your film costs to less than one half of the cost of ready-loaded cassettes and will allow you to use just the amount of film that is needed. If you have no cassettes, your dealer will be able to supply for a few pence each but make sure that they are in good condition and that the velvet light traps are clean and free from dust. A clean, discarded toothbrush is ideal for this. In any case, discard a cassette when it has been used about 6 times, it has repaid its cost by then. A bulk film loader such as that manufactured by Burke and James, and sold under the name of 'Watson' is a very useful accessory for loading film if you have much work to do, but is by no means a necessity.

Similarly with chemicals. Buy these fresh and make them up according to the manufacturers instructions. Above all else, do not store film and chemicals together, something or other unpleasant is bound to happen. With a bit of luck, a suitable corner of the home can be found that is cool and dry for storage. Remember that photographic chemicals are not for consumption, so no developer or fixer in old gin bottles in the sideboard, and keep all film and chemicals away from

children. Whilst film is not poisonous, the sight of a three-year-old
playing yo-yo with 5 metres of previously unexposed FP4 can promote the
most unpredictable behaviour in the quietest astronomer.

(c) APPARATUS AND EXPOSURE

The range of apparatus that might be used to photograph double
stars is so wide that it would be impracticable to attempt to cover
every possibility. For those who have not attempted stellar photography
before, the following table may prove useful. All of the data in it is
taken from exposures made by the writer, not specifically for double
star work, but it will give a fairly good idea of what may be expected
from various instruments. In each case the star taken as the example is
approximately two magnitudes above the absolute threshold of the
exposure. The film used was FP4, processed in Hyfin.

Table 5.   Magnitude and Image Diameters with various Apertures.

Objective and F.L.		Lin. Aperture.	Exp.	Mag.	Diam.(")
Telephoto lens	135mm	34 mm	2 mins.	7	45
Telephoto lens	400 mm	63 mm	2 mins.	9	21
Speculum	1400 mm	216 mm	1 min.	10	7
Object Glass	3200 mm	204 mm	2 mins.	11	3

The above figures are not completely comparable, as the observing
conditions were not necessarily identical on each occasion, but they
will suffice to indicate the results to be expected.   If anything the
magnitude figures are conservative.

The limiting magnitude that might be expected is dependent on many
factors, not least of which is the sky brightness. Obviously the best
combination is a large aperture, long focal length and accurate guiding.
This will give a large scale, minimise sky brightness and give access to
fainter stars. Unfortunately, to meet these requirements the accuracy
of guiding needed is high, and needs an equatorial head that is in
accurate adjustment and a drive with very smooth operation and control.
Except near the zenith, changes in refraction may well affect the
result; as the last entry in the above table illustrates, with an image
only 3 arc sec across, an error of only 1 arc sec will produce a
decidedly elliptical image. This effect can be minimised by making
exposures as near to the meridian as possible.

As a general guide, with a head in good adjustment, and good driving apparatus, with smooth differentials, or frequency control in the case of variable frequency drives, it ought to be possible to give an exposure in which the product of focal length in mm and the exposure in minutes is anything up to about 18,000 with little guiding correction, if any. According to the accuracy of setting of the head, nearness to the meridian and smoothness of control of drive, this figure can, of course, be considerably exceeded, although it must be remembered that we are only considering guiding problems. Sky brightness may well prove to be the limiting factor.

So far as the type of exposure that may be given, the simplest is to expose in the focal plane, which will record the double as two dark circular images on the film. If one wishes to make some measurements, then it is necessary first to determine the precise scale at the focal plane, and for this purpose the Pleiades are probably the best objects in the sky. They are bright, so that exposures may be short, and guiding problems are at a minimum, and their positions are known accurately. Failing this, photograph several well-known fixed doubles (see Appendix 1), and obtain the scale from the resultant exposures. If you use a Barlow lens be sure that you replace it in exactly the same place each time. If not, you will need to take a calibration exposure of a fixed double star at the beginning of each night's photography. Measurement of the exposures, either with a compound microscope with eyepiece micrometer, (a simple graticule is sufficient), or by projection with a lens of known, good linearity (probably an enlarging lens of the highest grade) will give the separation, provided that the centres of the images are estimated accurately. Each measurement should be made several times and the average taken.

If the exact effective focal length of the optical system in use is known, then the image scale may be determined from the formula:

$$s = 206265/f$$

where f = focal length in mm and s = scale at the focal plane in arc seconds per mm.

No reference is made in this section to the means of placing the film in the focal plane. Much has been written elsewhere, and the reader is referred to the bibliography at the end of this book (Sidgwick (1952), Rackham (1959)). However, the single lens reflex system, or some other arrangement that allows the observer to see the image about to be photographed has so much to recommend it that it may be considered almost an essential. This does not mean that good work cannot be done without such a system, but the ease of working means that much more work can be done. Suitable single lens reflex bodies may be obtained second-hand very reasonably, and the addition of a suitable lens at a later date will provide the observer with a general purpose camera.

The type of exposure that has been discussed so far is merely that of the images of the two components of the double, together with the images of any other stars in the field. To determine position angle, two courses are open. The first is the more accurate if one of the stars is bright enough to leave a trail with the telescope drive stopped. In this case, with the driven exposure completed, (the star having been placed towards the following side of the field), the exposure is interrupted for, say, 5 seconds, with a dark card over the aperture and the drive stopped. The card is then removed and the star allowed to trail out of the field.

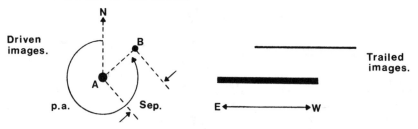

Fig 31.   Measurement of Position Angle.   (Trail method).

Unless the exposure is very close to the Pole, or the field of view very large, the result will be to all intents a straight line which will define the E-W direction. Make sure that the trail will not obscure either of the images, as may occur where the position angle is near 90 or 270 degrees, and also try to assess the effect of the trails that will be left by any other stars in the field.

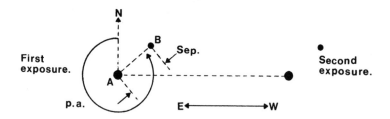

Fig 32. Measurement of position angle. (Double Image Method).

To get a brighter image, do not merely slow down the telescope drive. Unless this is perfectly in an E – W direction, the result will be to compound the movement of the telescope with the diurnal motion of the star and give a false E – W direction.

If neither star is sufficiently bright for the preceding method, after having made the first exposure, and with the exposure interrupted with the drive stopped, restart the drive and make a second exposure as far from the first as the field will allow. A line joining the same stars in the double exposure will define the E - W direction. This method is very dependent on having a telescope mounting that can be stopped and started precisely, and with absolutely no movement in N - S direction during stopping and starting, since this will give a completely wrong result.

With reference to guiding, it ought not to be necessary to correct in declination for exposures of the order of which we are speaking. Unless such corrections are made continuously the result will be painfully apparent. The answer lies in getting the equatorial head into really accurate alignment, and eliminating any flexing or movement between the camera and the guide instrument. It is preferable to make this guide instrument adjustable, so that it can be offset to guide on an adjacent bright star. This can be thrown out of focus and the resulting circular image kept carefully quartered on the crosswires of the guiding eyepiece, which in this manner of use require no illumination. It may be noted that with a guide instrument of 11-cm aperture a magnification of x40 is suitable when the camera in use is fitted with a telephoto lens of 400mm focal length, and of x225 when making exposures at the prime focus of a 216mm speculum of basic focal length 1,400mm used in conjuction with a x2 barlow lens. Stars down to magnitude 7 are sufficiently bright to be thrown sufficiently out of focus to be suitable for guiding.

(d) CONCLUSIONS

All astronomical photography is more or less experimental, and this applies more to the photography of double stars than to any other field. It is necessary to make test exposures, to determine the magnitude limits available with your equipment, the scale of the image and the effect of sky darkening. Remember that a Barlow lens will help in the last case with a reflector of short focal ratio. If your funds will run to it, and assuming that you are using a single lens reflex camera body, the use of the 'tele-extender' of x2 has the double advantage that it will be a highly corrected lens, (although being usually of 4 element construction will introduce a certain light loss), and that if used with the correct adaptors to suit the eyepiece focussing mount and the camera body, will always occupy the same position, thereby providing a constant scale.

In general, filters are not of great use in this type of work, but in one case the use of the correct filter can be invaluable. Increasing areas are being illuminated by sodium lighting and this constitutes a major factor in background darkening on exposures. However, except in the case of the high pressure type of lamp, (which has light of a pinkish tinge), almost all of the light is contained in a very narrow band of the spectrum in the yellow, (the 'D' lines). The use of neodymium filters (also called didymium filters), which are opaque to a narrow band containing these lines can eliminate this, but such filters are comparatively expensive and are fairly opaque to the remaining light, necessitating long exposures. A better alternative is to use a blue filter, such as the Kodak Wratten 44 or 44A. The latter is preferable, since it has a better transmission up to the cut-off point, which is just short of the 'D' lines, but is usually a special order item. Both of these filters are available in Gelatin, and are inexpensive. They must be handled carefully and not allowed to become damp or dewed up, but if they do suffer damage they are cheap to replace. Either the 44 or 44A will reject more than 99% of sodium lighting whilst exposures require increasing by about 1.7 for the 44A and around 2.2 for the somewhat denser 44. It will therefore be seen that there is an effective gain of not less than 4 magnitudes over the background if this is only due to sodium lighting.

The use of a blue filter alters the spectral response of the emulsion of course, and it is the experience of the writer, that either of the filters mentioned, use in conjunction with either HP4 or FP4 film will result in images being recorded in a similar manner to that which would obtain with a non-colour sensitive emulsion as used in the early days of photography, and the classic colour index applies sufficiently closely.

So far separation attainable has not been mentioned. With due precaution and a sufficient focal length it should be possible to record photographically two equal stars in the 'two magnitude above' threshold range which are of the order of 2 or 3 times the Dawe's limit for the aperture. The essential is to use a sufficiently large scale to minimise the effect of the enlargement of the image due to structure of the emulsion. As a limiting case, an example that can be quoted is the definite elongation into a pear-shaped image of a star with components of magnitude 4 and 8 separated by 70 arc seconds on a negative in which the scale was only 2.4mm per degree. This exposure was made with a quite ordinary telephoto lens of 135mm focal length and a linear aperture of 34mm on HP4 film.

Whilst photography cannot compete with the visual micrometer for absolute accuracy, it does have the advantage of providing a permanent record of the observation. There are a great number of double stars suitable for the camera, as a study of Webb's writings will reveal. Had Webb had the apparatus and materials that are available today he would have certainly tried his hand at photographing double stars, and it is hoped that the information in this chapter will prompt the reader to active work in this field.

7. BRIEF BIOGRAPHIES OF DOUBLE STAR OBSERVERS

In the first version of this Handbook a number of biographies of leading double star observers were included. The opportunity has been taken of including several major figures who were left out of the first edition. A list of the measurements made by each observer is also given, courtesy of Charles Worley of the United States Naval Observatory. An asterisk indicates that the observer is still active and the number represents the latest estimate of measurements made (April 1984). At the time of writing, the data for some of the 19th century observers has not been accessed for inclusion in the WDS catalogue but it seems clear that none of them will turn out to be major contributors. The number attributed to Burnham is an estimate only, and the observations by Otto Struve have not yet been fully assessed but are in excess of 10,000.

Observer	Observations	Observer	Observations
van den Bos W H	73940	Espin T E H	11630
Rabe W	36971	Struve F G	11330
van Biesbroeck G	35915	Schiaparelli G	10897
Worley C E*	>35000	Holden F	10218
Heintz W D*	>33000	Olivier C	10197
Aitken R G	26650	Dawson B H	9767
Voute J.G.E.G.	26126	Hussey W.J.	9563
Baize P.	24154	Bowyer W.	8898
Rossiter R.A.	23883	Walker R.L.*	8291
Burnham S.W.	22000	Muller P.*	8275
Couteau P.*	21000	Leavenworth F.	7354
Doolittle E.	20999	Innes R.T.A.	7126
Dembowski E.	20678	Siminov G.	6954
Finsen W.S.	15471	Duruy M.V.	6422
Doberck W.	14187	Knipe G.	6041
Fox P.	13749	Lewis T.	3928
Barton S.	12070	Secchi A.	3008
Jonckheere R.	12069	Milburn W.	2937

Robert Grant Aitken (1864 - 1951)

R G Aitken was born in Jackson, California on December 31, 1864 and was educated at Oakland High School. After graduating from Williams College in 1887, Aitken became an instructor in mathematics at Livermore College. Between 1891 and 1895 he was Professor of Mathematics at the University of the Pacific at San Jose in California. At this time he became Assistant Astronomer at Lick Observatory and his earliest work in the field of double star observation consisted of measuring, with the

12-inch refractor, a list of pairs selected by Professor E E Barnard.

After the work carried out by the Struves, it had generally been supposed that there were few new double stars left to be discovered, but this idea was soon dispelled by Burnham who was continually adding to his catalogues. Aitken had realised, however, that Burnham's discoveries had not been the result of a systematic search as had those of the Struves. He was therefore convinced that given the excellent observing conditions at Lick, the great resolving power of the 36-inch O.G. and the advantage of systematic work, a large number of systems could still be discovered. It was in July 1899 that Aitken and W J Hussey (who arrived in January 1896) combined forces and began to examine all the stars of the B.D. down to magnitude 9.0. (Hussey included those of magnitude 9.1) north of -22 . When Hussey left in 1905, Aitken continued alone, finishing in 1915.

In addition to his observational work, Aitken computed many orbits and in 1920, after the death of Doolittle, took over the supervision of the extended Burnham card index. This was used in the compilation of his great double star catalogue, the ADS, in 1932. It was in this year that Aitken was awarded the Gold Medal of the Royal Astronomical Society.

He was also the first President of Commission 26 of the IAU and when succeeded by Ejnar Hertzsprung in 1928, he was elected Honorary President. In 1930 he became Director of Lick Observatory and five years later Emeritus Astronomer and Director at Berkeley, where he retired and spent his remaining years.

In addition to double star work he enjoyed making measures of cometary positions and computing their orbits in addition to measuring the satellites of Mars, Jupiter, Saturn, Uranus and Neptune.

Paul Baize (1901 -   )

Dr Baize, after graduating as a medical practitioner in 1924 has worked as a specialist pediatrician during his long career. His astronomical work, although substantial even by professional standards, has been entirely amateur. He began serious double star observing with a 10.8 cm refractor in 1925, equipped with a micrometer of his own making. Between 1925 and 1932 he made some 3,834 measures of double stars which were published in 'Journal des Observateurs', some of them also being included in Aitken's 'General Catalogue of Double Stars' of 1932.

In 1933, Dr Baize began to use the 30.5-cm equatorial in the West Tower of Paris Observatory, with which he had completed 11,332 measures by 1949. From 1949 to 1971 he was able to work with the 38-cm equatorial in the East Tower and with this instrument he produced an additional 8,878 measures.

In addition to his observational work Dr Baize has calculated the orbital elements of some 200 binary stars and has published a number of articles in 'Annales d'Astrophysique', 'Bulletin Astronomique' of the Astronomical Society of France and 'Journal des Observateurs'. He has been a member of the Comite National Francais d'Astronomie since 1932, and served on Commission 26 of the IAU in 1936.

Sherburne Wesley Burnham (1838 - 1921)

S.W.Burnham was born in Thetford, Vermont on December 12, 1838. He began work as a shorthand reporter at first in New York and later with the Confederate Army in New Orleans. After the end of the Civil War, during which he first began to take an interest in astronomy, he continued in his profession and in 1892 became Clerk to the U.S. Circuit Court, a position which he held until 1910.

On a visit to London in 1861 Burnham purchased a 3-inch refractor which was designed more as a terrestrial than an astronomical telescope. In 1866 he settled down in Chicago, his home being just a few hundred yards from the Dearborn Observatory which had just been supplied with a new 18.5-inch refractor by Alvan G.Clark and Sons. At this time Burnham was changing telescopes regularly, never being satisfied with his current acquisition.

In 1869 he chanced to meet Alvan G.Clark in Chicago and this resulted in the ordering of the 6-inch refractor which was to win world renown for its owner. He stipulated that "its definition should be perfect and that it should do on double stars all that it was possible for a telescope of that aperture to do". Burnham himself was unable to explain why his interest should have focussed on double stars, but perhaps it was because he had amongst his small library a copy of Webb's 'Celestial Objects for Common Telescopes'. Burnham began his work by looking for new double stars, and found his first new pair, BU 40 on April 27, 1870. When he had accrued a list of 81 probably new pairs he sent it off to the Monthly Notices of the R.A.S. This was followed a year later by two further lists, although at this time Burnham did not have a micrometer. Subsequent contact with the great Italian observer Dembowski resulted in the latter supplying measures of Burnham's early pairs.

In 1874 Burnham was able to use the 9.4-inch refractor of the Dartmouth College Observatory on 10 nights whilst spending a summer vacation in New Hampshire. On this trip he also observed with the great 26-inch refractor at Washington on one night and then added 14 pairs to his growing list. From then on, Burnham was able to use many of the large American telescopes, culminating in the 36-inch at Lick and the 40-inch at Yerkes. Apart from the period 1888 - 1892 when he was officially on the staff of Lick Observatory, he remained an amateur observer, following his profession during the day and at weekends making the long trip out to Yerkes.

Early in his career, the lack of really useful astronomical literature on double stars prompted him to make notes at every opportunity of all the measures of the known pairs - a task which later expanded to become the General Catalogue of Double Stars published in two volumes in 1906. This magnificent work contains a valuable collection of 10,000 measures of the more neglected doubles as well as generous measures of the binaries known at that time.

He continued to observe until 1913 and during his long career discovered 1,274 double stars, many of which are in orbital motion, and some of which are amongst the binaries of shortest known period. It is a tribute to Burnham's superb eyesight that some of his most difficult discoveries were first suspected with the 6-inch refractor and later confirmed with a larger telescope in which they were still difficult objects.

Burnham's fundamental contribution to astronomy did not go unnoticed and in 1894 he received the Gold Medal of the Royal Astronomical Society, followed ten years later by the Lalande Prize of the Paris Academy of Sciences. He also received honorary degrees from Yale and Northwestern Universities.

Paul Couteau (1923 -   )

Couteau was born in La Roche sur Yon in the Vendee in France. His mother stimulated an early interest in astronomy which was reinforced by the works of Flammarion and Father Moreux. By the age of 11 he had already decided that his vocation lay in astronomy.

He started his astronomical career in earnest in 1949 at the Astrophysical Institute in Paris, completing a doctoral thesis on white dwarfs. Andre Danjon, who was looking for someone interested in visual binaries, persuaded Couteau to go to Nice in 1951. From 1951 to 1967 observations of visual binaries were made with the 38-cm refractor resulting in 12,000 measurements which appeared in 'Journal des Observateurs'. In 1961, at the invitation of George van Biesbroeck, Couteau went to Yerkes Observatory and spent 5 months using the 40-inch refractor and also the 36-inch refractor at Lick Observatory.

At this time he was also able to negotiate the refurbishment of the 76-cm refractor at Nice which had been inactive since 1926. The telescope was restored and fully active again by May 1979. A 50-cm refractor replaced the 38-cm telescope and it was with this instrument that Couteau has discovered most of his pairs. Since 1965 he has systematically searched the BD stars in the zone +17 to +53 (Paul Muller covering the region between +53 to +90). Of the 170,000 stars in this band, 102,000 have been observed resulting in the discovery of 2,200 pairs by 1984. Half of these are separated by less than 1 arc second and a third are closer than 0.5 arc second. Many of these pairs contain red dwarfs and a number of the discoveries include companions to bright stars such as theta CrB and 39 Com.

Couteau intends to continue this survey and in the next few years will calculate the first orbits for some of the rapid binaries discovered during the course of the work.

William Rutter Dawes (1799 -1868)

A qualified medical practitioner and an Independent Congregational Minister, Dawes had been interested in astronomy from his youth. His first congregation was at Ormskirk in Lancashire and here in 1830 he set up his first telescope, a 3.8-inch Dolland refractor, and in the same year was elected a Fellow of the Royal Astronomical Society. Never in good health, Dawes was forced to resign his position, and in 1839 he moved to St John's Wood, London and took charge of the Observatory owned by Mr Bishop near Regents Park. He married for the second time in 1842 and moved to Camden Lodge in Cranbrook, Kent where he erected an observatory containing a Merz refractor of 8.5 feet focal length and 6 inches aperture. His health continued to cause him concern and he was forced to move to Torquay for a time in order to recuperate. His health improved and in 1850 he moved to Wateringbury near Maidstone and finally, in 1857, to Hopefield, Haddenham, Buckinghamshire where he lived for the remainder of his life.

The bulk of his observations are to be found in the 'Catalogue of Micrometrical Measures of Double Stars' forming part of Vol 35 of the Transactions of the Astronomical Society of London (R.A.S.), a series of measures of 121 pairs in Vol 8 of the R.A.S. Memoirs and the Ormskirk observations which appear in Vol 19 of the R.A.S. Memoirs.

Baron Ercole Dembowski (1812 - 1881)

Ercole Dembowski was born in Milan on January 12th 1812. His father, General Giovanni Dembowski came from a noble Polish family and was a member of the Italian Royal Army founded at the beginning of the 19th century by Napoleon I. Orphaned at the age of 13, Dembowski entered the Autrian Navy College in Venice. After an eventful career in which he distinguished himself, Dembowski retired from the Navy in 1843 probably on health grounds (he suffered frequent attacks of gout). He went to live at Naples and it was here that he met Antonio Nobile, an astronomer at Capodimonte Observatory. Nobile was undoubtedly a guiding influence and may have been responsible for Dembowski's purchase of the 5-inch Plossl dialyte with which he commenced his double star measurements. This instrument was set up at San Giorgio a Cremano in the Naples hinterland and observations commenced at the end of 1851.

In 1855 he published his first list; accurate measurements of 127
double and triple stars taken from F.G.W.Struve's Dorpat Catalogue.
Dembowski produced further revisions of the Dorpat Catalogue in 1860,
1864 and 1866. By the end of 1858 Dembowski had move to Gallarate
(between Milan and Varese) and it was here that he set up his 7-inch
Merz refractor. With this instrument he made a complete and thorough
revision of the Dorpat Catalogue, the final results being published,
after his death, in Rome in 1883 in the two volumes called "Misure
Micrometrice di Stelle Doppie e Multiple". In 1879 Dembowski moved from
Gallarate to a small house at Monte near Lake Maggiore. His attacks of
gout became more frequent and intense, and although he set up his
instruments and an observatory he was unable to use them and died on
January 19th 1881.

Dembowski received the Gold Medal of the R.A.S. in 1874 for his
double-star work which, from the beginning of his astronomical career
was celebrated for its thoroughness and accuracy.

Eric Doolittle (1869 - 1920)

The son of a Professor of Mathematics and Astronomy at Lehigh
University Pennsylvania, Eric Doolittle was born on July 26th, 1869 in
Ontario, Indiana. After schooling in Bethelehem, Pennsylvania he went
on to attend Lehigh University, graduating as a civil engineer in 1891.
Following Aitken and Hussey, he became instructor in mathematics at
Lehigh and the University of Iowa, and in 1894 commenced postgraduate
study at the University of Chicago. During this period of two years, he
did research on the "Secular Variations of the Orbits of the Four Inner
Planets" which was published as a Memoir in 1912.

In 1896 Doolittle returned to the University of Pennsylvania to
become instructor in Mathematics and in addition, assistant to his
father Charles, who was Director of the newly founded Flower
Observatory.   The main instrument was a fine 18-inch Brashear refractor
of 30 feet focal length. For most of the rest of his life, Doolittle
engaged in double star measurement, and between 1901 and 1914 published
four large volumes of measures. The first was "Measures of 900 Double
and Multiple Stars" followed by "Measures of 1,066 Double and Multiple
Stars" in 1905, "Catalogue and Re-measurement of the 648 Hough Double
Stars" in 1907 and "Measures of 1,954 Double Stars" in 1914. In fact
several thousand measures were made after 1914 but remained unpublished
in Doolittle's lifetime.

In 1913 S.W.Burnham, on his retirement, entrusted the additional
data for an extension of his General Catalogue (1906) to Doolittle, who
kept methodical full records of all the published measures of double
stars.   Doolittle did not live to see the completion of the work, which

was carried on by his friend Robert Aitken, but died on September 21st, 1920.

Maurice Victor Duruy (1894 - 1984)

Maurice Duruy, a qualified mining engineer of the Ecole Polytechnique and School of Mines in Paris, graduated from the University of Nancy. His whole career was spent working for the French Government as an Engineer and then as an Inspector of Security in Mines which involved travelling abroad, notably to Britain and South Africa. At the same time he took a teaching post in Applied Mechanics at the Mining Institute of the University of Nancy, training future mining engineers. He later became Director of the Institute and went on to become Administrator of three Mining Schools, retiring in 1965.

His astronomical career had started much earlier. The first visual observations date from 1907 and show Saturn below Pegasus where it was to return in 1937 and 1966. In 1910, at the age of 16 he acquired his first telescope, a 3-inch refractor and the first observing notes were made. These records describe the passage of the Earth through the tail of Halley's Comet on May 18, 1910 and the total eclipse of the Sun visible from Paris on April 17, 1912.

The second main period in his career started in 1934 when he obtained an 18-cm objective. The work carried out with it included drawings of Mars, Jupiter and Saturn as well as observations of double and variable stars and was published in Journal des Observateurs. This encouraged Duruy to order a larger refractor from Andre Couder which was completed in 1936. Observations with the new 27.5-cm objective continued until the war when the observatory was destroyed. Fortunately the lens was saved but could not be redeployed because of its long focal length. In June 1941 Duruy went to Lyons on business and was able to use the 16.2-cm and 32.5-cm refractors there until 1946. There followed a long period when no observing was possible but in 1962 he set up a 26-cm reflector in the Montlhery region near Paris and a 40-cm reflector was added in 1964 carrying out a program of variable and double star observing.

In 1966 Duruy retured to Central France and a 60-cm equatorial was added to his Observatory. The double star work continued until about 1976 and then reluctantly discontinued because the seeing was too poor. The majority of measures in the Catalogue Section of this Handbook are due to Maurice Duruy whose diffraction grating micrometer is currently being used by amateur observers in both Britain and France.

Thomas Henry Espinall Compton Espin (1858 - 1934)

Educated at Haileybury and Exeter College, Oxford, Espin took Holy Orders, and from 1888 until his death was Vicar of Tow Law in County Durham. He became interested in astronomy after seeing Coggia's Comet in 1874, and at Oxford he was allowed to use the 13-inch De la Rue telescope.

The first part of the work for which he became well-known was his observation and cataloguing of red stars, some 3,800 of which he had listed between 1885 and 1899.

In 1900 Espin started observing double stars with a 17-inch Calver reflector - the first observer to use a reflector for this type of work since the Herschels. Most of his discoveries were confined to comparatively wide pairs (5 to 10 arc seconds separation) and these were found whilst re-examining the stars of the B.D. Catalogue. The total number of discoveries which he made, according to his own numbering was 2,575.

One observation of a different kind was his discovery of Nova Lacertae on Dec 30, 1910.

Espin was very friendly with Webb and assisted him with producing some of the earlier editions of 'Celestial Objects'. After Webb's death, it was Espin who published the 5th and 6th editions of this famous handbook.

In 1914 Espin acquired a 24-inch Calver reflector and from that date the 17-inch was used by W Milburn, Espin's assistant and pupil.

William Stephen Finsen (1905 - 1979)

Although born in Johannesburg, Finsen was of Icelandic descent, being the nephew of Niels R.Finsen winner of the 1903 Nobel Prize for Medicine and founder of the Finsen Institute in Copenhagen.

His early years were spent in Denmark , but in 1912 he returned to South Africa, studying at the King Edward VII School in Johannesburg. Finsen went on to obtain a B.Sc. at the University of South Africa in 1930. Further degrees of B.Sc. Honours and M.Sc. were awarded in 1936 and 1937 by the University of the Witwatersrand and in 1951 he received a D.Sc. from the University of Cape Town.

Finsen assisted van den Bos in the Union Observatory survey of southern double stars. Later, he specialised in observational and theoretical work on double stars, but was for some years in charge of the Time Department of the Observatory. In 1933 he began tests with the Anderson double star interferometer and in 1950, designed and constructed an eyepiece interferometer for the 26.5-inch refractor. With this instrument more than 13,000 examinations of 8,117 stars between declinations -75 and +20 were made. As a result 73 new pairs were found, 11 of which have orbital periods ranging from 21 years down to 2.65 years. In addition 6,000 measures of pairs too close for the micrometer were made.

Finsen also discovered the "splitting" of Nova Pictoris in 1928, studied the rotation of Eros visually in 1931 and during the oppositions of Mars in 1954 and 1956 took many fine photographs which were extensively reproduced in journals and books.

He became Assistant Director in 1941, Director in 1957 and retired in 1965 but continued to carry out private research after that time. He was the author of some 135 papers and reports including three editions of a catalogue of visual binary star orbits (the last with Charles Worley of U.S.N.O. in 1970).

Wulff Dieter Heintz (1930 -   )

Heintz was born in Würzberg in West Germany and graduated from Munich University and Munich Technological University. He went on to carry out astronomical research in Australia and West Germany.

His work on double stars began in 1954 and at the time of writing (April, 1984) he had accumulated more than 33,000 double star observations. In addition he has computed more than 300 orbits which is a world record, and has discovered 250 new pairs.

In 1968 Dr Heintz was appointed Professor of Astronomy at Swarthmore College in Pennsylvania, U.S.A. where he is still based. His publications include 120 research papers which reflect his interest in multiple systems, combined astrometric/spectroscopic and visual systems, parallaxes and mass ratios and low mass objects. In 1978 he wrote 'Double Stars', a monograph covering all aspects of double star astronomy. Together with Charles Worley he is responsible for a new Catalogue of visual binary orbits which is currently in press.

Sir Frederick William Herschel (1738 - 1822)

As in other branches of astronomy, in double star observation, William Herschel was a magnificent pioneer. His first observations, of close unequal pairs, were designed to obtain a value for stellar parallax and, beginning in 1779, he soon produced a list of 269 pairs, only 42 of which had previously been observed as double. Eventually, Herschel, after making numerous accurate measurements of distance and position angle, was forced to the conclusion that the changes he detected were due not to parallactic shift but to actual orbital movement of the pairs.

This extremely important conclusion was revealed in his Phil. Tran. paper of 1803, and this date represents the real beginning of double- star astronomy. It should be remembered, too, that at the time, this evidence of true binary orbital motion showed that the principles of Newtonian gravitational theory could be extended well beyond the solar system, and strongly supported the view that this was a truly universal law.

In his double star measurements, as in all his work, William Herschel displayed his genius: where equipment and instruments, as he found them, were inadequate for the task in hand, he improved them and used them with consummate skill; when the evidence his observations revealed was at variance with the original hypothesis he accepted it without question, and immediately drew the correct conclusion and revealed a new and vitally important aspect of the heavens.

Sir John Herschel (1792 - 1871)

When John Herschel was persuaded by his father to give up his law studies and devote himself to astronomy, he began his work in 1816 on purely double-star observations. His object was to re-measure some 364 of his father's discoveries in order to accrue more evidence in support of the binary orbital motion which had been adduced earlier.

John Herschel then began a fruitful collaboration with James South (later Sir James South) at Southwark which resulted in the publication of a catalogue of 380 new pairs. For this work, Herschel and South were jointly awarded the Gold Medal of the R.A.S. in 1826.

John Herschel's expedition to the Cape of Good Hope (1834 - 1838) was one of the most fruitful in the history of astronomy and although in these southern observations, double stars were only of "subordinate interest", he nevertheless managed to catalogue some 1,202 pairs.

After his return from the Cape, he devoted his time to publishing the results of his visit, which occupied him until 1847. He made few astronomical observations after this time but his pioneer observations with South were of great interest in double-star astronomy.

William Joseph Hussey (1862 -1926)

Hussey graduated at Ann Arbor University in 1889. Between 1889 and 1891, he was, like Aitken, an instructor in mathematics, and the following year became Assistant Director of the Detroit Observatory of the University of Michigan, unitl Professor Asaph Hall took up his appointment as Director.

Hussey then went on to the Leland Stanford Junior University at
Palo Alto where he became Professor of Astronomy. Whilst here he would
make frequent visits to Lick, and in 1896 joined the staff as
Astronomer. In the years 1898 and 1899 he re-observed all of the
Poulkova stars of Otto Struve, the results appearing in the Publications
of the Lick Observatory, Vol V, 1901. This very valuable work also
contains a complete collection of every other measure published of these
pairs, together with their respective references.

During his co-operative program with Aitken he found 1,327 pairs in
six years, for which he was awarded the Lalande Gold Medal of the Paris
Academy of Sciences.

In 1905 he returned to Ann Arbor to become Professor of Astronomy
and Director of the Detroit Observatory, and during this time designed a
37.5-inch reflector which was subsequently built almost entirely in the
workshops of the University. In 1911 he became Director of the
Observatory of the University of La Plata in Argentina whilst retaining
his post at Ann Arbor. He made four trips out to Argentina, and using
the 17-inch refractor there added another 323 pairs to his catalogue of
discoveries.

Hussey's great ambition was to see the establishment of an
observatory in the Southern Hemisphere for the discovery and measurement
of double stars. His early college friendship with R.P. Lamont led to
the financial support of the latter for a 24-inch refractor. The
interruption of the war delayed the delivery of the blanks for the
objective but in 1923 two 27-inch blanks were obtained from Jena. In
the same year Hussey journeyed to Bloemfontein to look for a suitable
site for a new observatory. In October 1926 while in London on his way
to South Africa to supervise the erection of the telescope, he died
suddenly.

Although, tragically, he did not live to see the completion of the
project, the telescope was soon in working order under the supervision
of Professor R.A.Rossiter, and it has since fully justified Hussey's
expectations.

Robert Thorburn Ayton Innes (1861 - 1933)

Innes was born in Edinburgh and went to school in Dublin, but all
his astronomical work was carried out in the southern hemisphere.
Beginning purely as an amateur, he soon became well known in Australia
for his discovery and measurement of double stars, besides gaining a
reputation for his ability in mathematical astronomy, including
celestial mechanics.

In 1896 he moved to South Africa where he became secretary to Sir David Gill at the Cape Observatory. Here he used the 7-inch and 18-inch equatorials for the observation of both double and variable stars and in 1899 compiled a "Reference Catalogue of Southern Double Stars".

In 1903 Innes became Director of the Transvaal Observatory at Johannesburg: here, in addition to photographic work with the twin 6-inch and 7-inch Franklin-Adams refractors, he made a thorough and systematic survey of the southern skies with the 26.5-inch refractor for the discovery of new double stars. Together with B.H.Dawson of La Plata Observatory and W.H. van den Bos, Innes compiled and published a "Southern Double Star Catologue" in 1927. In this important work, Innes contributed 1,613 new pairs, van den Bos more than 2,000 and Finsen more than 300.

R.T.A. Innes made many other contributions to astronomy, including the confirmation (from a reduction of all known transits of Mercury) that the rotation of the Earth is not constant, and that Proxima Centauri is our nearest stellar neighbour.

Robert Jonckheere (1889 -1974)

Jonckheere began his long career as a double-star observer in 1905 using a 3-inch refractor. This instrument was followed by a 4-inch and 5-inch, and in 1907, by a 9-inch equatorial refractor fitted with a micrometer. This work was carried out at a private observatory on the roof of a house in Roubaix but soon Jonckheere decided that he needed more formal instruction in astronomy and he took a course at Strasbourg Observatory where he used a 6-inch equatorial. With this instrument he discovered 40 new pairs which were included in a list he published in the Bulletin Astronomique in December 1908.

Jonckheere now set about the task of setting up a Belgian Observatory and this was successfully established at Hem near Lille and eventually was attached to Lille University. Double-star observation was a major program at Lille, but at the beginning of World War I when the country was over-run Jonckheere took refuge in England. Here, he was able to use the 28-inch refractor at Greenwich Observatory and by the end of 1916 he had compiled a catalogue.

In 1919, Jonckheere was able to return to Lille Observatory to continue his double-star work without further interruption. In 1930 he retired and moved to central France: his retirement, however, was only nominal, for during the next 30 years, he was able to use various instruments at the Observatories of Marseilles, Nice, Toulouse and Strasbourg.

Eventually, in 1962 he published his major work, the "General Catalogue" which contains, among other observations, no less than 3,355 new double and multiple stars discovered by him since the beginning of his career in 1906.

Although his life-long interest lay in double-star observation Jonckheere made many observations of planetary nebulae, red stars and novae. His published papers amount to more than 40 and represent the devotion to astronomy of a long and fruitful life. He died on June 24th, 1974.

Thomas Lewis (1856 - 1927)

Lewis joined the staff of the Royal Observatory early in 1881. Initially his work involved the reduction of zenith distance observations made with the Transit Circle (8.1-inch aperture, focal length = 11 feet 7 inches) but later in 1881 became Superintendent of the Time Department, a post which he occupied until his retirement in 1917.

Lewis spent several years observing with the Transit Circle, the altazimuth (3.75-inch aperture for lunar observations) and the Small Equatorial. In 1893 he began to measure double stars with the Great Equatorial, a refractor with a 12.8-inch Merz object glass of 17 foot 10 inches focal length. The new 28-inch refractor was delivered in the same year, and Lewis spent most of his observing hours using this telescope for double star measures.

He concentrated on the pairs of F.G.W. Struve and is most remembered for his great volume "Measures of the Double Stars contained in the Mensurae Micrometricae of F.G.W. Struve" which was published in 1906. This earned him the Lalande prize of the Paris Academy of Sciences the following year.

He retired in September 1917 and lived at Wivenhoe in Essex until his death in June 1927.

Paul Muller (1910 -   )

Born in 1910, Paul Muller joined the Observatory of Strasbourg in 1931. His interest in double stars began after he had constructed the double image micrometer with which his name is now associated. He has used this micrometer on many telescopes from 1937 to the present day (with the exception of the war years) including the 16, 21 and 49-cm telescopes at Strasbourg, the 24 and 83-cm refractors at Paris-Meudon and the 50-cm refractor at Nice. In addition it has also been taken to Pic-du-Midi (60-cm refractor) and to the great refractor at Lick (91-cm). Equipped with a differential photometer the micrometer has furnished Dr Muller with accurate measurements of m and differences in colour for pairs as close as 0".5 and these remain the only existing determinations.

His total of measures amount to more than 11,000 of which 5,500 were made at Strasbourg between 1937 and 1956, 1,500 at Paris-Meudon (1956 - 1974) and a further 4,500 at Nice from 1974 onwards. Photometric measurements have been made on 400 pairs whilst colours have been determined for about 100.

Dr Muller has calculated 90 orbits and in 1953 published the first ephemeris catalogue, followed by a supplement in 1954. The second and third editions were produced in conjunction with G Meyer in 1964 and 1970 and the fourth catalogue (with positions every year from 1978-1988) was published with Paul Couteau in 1979.

In 1969 Dr Muller started to survey the stars in the declination zone +52 to +90 and this has complemented the survey being carried out by Couteau at Nice. It is now about 95% complete and has yielded about 680 new pairs which have a mean separation of 0".5.

Paul Muller has been President of Commission 26 (Double Stars) of the I.A.U. on two occasions; from 1952 to 1958 and again from 1976 to 1979. In 1954 he founded the Information Circulars of this Commission and was responsible for the appearance of this bulletin three times a year for 30 years, being succeeded in November 1983 by Paul Couteau.

Richard Alfred Rossiter (1886 - 1977)

One of the great practitioners of Southern Hemisphere double-star astronomy, Rossiter was born in Oswego, New York State on December 19th, 1886. He studied at Wesleyan University and graduated in 1914, going on to teach mathematics at Genesee Wesleyan Seminary for 5 years. At the University of Michigan he did research in stellar spectroscopy and was the first to demonstrate the existence of stellar rotation in the star Beta Lyrae. The head of the Astronomy Department at that time was W.J. Hussey who saw Rossiter as a key figure in his scheme to set up a Southern observing station.

In 1926 Rossiter and his family accompanied Professor and Mrs Hussey to London en route to Bloemfontein. Tragically Hussey died unexpectedly in London, and the Rossiters continued on to South Africa. The task of choosing a site and superintending the erection of the telescope now fell fully on Rossiter. With the financial help of the Bloemfontein City Council the Observatory was erected, and Rossiter was installed in rent-free accommodation. By April 1928 the telescope was ready to start work. Assistance had arrived several months previously in the shape of H.F. Donner and M.K. Jessup, both graduates in electrical engineering from the University of Michigan. By May 1928, Rossiter with Donner and Jessup had started observing, and this program was continued until the end of 1952, the last 19 years being carried out by Rossiter alone.

The result was 7,368 pairs of which 5,534 were discovered by Rossiter, a record which has not been approached since, let alone equalled. After retirement, Rossiter moved to Pietermaritzburg returning to Bloemfontein again in 1975 where he died on January 26th, 1977.

Father Angelo Secchi (1818 - 1878)

Although best-known for his pioneer study of stellar spectra and their classification into four types, Secchi made a significant contribution to double-star work. Using the 9.6-inch Merz refractor of the Observatory of the Collegio Romano (where he was Director), Secchi observed double stars between 1854 and 1859, publishing the results in his "Catalogo do 1,321 Stelle Doppie..." of 1860. In this work, Secchi also attempted a statistical analysis of the proportion of binary stars to the total in F.G.W. Struve's "Mensurae Micrometricae" and related to the degree of separation of the pairs. The Lick Index of Double Stars (IDS) lists only four pairs against Secchi.

Admiral William Henry Smyth (1788 - 1865)

The son of an American loyalist emigre, he started his career in the Royal Navy as a boy. He obtained a commission from the lower deck and commanded a brigantine in the Mediterranean during the Napoleonic wars.

Smyth owes the intense interest in astronomy of his later years to a meeting with Piazzi in 1817 at Palermo Observatory. His first astronomical telescope was a fine 5.9-inch refractor by Tulley which he set up in his small observatory at Bedford in 1830. He took a special interest in double-star observation. By 1839 he had catalogued many celestial objects, including some 350 double and multiple stars, some of his binaries being measured annually. After this date Smyth sold his equipment which was installed in an observatory belonging to a Dr. Lee-Smith at Hartwell near Aylesbury.

Smyth retained access to the observatory at Hartwell and by 1843 had made measures, accurate for his day, of some 680 pairs. In the following year 1844, Smyth published his "Cycle of Celestial Objects", the work for which he is generally remembered and for which he was awarded the Gold Medal of the R.A.S. in 1845. In 1860 he published another book, "Speculum Hartwellianum", which, although not as popular as his "Cycle", contains a large number of double-star measures.

Sir James South (1785 - 1867)

South was a qualified surgeon who became interested in astronomy and, after acquiring a fortune by marriage, spent his whole time and considerable sums of money on his chosen hobby. He began double-star observations with a 5-inch refractor at his observatory in Blackman Street, Borough, London. He became a founder member of the newly-formed Astronomical Society of London and through his influence obtained Royal recognition of the Society.

His friendship ith John Herschel led to their collaboration in re-measuring William Herschel's doubles, and their joint catalogue of 380 pairs was presented to the Royal Society in 1824.

Immediately after this, South moved to Passy, near Paris where he began a further series of double-star measures, but by 1826 he had returned to England, establishing a very well-equipped observatory at Campden Hill, Kensington. Here, South had ideas of making a comprehensive double-star survey and he spent a great deal of money in obtaining a 11.75-inch Cauchoix objective and getting it mounted by Troughton. He soon became dissatisfied with the telescope and refused to pay Troughton's bill. Many law-suits followed, much of the trouble being due to South's intemperate behaviour - and he abandoned his double-star ambitions and destroyed his equipment. The Cauchoix objective was saved however, and eventually found its way to Dunsink Observatory where it is still in use.

Friedrich Georg Wilhelm Struve (1793 - 1864)

F.G.W. Struve was one of the greatest double-star observers, and, after the Herschels, a pioneer in the field. He was born near Hamburg in Altona on April 15th, 1793. In 1808 he went to the University of Dorpat where he studied philology with his older brother Karl. He also studied mathematics and in 1811 turned his interest to astronomy, receiving a doctorate two years later for a thesis in which he determined the latitude and longitude of the Observatory at Dorpat. He started measuring double stars with a small refractor and the transit instrument which resulted in the publication in 1822 of his "Catalogus 795 Stellarum Duplicium".

In 1824 Struve obtained a superb telescope, a 9.6-inch Fraunhofer refractor, then the largest in the world, equipped with an equatorial mounting and driving clock. With this instrument he began his monumental survey of double stars down to declination -15 . In a little over two years, Struve, with his assistants, Preuss and Knorre, completed no less than 10,448 measures of some 3,112 pairs and multiple stars of which 2,343 were new discoveries.

The results of this great work were published in 1837 as "Mensurae Micrometricae Stellarum duplicum et multiplicum" a catalogue which was to prove the foundation for many subsequent observers to build upon.

In 1839 Struve became Director of the newly-established Poulkova Observatory where the principal instruments were a 15-inch refractor and a 7.6-inch heliometer. The main programme consisted of a comprehensive general survey of Northern Hemisphere stars down to magnitude 7 and a positional survey of equatorial stars. In this work he was assisted by his son Otto.

In 1852 Struve published the accurate meridian positions of each of the primary stars in his Catalogue and also many single stars.

Ill health forced him to turn over the running of the Observatory to his son, Otto and he died on November 23rd, 1864 having retired to the estate which the Tsar had granted him in gratitude for his astronomical work.

Otto Wilhelm Struve (1819 - 1905)

Otto Struve was born on May 7th 1819 at Dorpat and at the age of 18 he became assistant to his father in double-star work at the observatory whilst still a student at the University. After taking a degree, Struve along with C A F Peters was appointed to the post of Assistant Astronomer at Poulkova. His initial work involved the determination of the constant of precession and the proper motion of the solar system which eventually led to the award of the Gold Medal of the R.A.S., an honour which was also given to his father and his son, Herman. In 1862 he succeeded his father as Director at Poulkova and dedicated himself to double stars and fundamental astronomy. One of his major projects was the Zone Catalogue of the Astronomische Gesellschaft (A.G.). His double star work included the discovery of 547 pairs with the 15-inch refractor and included amongst them delta Equulei which, with a period of 5.70 years, is even today surpassed in shortness of period by only 2 or 3 stars. He was very interested in the effect of personal equation on observations of double stars and undertook a major investigation in this field. He himself had an unusually large personal equation, but by numerous experiments with artificial double stars was able to make satisfactory corrections to his measures.

He retired from the post of Director at Poulkova in 1889 and spent his remaining years at St Petersburg (now Leningrad) and Karlsruhe where he died on January 14th, 1905.

Georges Achille van Biesbroeck (1880 - 1974)

Among double-star observers, George van Biesbroeck must be considered as one of the greatest. He was an active observer for more than 70 years and the major part of his work was devoted to double-star astronomy. Although he started his working life as an engineer, graduating from the University of Ghent in 1902, he soon transferred his energies to astronomy, beginning as a volunteer observer at the Belgian Royal Observatory at Uccle. Using a 15-inch refractor, his careful micrometer measurements of close doubles earned him immediate recognition.

In 1906 he obtained a Fellowship at Heidelburg University and continued his double-star measures with the 12-inch refractor until 1908, when he returned to Uccle. Like many European astronomers, van Biesbroeck found life and work greatly hampered by World War I but in 1915 he was fortunate in obtaining a Visiting Fellowship at Yerkes Observatory and in the following year he and his family emigrated to Wisconsin.

At Yerkes he found in the famous 40-inch refractor an ideal instrument for the study of doubles that were both close and faint, and in his first programme he re-observed most of the 1,200 or so doubles which W.J. Hussey had discovered earlier at Lick Observatory. As might be expected, many of these close pairs showed fairly rapid change since Hussey's time, and van Biesbroeck was able to compute reliable orbits for many of them.

During the mid-1930's van Biesbroeck took part in the engineering work for the new 82-inch reflector at McDonald Observatory and after its completion soon showed that a good reflecting telescope was just as effective as a refractor for double-star measures.

Although he discovered some new doubles during his long career, van Biesbroeck concentrated his attention on the continuing observation and precise measurement of close doubles which were already known, thus providing reliable data from which orbital elements could be obtained.

In 1945, van Biesbroeck, now aged 65, officially 'retired' but in fact he continued observing: he took part in eclipse expeditions to Brazil in 1947 and the Sudan in 1954, and in 1964 worked with the large reflectors of Kitt Peak and Steward Observatories.

Besides his outstanding double-star work he made many observations of comets, minor planets (two of the former and one of the latter bear his name) and other objects. One of the interests linked to his double-star work was the search for companions to stars of large proper motion. In 1944 he discovered a faint companion to BD +4 4048. 'Van Biesbroeck's Star' as it is now called, has an absolute magnitude of +19 and is still the least luminous star known.

Van Biesbroeck died on February 23, 1974:   he   lived   a   long   and
fruitful life during which his 35,915 double-star measures of the
highest quality have put him amongst the foremost double star observers
of all time.

Willem Hendrik van den Bos (1896 - 1974)

Dr. van den Bos was born in Rotterdam on September 25th, 1896. He
was attracted to astronomy and in particular double stars at an early
age. In 1913 he commenced study at the University of Leiden and whilst
there was taught by such eminent men as Hertzsprung and de Sitter. In
1925 van den Bos received his doctorate in Physics and Mathematics from
Leiden, and in August of that year arrived at the Union (later Republic)
Observatory at Johannesburg in South Africa as a guest observer.   He
played a major part in the systematic search for new double stars in the
Southern Hemisphere, which continued the work of Aitken and Hussey at
Lick.

In 1930 van den Bos joined the staff of the Union Observatory and
remained there until his retirement in 1956. However he continued his
researches in a private capacity until ill-health forced him to stop in
1966, at which point he had made nearly 74,000 visual measures,
discovered some 2,900 new pairs and computed 150 orbits. In addition to
the 26.5-inch and 9-inch refractors, Dr van den Bos used the 27-inch at
the Lamont Hussey Observatory, the 24-inch and 14-inch at Bosscha, Java,
the 36-inch at Lick, the 40-inch at Yerkes and the 10.5-inch at Leiden
(all refractors) as well as the 36-inch and 82-inch reflectors at the
McDonald Observatory in Texas.

He was a visual observer of great skill and could make accurate
measures with amazing rapidity, sometimes completing as many as twenty
in an hour of favourable viewing conditions.   This great double-star
observer died on March 30th, 1974.

Joan George Erardus Gijsbertus Voute (1879 - 1963)

Voute was born in Madioen, Java on June 7th, 1879 and was educated
in Holland, graduating in civil engineering at Delft. In 1908 he
started work at Leiden Observatory having taken an interest in astronomy
at Delft and in his first year produced a double-star orbit which was
published in the Monthly Notices of the R.A.S.

He realised that the future of double star astronomy lay in opening
up the southern skies as the large American telescopes had done for the
North. J.C.Kapteyn helped him to obtain a post at the Cape Observatory
in South Africa where he worked mainly on double stars and parallaxes.

On returning to Java in 1919 Voute, along with his wealthy friends K.A.R. Bosscha and R.A. Kerkhoven and others, set up the Nederlandsch Indische Sterrnkundige Vereeniging with the express intent of setting up and maintaining an astronomical observatory in Java. On his appointment as Director, Voute chose a site at Lembang located on the side of the Tangkoebuu Prahoe volcano at an altitude of 1300 metres. A double Zeiss refractor of 24-inch aperture was set up mainly due to the generosity of Bosscha.

Voute made many measures of double stars at Lembang, and continued his researches in Australia after the Second World War during which he suffered for a time as a Japanese prisoner-of-war. Towards the end of his life he returned to Holland and he died in The Hague on August 20th 1963.

His total of 26,126 measures rank him amongst the most prolific observers of all time and his concentration on close and difficult pairs placed him, according to Aitken, amongst the very front rank.

Charles E Worley (1935 -   )

Worley began double-star observations in 1954 at Lick Observatory and whilst attending university continued until 1961. He then joined the staff of the United States Naval Observatory where he has remained to this day. Working mostly with the 26-inch Clark refractor at Washington, he has also used the 36-inch and 60-inch reflectors at Cerro Tololo Interamerican Observatory in Chile.

Since 1965 Dr Worley has been in charge of the data base of double-star observations which has now grown to a total of more than 400,000 observations of 73,609 pairs. One of the most significant parts of this project was to get all of the observations from the Lick Index catalogue, previously on cards, transferred onto computer. This huge task is now almost complete, and April 1984 saw the issue of the WDS or Washington Double Star Catalogue which is the successor to the IDS.

8. COLOURS OF DOUBLE STARS

Brief history

The ability of different eyes to see different colours in the same star has long been a subject for discussion. According to Smyth (Sidereal Chromatics) the ancients recognised no blue stars; they spoke of red or white ones. Both Ptolemy and Seneca recorded Sirius as reddish giving rise to the possibility of secular variation of colour. Zahn, in 1694, compared the colours of the stars to those of the planets classifying them as Saturnine i.e. dullish, Jovian (bright and white) and Martial (reddish). Solar stars were partly yellow and partly red, whilst lunar stars were pale and dim and those of Venus were called 'box-coloured'. In the case of double stars it is certain that contrast plays an important part in the apparent colour that each component registers on the eye. Arago considered that that the light of fainter companions was absorbed by the atmosphere of the primary star. In other words the fainter star would always be redder than the brighter. Smyth showed that this was not the case and some stars did have primary stars which were redder than their secondaries.

In the post-telescopic era the most notable recorders of colours were William Herschel, F.G.W.Struve and W.H.Smyth. The first two recorded colours in double stars as a matter of course. Struve was particularly enthusiastic and went as far as inventing his own system of chromatic designations ranging from obscurissima through alba, flava and caerulea to rubra. His most famous epithet was olivacea subrubicunda which means pinkish-green! In a recently published book, David Malin and Paul Murdin (1984) have shown that the colours of both Herschel and Struve correlate with stellar spectral class and thus with surface temperature.

The greatest part of this chapter is taken up by the results of a program by four American amateur astronomers: Joseph J. Kaznica, James F. Russell Jr, Sandra T.(Keen) Kaznica, and Billie Westergard. They have used the 24-inch (60-cm) reflector of the Mount Cuba Observatory at Wilmington, Delaware, U.S.A. to determine the photographic colours of 200 wide pairs of double stars.

Introduction

At the Mount Cuba Astronomical Observatory we have been engaged in the development and evolution of a colour photographic technique to determine the colours of double stars and relate them in a semi-quantitative manner to spectral class. The purpose of the programme is to make colour determinations of 200 double stars commonly observed by astronomers.

There is a great deal of variability in visual reports of colours of double stars. Since visual observations are biased by the type of instrument, observer, seeing conditions, brightness of the stars and lack of colour reference, these variations are understandable. Most of these parameters are related to the function of the human eye, and bias is introduced simply because the human eye is not well suited to determining star colours. The retina of the eye is furnished with a layer of specialised cells called rods and cones which are sensitive to light. The rods are adaptable to low light conditions and are responsible for the 'averted vision' phenomenon with which all astronomers are familiar. However, the rods see only in black and white. The cones, which perceive form and colour, are designed to operate under normal daylight conditions, but are poorly suited to determine colour from very bright or very dim point sources under dark-adapted conditions.

Existing colour-index systems, such as photographic magnitude versus visual magnitude and the UBV photometry system, generate numerical values of colour. The element that is missing from these colour indices is a description of the intrinsic star colour recognisable in terms of human colour perception. Stated another way, these colour index systems generate a number and not a colour.

We wondered whether another colour-index system could be developed which would relate intrinsic star colour to spectral class, a system having more relevance to the visual observer. Naturally we thought of using colour film. Although colour film is not a perfect match for the eye, and the various dyes have different reciprocity characteristics, we felt that Kodak Ektachrome film would be successful in reproducing star colour, especially if the exposure times were kept short. Originally we experimented with Kodak Ektachrome ASA 64 film as we found a more uniform grain dispersal and distribution of colour using the slower, finer grained film. We developed an exposure curve by theoretical and empirical methods that permits us to make a correct exposure for a star of given magnitude. For example, a sixth magnitude star would be exposed for 5 seconds.

All exposures are made at the f/16 Cassegrain focus of the 24-inch (61-cm) Mount Cuba reflecting telescope. This eliminates any chromatic aberrations and no filters are used. On each roll of film there is an exposure of a colour reference chart taken in daylight.

Our choice of a colour reference chart is the MacBeth ColorChecker, an accepted standard in the photographic industry. This chart represents the internal standard, and variations in colour during the development of the film can be ignored since the internal standard will always correspond to the master copy of the ColorChecker. The ColorChecker is a 4 x 6 array of colour patches. There are 18 colour squares of various hues corresponding to different dominant wavelengths ranging from vivid purplish blue to red. The bottom row is a series of well spaced neutral patches. Each square is identified by an ISCC/NBS name and by its colorimetric designation in the CIE and Munsell systems. For our colour determinations we use the ISCC/CIE names.

At the telescope each double star requires at least two exposures - one for the primary star and one for the secondary - except where both stars are essentially the same magnitude and a single exposure will do.

To determine star colour, the internal standard ColorChecker is projected onto a screen, and then the star images are projected onto the same screen using a second projector. One observer positions the star images next to the colour squares, while two other observers stand close to the screen and compare colours for determination.

In most cases the stars have had colours closely matching one of the nine colour squares; strong purplish blue, moderate blue, strong greenish blue, light bluish green, strong yellowish green, vivid yellow, strong orange yellow, strong orange and strong red.

Once the stars have had their colours determined by this procedure they are photgraphed a second time, on a different night, and determined again. A finalised star colour, by our method, is dependent on reproducibility of a determined colour.

The stars are described in terms of the National Bureau of Standards colours and in accordance with the following table:

Table 6. The Munsell Color System.

Colour index	Colour	Hue	Value/Chroma
1	Strong purplish blue	7.5 PB	4/10.7
2	Moderate blue	4.3 PB	4.95/5.55
3	Strong greenish blue	5 PB	5/8
4	Light bluish green	2.5 BG	7/6
5	Strong yellow green	5 GY	7.08/9.01
6	Vivid yellow	5 Y	8/11.1
7	Strong orange yellow	10 YR	7/10.5
8	Strong orange	5 YR	6/11
9	Strong red	5 R	4/12

We offer in Table 9 a list of determined colour versus spectral class as evidence that our technique should be given serious consideration in describing the colours of stars in terms of human colour perception.

Let us examine this table in detail. Across the top we find the colours listed by National Bureau of Standards name. Below each colour name we find the colour index number which simply enables us to identify the colour of a star by a number. At left is spectral class by sub-class and to the right is shown the total number of stars in each sub-class. Our study totals 406 individual stars comprising 95 doubles, 4 triples and 1 quadruple star system. This table consists of 349 individual stars leaving 57 to be omitted because a spectral classification was not available and these are all secondary or tertiary stars.

Note the overall trend going from blue to red as the stars are listed from the hottest, spectral class O to the coolest, spectral class M. We do show a rogue point for spectral class A0 to A4 showing one star as strong orange. This is the secondary star of iota Bootis which is given as spectral type A2 in Robert Burnham's 'Celestial Handbook'. The literature on this star is confusing. It is given in the Lick Catalogue as magnitude 7.5 but in the Becvar Catalogue it is magnitude 8.3. We have photographed this star a number of times and have determined that the Becvar value is the correct one and that the colour is indeed strong orange. Burnham's reference for the spectral type is from a European source and we have written to him for clarification.

Spectral class O and B stars we would expect to be bluish and our technique describes them as such. G class stars are determined as yellow or yellowish and K and M stars are described as being mostly orange. For these spectral class stars the determined colour ranges over only three or four colours while for spectral class A and F the determined colours range over five or six colours. This difference of determined colour range is in agreement with that determined by the UBV colour system and is also expected. We would expect that the colours determined for A and F class stars would range from bluish through greenish to yellowish as they are midway between the very hot and very cool stars. Again our technique agrees with this premise.

Based on this correlation of observed colour with spectral class we have confidence in our technique describing star colour in terms of human colour perception. We developed this technique in order to give the visual observer an idea of colours of the double star pairs discussed if the eye was compensated for all of the variables discussed in our original article. These variables render colour determination at the eyepiece a haphazard guess at best.

Conclusions

First of all let me say that I consider our sample of double stars to be a random sample. They are distributed fairly evenly throughout the sky. My choice was simply based on "Pretty Pairs" that observers would enjoy. I was limited by our photographic technique of choosing pairs of the same magnitude wider than 3.5 arc seconds and pairs of unequal magnitude wider than 6.5 arc seconds. To use our catalogue with small telescopes I chose most of the classic wide pairs so that the average separation of the 195 double stars in the survey is 22.8 arc seconds. The 5 multiple stars have similar separations. Most of the stars have common proper motion and are usually referred to as relatively fixed. Only 10 show orbital motion and a further 10 are optical pairs.

We classified a star as belonging to one of the nine colour classes which are given on page 45 and each component of a double or multiple system was examined separately. The Table given below shows the frequency with which various differences in colour occurred in double star pairs.

Table 7. Observed colours of 195 double star pairs

Colour Category Difference	Number of Pairs	Fraction of total
Same colour	101	52%
Difference of one colour	36	18%
" two colours	22	11%
" three colours	18	9%
" four colours	4	2%
" five colours	7	4%
" six colours	4	2%
" seven colours	3	2%

Table 7 shows a high probability that a given double star will have components of the same colour or very similar colours. In 52% of the pairs the colours are the same whilst 81% showed differences of two colour categories or less. The 5 multiple stars show similar results. The famous pairs with great colour contrast such as Albireo (beta Cygni) thus appear to be the exception rather than the rule.

We also looked for a correlation between stars which appeared to have the same colour and the angular separation. The average separation of 195 pairs is 22.8 arc seconds and the results are given below.

Table 8. Distribution of colour difference with angular separation.

Colour Category Difference	Average Separation
Zero or one	20.5 arc secs.
Two or three	25.1 arc secs.
Four or more	34.1 arc secs.

The 5 multiple stars show a similar correlation.

Table 8 indicates that the smaller the separation of a pair the greater the probability that the colours will be the same. There are, of course, some striking exceptions to this rule. In the pair Almach (gamma Andromedae) the stars are six colour categories apart but they are separated by only 10 arc seconds, whilst Aldebaran (alpha Tauri) the stars have the same colour but the separation is 121 arc seconds.

Since colour is an indication of star spectral type the analysis of our data shows that the components of a double star system, even wide common proper motion pairs tend to be similar in type. The data base here is small and these correlations are based on a quantitative technique but there does appear to be some very specific trends in the data. Hopefully this information will lead to a better understanding of double stars.

Table 9. Summary of Mt. Cuba star colour determinations
and relation to spectral class

ISCC NBS Name Col.	Str. Purp. Blue Index	Mod. Blue 1	Str. Grn. Blue 2	Lt. Blue Grn. 3	Str. Yell. Grn. 4	Viv. Yell. 5	Str. Or. Yell. 6	Str. Or. 7	Str. Red 8	Sub Class Tot 9
05-09	2	2	1							5
B1-B4	1	5	7	1						14
B5-B9	8	11	14	4						37
A0-A4	2	26	21	24	3			1		77
A5-A9		7	1	8	2	3				21
F0-F4		1	1	19	12	12				47
F5-F9			1	10	11	16	7	2		47
G0-G4					5	11	5			21
G5-G9					2	6	11	10		29
K0-K4					5	18	14	1		38
K5-K9						4	3	1		8
M0-M5						1	2	2		5

Table 10. Double Star Colour Observations

Constellation	Double Star	Comp A	Comp B	Comp C	Comp D
Andromeda	gamma (STF 205)	7	1		
	pi(STT 4 App)	1	1		
	59	3	3		
	STF 79	4	4		
	STF 2985	5	6		
	STF 1 App I	6	7		
	STT 547	9	9		
Aquarius	94 (STF 2998)	7	8		
Aquila	5 (STF 2379)	4	6		
	15 (HJ 598)	8	8		
	STF 2449	6	6		
Aries	lambda (STT 21 App)	2	5		
	gamma (STF 180)	2	2		
	30 (STF 5 App I)	4	4		
	33 (STF 289)	2	4		
	STF 326	6	8		
	STF 394	5	3		
Auriga	14 (STF 653)	2	4		
	26 (STF 753)	5	4		
	41 (STF 845)	4	4		
	STF 698	6	4		
	STF 718	4	4		
	STF 764	2	2		
	STF 872	4	4		
	STF 933	3	3		
Bootes	pi (STF 1864)	2	5		
	iota (STF 26 App I)	2	8		
	kappa (STF 1821)	2	4		
	xi (STF 1888)	7	8		
	STF 1850	2	2		
	STF 1921	2	2		
Camelopardalis	1 (STF 550)	4	4		
	STF 396	4	5		
	STF 618	6	6		
	STF 1625	6	6		
	STF 1694	2	2		
	Piazzi III 97	8	3		
Cancer	iota (STF 1268)	6	3		

Constellation	Double Star	Comp A	Comp B	Comp C	Comp D
Cancer	phi 2 (STF 1223)	4	4		
	24 (STF 1224)	4	4		
	STF 1245	5	8		
	STF 1311	5	4		
Canes Venatici	alpha (STF 1692)	3	4		
	2 (STF 1622)	8	8		
	STF 1645	6	6		
Canis Major	nu (HJ 239)	8	5		
	HJ 3945	9	7		
Cassiopeia	alpha (H 18)	7	7		
	eta (STF 60)	6	8		
	35 (S 397)	2	9		
	STF 30	2	4		
	STF 3053	7	2		
Cepheus	beta (STF 2806)	2	2		
	kappa (STF 2675)	2	5		
	xi (STF 2863)	4	5		
	delta (STF 58 App I)	7	3		
	STF 2840	3	3		
	STF 2873	6	7		
	STF 2883	5	8		
	STF 2893	7	3		
	STF 2903	7	3		
	STF 2947	5	5		
Cetus	26 (STF 84)	6	7		
	37 (STF 3 App I)	7	7		
	66 (STF 231)	6	7		
	STF 274	2	2		
	STF 6 App I	6	6		
Coma Berenices	2 (STF 1596)	2	4		
	12 (SHJ 143)	5	4		
	17 (STF 21 App I)	2	4		
	24 (STF 1657)	7	4		
	STF 1633	4	4		
	STF 1678	2	5		
	STF 1685	4	5		
Corona Borealis	zeta (STF 1965)	3	1		
	sigma (STF 2032)	6	6		
Corvus	delta (SHJ 145)	3	8		
	STF 1669	6	6		

Constellation	Double Star	Comp A	Comp B	Comp C	Comp D
Cygnus	beta (STF 43 App I)	8	1		
	16 (STF 46 App I)	6	6		
	17 (STF 2586)	5	8		
	61 (STF 2758)	7	8		
	STF 2486	6	6		
	STF 2578	3	3		
	STF 2687	3	3		
	STT 191 App	8	3		
Delphinus	gamma (STF 2727)	6	4		
	S 752	3	3		
Draco	nu (STF 35 App I)	2	2		
	psi (STF 2241)	6	6		
	omicron (STF 2420)	8	9		
	40-41 (STF 2308)	6	6		
	STF 1362	6	6		
	STF 2273	6	6		
	STF 2348	7	2		
	STF 2573	4	7		
Eridanus	32 (STF 470)	8	1		
	55 (STF 590)	8	3		
	STF 570	4	4		
Gemini	15 (HJ 223)	7	7		
	20 (STF 924)	5	5		
	38 (STF 982)	5	6		
	STF 1108	7	5		
Hercules	kappa (STF 2010)	7	6		
	rho (STF 2161)	2	1		
	95 (STF 2264)	7	2		
	100 (STF 2280)	2	2		
	STF 2063	3	7		
Hydra	17 (STF 1295)	4	4		
	STF 1270	7	7		
	STF 1329	8	7		
Lacerta	8 (STF 2922)	2	2		
Leo	alpha (STF 6 App II)	2	8		
	gamma (STF 1424)	8	7		
	tau (STF 19 App I)	8	5		
	6 (SHJ 107)	7	5		
	54 (STF 1487)	2	2		
	83 (STF 1540)	7	7		
	88 (STF 1547)	6	9		

Constellation	Double Star	Comp A	Comp B	Comp C	Comp D
Leo	90 (STF 1552)	3	4	4	
	STF 1552	5	6		
Libra	STF 1962	7	7		
Lynx	19 (STF 1062)	4	4		
	20 (STF 1065)	4	4		
	STF 958	6	6		
	STF 1009	4	4		
	STF 1282	7	7		
	STF 1369	5	5	5	
Lyra	beta (STF 39 App I)	1	1		
	eta (STF 2487)	3	2		
	zeta (STF 38 App I)	4	5		
	STF 2372	3	3		
	STF 2459	3	3		
	STF 2470	3	4		
	STF 2474	4	4		
Monoceros	epsilon (STF 900)	6	6		
Ophiuchus	61 (STF 2202)	2	2		
Orion	delta (STF 14 App I)	3	3		
	lambda (STF 738)	2	2		
	iota (STF 752)	1	1		
	sigma (STF 762)	2	3	3	2
	23 (STF 696)	1	3		
	STF 627	4	4		
	STF 697	2	3		
	STF 747	2	3		
	STF 855	1	1		
Pegasus	epsilon (S 798)	8	6		
	1 (STF 1 App II)	7	8		
	3 (STF 56 App I)	2	2		
	STF 2841	7	4		
	STF 2978	4	4		
Perseus	eta (STF 307)	8	2		
	epsilon (STF 471)	3	3		
	STF 331	2	2		
	STF 336	7	4		
	STF 552	3	3		
Pisces	psi (STF 88)	3	3		
	zeta (STF 100)	6	6		
	35 (STF 12)	4	4		

Constellation	Double Star	Comp A	Comp B	Comp C	Comp D
Pisces	55 (STF 46)	7	4		
	65 (STF 61)	4	4		
	77 (STF 90)	6	6		
	STF 98	3	3		
Sagitta	theta (STF 2637)	5	8	7	
Serpens	delta (STF 1954)	4	4		
	theta (STF 2417)	4	4		
	49 (STF 2021)	6	6		
	STF 1919	6	7		
	STF 1931	5	7		
Sextans	35 (STF 1466)	7	7		
Taurus	alpha (STF 2 App II)	8	8		
	chi (STF 528)	3	5		
	118 (STF 716)	3	4		
	STF 401	5	5		
	STF 422	7	7		
	STF 494	2	2		
	STF 548	5	4		
	STF 572	4	4		
	STF 645	4	5		
	H VI 98	6	6		
Triangulum	iota (STF 227)	7	4		
	STF 239	4	5		
Ursa Major	zeta (STF 1744)	3	3		
	65 (STF 1579)	2	2	4	
	STF 1315	4	4		
	STF 1415	4	4		
	STF 1520	5	5		
	STF 1561	6	8		
	STF 1603	5	5		
Ursa Minor	alpha (STF 93)	6	6		
	pi (STF 1972)	7	8		
Virgo	gamma (STF 1670)	5	5		
	theta (STF 1724)	2	5		
	17 (STF 1636)	8	8		
	54 (HJ 412)	3	3		
	STF 1575	7	5		
	STF 1627	6	6		
	STF 1740	7	8		
Vulpecula	STF 2769	2	3		

PART TWO

PART TWO

A CATALOGUE OF DOUBLE STARS

INTRODUCTION

The measures in this catalogue were made by a number of observers and details are given later. The large majority were made by Maurice Duruy, and his contribution amounts to 3,499 measures of 420 systems out of a total of 5,035 measures of 685 systems. These measures were made between 1941 and 1975 but are not continuous, being divided into two distinct periods;
(a) 1941 - 1945

During this time the 32·5-cm Coudé refractor of the Observatory of Lyon at St. Genis Laval was used. The micrometer was a filar with a screw constant of 7·43 arc secs per revolution.

(b) 1963 - 1975

Reflectors of 26-cm, 40-cm and 60-cm aperture were used and observations were made from two different sites.

(i) 26-cm reflector.

This telescope was situated at Montlhery, near Paris (altitude 80 metres) where Duruy reported that the seeing was such that measures could be made on more than 95% of clear nights. Between 1962 and 1964, measures of distance were made using the binocular micrometer which utilises a pair of artificial stars, whilst a wire in the eyepiece and a graduated circle were used for the measurement of position angle. From early in 1964 to early 1965, the grating micrometer was used for pairs wider than 1 arc sec, whilst below this separation, the binocular micrometer was used as before.

(ii) 40-cm reflector.

This was also set up at Montlhery, the first measures being made in early 1965. Again the binocular micrometer was used for the great majority of measures. In mid-1966, M.Duruy moved to Le Rouret which is 25 kilometres west of Nice. Mountains rise to 2000 metres some 16 kilometres north of the site, and the Mediterranean is the same distance to the south. The Mistral frequently reduced the seeing to 5 arc seconds, making the measurement of close pairs impossible.

(iii) 60-cm reflector.

The 40-cm was transferred to an alt-azimuth mounting, and the original equatorial, after reinforcement, was used to carry the 60-cm.

The telescope is housed in an observatory with a divided roof which opens to the east and west. At low declinations the 60-cm can see objects from 1 hour west to 2 hours east, whilst at high declinations the limits are 2 hours west and 3 hours east.

Duruy noted that the seeing often prohibited the use of the telescope on double stars. A plane parallel window was added in 1970 and on nights of good seeing, stars as close as 0·20 arc seconds could be measured.

The measures made by Argyle were obtained in two short periods in 1970 and 1972 - 1973. These were made using:

(i) The 28-inch refractor at the Royal Greenwich Observatory.

These measures were made between May and September 1970. For pairs below 4 arc secs, the comparison image micrometer (C.I.M.) was used exclusively for separation, whilst the filar was used for all measures of position angle and those separations greater than 4 arc secs. The constant of the C.I.M. was 1mm = 0·0794 arc secs, and that of the filar was 6·11 arc secs per revolution with a x2 Barlow lens fitted, and 12·16 arc secs per revolution without.

(ii) The 6-inch Cooke refractor at the Royal Greenwich Observatory.

This instrument was used between November 1972 and March 1973. A filar micrometer with a screw constant of 23·70 arc secs per revolution was used for all measures.

EXPLANATORY NOTES

The following abbreviations are used:

A	– R.G. Aitken	HU	– W.J. Hussey
AC	– Alvan Clark	J	– R. Jonckheere
AGC	– Alvan G. Clark	KRU	– A. Kruger
BU	– S.W. Burnham	KUI	– G.P. Kuiper
COU	– P. Couteau	P	– C. Piazzi Smyth
D	– E. Dembowski	SE	– A. Secchi
DA	– W.R. Dawes	SHJ	– J. Herschel/J. South
ES	– T.H.E.C. Espin	STF	– F.G.W. Struve
H	– W. Herschel	STF App –	" (appendix)
HJ	– J. Herschel	STT	– O. Struve
HLD	– E.S. Holden	STT App	" (appendix)
HLM	– E. Holmes	WNC	– A Winnecke
HO	– G.W. Hough		

The Right Ascension for 2000, tne magnitudes, the original measures and the notes on comites were taken from the IDS. The periods of binaries and the ephemeris positions for 1985.0 come from Muller and Couteau (1978).

An "e" beside the measures of separation indicates that the pair was elongated. The number of nights on which measures were made is denoted by "N". If two figures are shown, the former refers to the number of measures of position angle and the latter to the number of measures of separation.

The codes in the extreme right-hand column in the catalogue refer to the observer and the telescope used, and are as follows:

D1	M.V.Duruy	32·5-cm refractor	St. Genis Laval
D2	M.V.Duruy	26-cm reflector	Montlhery
D3	M.V.Duruy	40-cm reflector	Montlhery
D4	M.V.Duruy	60-cm reflector	Le Rouret
A1	R.W.Argyle	6-inch refractor	Herstmonceux
A2	R.W.Argyle	28-inch refractor	Herstmonceux
RW	R.S.Waterworth	25-cm reflector	Pickering
KS	K.M.Sturdy	21-cm reflector	York
RF	R.Frangetto	4-inch refractor	Sao Paolo
DG	D.Gellera	11-cm refractor	Lodi
CP	C.M.Pither	30-cm reflector	Bournemouth

In many of the wider pairs, the colour of each component has been estimated by members of the Webb Society Double Star Section. In order to make the notes more compact, the observed colours have been abbreviated thus:

w - white   b - blue   o - orange   y - yellow   p - purple
g - grey   r - red   l - lilac   g - green   a - gold

Intensities are noted by: P - pale, D - deep.

A tendency towards a particular colour is indicated by: ysh (yellowish) bsh (bluish) etc, and intermediate colours are shown by combinations of letters from the table above, viz: yw (yellow-white), bw (blue-white).

Colours were observed by the following: A.Tuck, D.A.Allen, B. Szentmartoni,(Hungary), A.Fahy, A Curran, J.E.Isles, I. Genner, A. Walker, E.R.Hancock, G.Gough, A Northcott and R.W.Argyle.

(i) Measures

PAIR	RA 2000 DEC		MAGS	PA	SEP	DATE	N	OBS
STT 547	0005.4	4549N	9.4,9.4	167.9	5.36	67.61	4	D3
				169.3	5.80	73.59	3,1	D4
STF 3062	0006.2	5826N	6.4,7.5	150.8	0.51	43.68	5	D1
				167.7	0.6	45.19	1	D1
				177.7	0.62	45.86	6	D1
STF 3062	0006.2	5826N	6.4,7.5	255.4	1.27	65.61	6,5	D3
				260.8	1.28	67.63	3	D4
				271.4	1.31	72.53	3	D4
				272.0	1.40	73.54	3	D4
BU 255	0011.9	2825N	8.5,8.8	round		66.0	1	D3
BU 1026	0012.2	5337N	7.2,8.0	round		66.0	1	D3
STF 12	0014.9	0849N	6.1,7.7	147.5	11.6	72.9	1	A1
				149.3	11.47	81.66	4	WS
STT 4	0016.7	3629N	8.2,8.9	213.3	0.4	44.88	1	D1
				187.6	0.49	65.60	3	D3
STF 23	0017.5	0019N	7.9,10.2	278.3	3.75	42.90	2	D1
STF 24	0018.5	2608N	7.6,8.4	252.0	5.33	41.99	1	D1
STT 12	0031.8	5432N	5.5,5.8	177.7	0.56	65.70	6,5	D3
				179.1	0.52	70.64	3	A2
				176.2	0.55	73.62	2	D4
STF 39	0034.5	0433S	7.0,10.2	46.8	20.12	82.95	2	KS
STF 40	0035.2	3650N	7.0,9.0	311.5	12.0	72.9	2	A1
HJ 323				286.8	62.64	82.95	2	KS
STT 4 APP	0036.8	3343N	4.4,8.9	173.4	36.1	72.9	3	A1
STF 1 APP	0046.5	3057N	7.4,7.6	47.9	48.5	72.9	2	A1
				48.1	46.98	82.83	2	KS
STF 60	0048.8	5750N	3.6,7.2	284.1	9.66	43.97	2	D1
				286.1	10.00	45.92	1	D1
				294.	10.22	62.9	1	D2
				297.6	11.05	64.6	2,3	D2
				299.9	11.25	66.0	3,5	D3
				300.7	11.64	73.62	5	D4
				306.3	12.28	77.45	9,7	WS
STF 61	0049.8	2743N	6.3,6.3	295.0	4.42	42.09	10	D1
				296.7	4.43	68.58	1,2	D3
				297.7	4.36	77.95	3	GH
BU 232	0050.4	5038N	8.5,9.0	225.0	0.72	65.59	3	D3
				244.	0.7	71.03	1	D4
STT 20	0054.6	1912N	6.1,7.2	238.7	0.42	65.90	5	D3
				238.8	0.47	67.66	5,4	D3

PAIR	RA 2000 DEC		MAGS	PA	SEP	DATE	N	OBS
STT 20	0054.6	1912N	6.1,7.2	237.0	0.5	71.02	2	D4
				226.7	0.48	73.71	4	D4
STF 73	0055.0	2338N	6.1,6.7	132.6	0.61	43.99	3	D1
				140.0	0.57	45.88	3	D1
				200.7	0.58	65.6	4	D3
				211.9	0.74	67.48	4	D3
				218.5	0.58	70.69	3	A2
				217.5	0.80	71.01	3	D4
				231.0	0.69	72.57	1	D4
				229.7	0.66	73.71	6	D4
BU 500	0055.4	3039N	8.7,8.7	303.	0.4	71.03	1	D4
BU 1099	0056.8	6022N	6.0,6.7	round		65.6	1	D3
BU 302	0058.3	2125N	6.7,8.1	124.7	0.57	42.92	2	D1
				141.8	0.65	65.64	3	D3
				152.0	0.45	73.88	3	D4
STF 79	0100.0	4442N	6.0,6.8	194.3	7.93	44.62	3	D1
				194.3	8.03	77.69	3	GH
				191.4	7.62	81.60	2	WS
STT 21	0103.0	4722N	6.7,8.0	172.0	0.68	65.7	3	D3
STF 88 AB	0105.6	2128N	5.6,5.8	159.7	30.5	72.9	2	A1
				161.0	30.0	82.16	2	RW
AC			,11.2	72.9	108.2	72.9	1	A1
STT 515	0109.3	4715N	4.5,6.1	150.6	0.49	65.7	7,6	D3
				142.1	0.46	70.71	2	A2
BU 303	0109.6	2348N	7.3,7.5	289.0	0.67	67.65	2	D3
BU 235	0110.6	5101N	7.5,7.9	119.5	1.06	65.8	7	D3
A 655	0111.3	4113N	8.5,8.9	round		65.8	1	D3
STF 98	0112.9	3205N	7.0,8.0	248.0	19.90	78.01	3	GH
STF 100	0113.7	0733N	5.6,6.5	63.7	23.0	72.9	2	A1
				62.4	22.73	78.05	3	GH
BU 1100	0114.7	6057N	8.3,8.3	43.	0.37	65.1	4	D3
				40.6	0.38	67.64	1	D3
STF 102	0117.8	4901N	7.1,8.3	284.5	0.45	65.63	4	D3
				278.8	0.42	71.03	3	D4
BU 4	0121.3	1132N	7.4,7.9	round		65.9	2	D3
STF 117AB-C	0126.0	6807N	9.4,10.0	121.2	21.64	82.94	3	KS
CD				73.2	2.98	42.93	2	D1
STF 121	0127.6	6428N	8.6,9.6	269.9	11.37	81.87	2	KS
STF 131	0131.2	6040N	7.4,10.6	143.8	14.20	82.99	2	KS
A 816	0135.7	7226N	8.5,8.6	307.5	0.57	42.97	2	D1

PAIR	RA 2000	DEC	MAGS	PA	SEP	DATE	N	OBS
A 816	0135.7	7226N	8.5,8.6	310.1	0.62	43.99	2	D1
				308.2	0.53	73.89	4	D4
STF 138	0136.0	0739N	7.7,7.7	47.3	1.59	41.96	3	D1
				51.0	1.43	73.63	3	D4
HU 1030	0138.9	7644N	8.8,9.0	321.	0.6	43.97	1	D1
DUN 5	0139.7	5612S	6.0,6.0	195.7	11.19	80.00	4	RF
HJ 3461	0145.7	2503S	5.5,8.3	29.6	4.73	82.13	3	RF
STF 162	0149.2	4754N	6.5,7.0	204.9	1.97	66.0	4,3	D3
STT 34	0149.9	8053N	7.9,8.1	258.5	0.35	66.0	1	D3
				259	0.31	67.65	1,2	D3
STF 174	0150.1	2217N	6.2,7.4	168.0	2.77	42.39	7	D1
				164.8	2.97	66.1	1	D3
				168.2	2.80	73.62	3	D4
				166.0	3.16	77.74	3	GH
HO 311	0151.2	2439N	7.6,7.8	200.5	0.3	71.02	1	D4
STF 163	0151.2	6452N	7.1,9.1	37.4	36.43	81.98	2	KS
STF 180	0153.5	1918N	4.8,4.8	359.3	7.61	64.0	1,4	D2
				0.0	7.88	64.6	1,7	D2
				0.3	7.87	67.89	1,2	D3
				180.5	8.11	76.87	3	GH
				359.0	7.79	81.71	3	WS
STF 183	0155.1	2847N	7.8,8.5	round		65.6	2	D3
				round		73.63	1	D4
STF 186	0155.8	0151N	7.0,7.0	56.2	1.37	73.63	1	D4
STF 4 APP	0156.1	3716N	5.8,6.0	298.3	196.6	73.0	2	A1
				297.4	199.44	81.84	3,2	KS
STF 182	0156.4	6116N	8.1,8.1	124.3	3.67	41.97	3	D1
STT 21 APP	0158.1	2335N	4.9,7.7	47.1	38.5	72.9	2	A1
HJ 1100	0159.5	6437N	5.2,9.5	310.3	42.02	81.96	2	KS
BU 513	0201.9	7054N	4.7,7.2	277.0	0.77	43.99	3	D1
				281.3	0.91	45.30	3	D1
STF 202	0202.0	0246N	4.3,5.2	294.2	2.38	63.0	3	D2
				291.7	1.95	65.6	3	D3
				291.7	1.97	67.05	7,10	D3
				288.4	1.82	73.58	3	D4
				286.5	1.91	75.09	3	D4
				285.0	1.76	77.43	8,5	WS
STF 205	0203.5	4223N	2.3,5.0	63.	9.96	64.5	1	D2
				64.7	9.63	70.7	1	A2
				63.9	9.45	77.	3	GH

PAIR	RA 2000 DEC	MAGS	PA	SEP	DATE	N	OBS
STF 205	0203.5 4223N	2.3,5.0	63.9	9.43	81.98	5	RW
STT 38	" "	5.1,8.3	101.1	0.4	42.27	2	D1
			97.	0.4	44.02	1	D1
			115.	0.46	65.8	4	D3
			112.8	0.53	67.43	5	D3
			113.4	0.48	70.71	2	A2
STF 222	0210.8 3903N	6.0,6.7	35.9	16.8	72.9	2	A1
			35.1	15.61	77.88	3	GH
			35.	17.5	82.11	1	RW
STF 227	0212.4 3018N	5.2,6.6	73.8	3.85	41.98	2	D1
			74.3	3.88	66.0	1,2	D3
			70.9	3.97	77.09	4	WS
STF 231	0212.7 0224S	5.8,7.6	235.4	16.85	78.05	5,3	WS
			232.9	15.97	82.46	2	KS
STF 228	0214.1 4729N	6.4,7.3	210.2	0.47	44.02	4	D1
			252.6	0.81	65.64	3	D3
			254.6	0.87	67.47	3	D3
			260.9	1.06	73.60	4	D4
STF 234	0217.4 6121N	8.5,9.4	245.5	0.73	66.59	3	D3
STF 239	0217.4 2845N	7.0,8.0	212.6	13.51	78.08	3	GH
STF 249	0221.6 4435N	7.2,9.2	195.4	2.23	42.98	2	D1
STF 257	0225.7 6133N	7.6,8.1	17.	0.30	65.64	1	D3
			24.	0.28	67.92	5	D3
			230.	0.25	71.35	3	D4
			45.6	0.22	73.64	1	D4
STF 271	0230.5 2515N	5.9,10.4	181.4	12.5	72.9	1	A1
STF 274	0231.5 0104N	7.3,7.8	219.2	14.17	78.47	6,3	WS
STF 93	0231.6 8916N	2.1,9.1	216.4	17.8	73.2	3	A1
STT 42	0233.3 5218N	7.0,7.5	271.5	0.29	67.62	6	D3
STF 5 APP	0237.0 2439N	6.6,7.4	275.6	38.3	73.0	2	A1
STF 285	0238.7 3325N	7.5,8.2	170.7	1.59	42.96	3	D1
			163.6	1.62	73.62	2	D4
STT 43	0240.7 2638N	8.3,9.9	30.4	1.14	44.02	1	D1
STF 299	0243.3 0314N	3.6,7.4	294.3	2.92	42.95	1	D1
STF 296	0244.2 4913N	4.2,10.0	301.8	18.36	42.99	1	D1
STF 305	0247.5 1922N	7.4,8.3	312.3	3.42	42.72	4	D1
			310.6	3.56	72.95	1	A1
			312.1	3.41	80.15	1	CP
STF 307	0250.6 5554N	3.9,7.9	300.9	28.4	73.0	2	A1
STF 314	0252.9 5300N	6.4,7.1	306.7	1.48	43.02	3	D1

PAIR	RA 2000	DEC	MAGS	PA	SEP	DATE	N	OBS
STF 314	0252.9	5300N	6.4,7.1	130.2	1.57	66.0	3	D3
BU 524	0253.7	3820N	5.6,6.7	344.8	0.25	73.64	3	D4
BU 525	0258.9	2137N	7.5,7.5	246.2	0.41	65.84	5	D3
				247.2	0.42	67.49	3	D3
				73.0	0.38	70.92	3	D4
				251.8	0.40	73.63	4	D4
STF 333	0259.2	2120N	5.2,5.5	205.3	1.57	65.9	2,1	D3
				207.6	1.52	78.04	2	GH
STF 331	0300.8	5221N	5.4,6.8	84.8	12.3	73.1	2	A1
				87.0	13.45	78.03	5,2	WS
STF 346	0305.5	2515N	6.9,6.9	round		44.02	1	D1
STF 320	0306.2	7925N	5.8,9.0	232.2	5.46	82.08	3	KS
STF 6 APP	0309.1	0728N	8.3,8.5	162.8	82.53	82.07	2	KS
HJ 3555	0312.0	2900S	4.0,9.5	294.7	4.11	80.10	4	RF
STF 360	0312.1	3712N	8.1,8.3	128.3	2.47	66.0	4	D3
STT 50	0312.5	7133N	8.5,8.5	175.0	1.27	66.0	3	D3
STF 367	0314.0	0044N	8.9,8.9	173.0	0.77	42.95	1	D1
				153.6	0.92	67.72	2	D3
STT 52	0317.5	6539N	6.9,7.5	80.7	0.42	66.0	6	D3
				63.2	0.47	73.63	2	D4
STT 53	0317.7	3838N	7.7,8.5	275.0	0.5	43.04	1	D1
				269.1	0.74	67.01	4	D3
				265.0	0.72	73.63	2	D4
STF 401	0331.4	2734N	6.4,6.9	269.5	11.1	73.1	2	A1
				267.2	11.84	77.90	3	GH
				269.6	10.49	79.18	1	CP
STF 396	0333.5	5846N	6.3,8.2	243.8	20.6	73.1	2	A1
STF 412	0334.5	2428N	6.6,6.7	46.0	0.4	43.16	1	D1
				13.8	0.50	67.06	4	D3
				8.2	0.62	73.64	1	D4
STF 400	0334.9	6002N	6.9,7.9	255.5	0.66	66.0	3	D3
				255.3	1.17	73.64	1	D4
BU 533	0335.6	3141N	7.6,7.6	43.7	0.87	42.96	2	D1
				46.5	1.11	67.73	2	D3
A 1535	0336.1	4221N	9.0,9.4	102.1	0.37	67.73	2	D3
STF 422	0336.8	0036N	6.2,8.4	259.0	6.74	43.10	3	D1
STT 37 APP	0338.3	4449N	8.0,8.0	95.7	41.3	73.1	2	A1
STF 430 AB	0340.5	0507N	6.8,9.8	57.4	26.3	73.1	2	A1
AC	"	"	,10.5	300.2	36.1	73.1	2	A1
STF 427	0340.6	2847N	7.3,8.1	207.5	6.77	43.10	3	D1

PAIR	RA 2000 DEC		MAGS	PA	SEP	DATE	N	OBS
P III 97	0342.7	5959N	6.0,8.6	35.2	55.0	73.2	2	A1
STF 452	0348.3	1109N	5.0,10.1	58.6	9.5	73.0	2	A1
STT 65	0350.4	2536N	6.0,6.3	209.6	0.70	67.39	6	D3
				215.	0.6	71.22	3	D4
				208.5	0.66	73.65	3	D4
KUI 15	0351.9	0633N	6.3,6.4	35.	0.35	42.95	1	D1
				34.	0.42	66.0	1	D3
				28.5	0.6	67.59	3	D3
				38.8	0.5	73.77	1	D4
STT 66	0352.1	4048N	8.0,8.5	145.2	0.80	67.05	3	D3
STF 470	0354.3	0257S	5.0,6.3	347.	6.76	43.15	2	D1
				349.2	6.64	78.38	5,2	GH
				348.	7.3	82.12	1	RW
STT 67	0357.2	6106N	5.3,8.5	49.8	1.41	66.0	2	D3
STF 471	0357.8	4001N	3.0,8.2	13.0	9.26	80.96	1	RW
STF 479 AB	0400.9	2313N	6.9,7.8	127.4	7.6	73.1	2	A1
AC "	"	"	,9.0	241.4	57.8	73.1	2,1	A1
STT 531	0407.5	3805N	7.3,9.0	76.6	0.87	66.0	3	D3
STF 495	0407.6	1509N	6.0,8.8	221.0	3.59	73.1	2	A1
STF 460	0410.1	8042N	5.6,6.5	98.7	0.87	66.0	3	D3
STT 77	0415.9	3142N	8.2,8.2	72.8	0.65	43.04	1	D1
STT 44 APP	0417.3	4613N	7.2,8.6	322.1	58.3	73.2	2	A1
STF 511	0417.9	5847N	7.4,7.9	124.1	0.36	67.07	3	D3
				130.	0.25	71.33	1	D4
STT 48 APP	0420.4	2722N	5.1,8.5	254.0	49.6	73.1	2	A1
STF 528	0422.6	2538N	5.5,7.6	25.7	19.6	73.0	2	A1
STT 82	0422.8	1504N	7.3,9.3	206.2	1.18	43.10	3	D1
HU 304	0423.9	0928N	5.9,5.9	211.6	0.29	67.73	2	D3
STF 534	0424.1	2418N	6.2,8.6	289.9	29.1	73.1	2	A1
STF 548	0428.9	3021N	6.5,8.5	36.5	14.7	73.1	2	A1
STF 552	0431.4	4001N	7.0,7.2	117.9	9.15	78.90	3	GH
				115.8	10.14	82.08	3	KS
STF 550	0432.0	5355N	5.7,6.8	307.6	10.0	73.1	2	A1
				308.1	10.21	77.91	2	GH
STF 559	0434.6	1801N	6.9,7.0	277.6	3.13	78.11	2	GH
STF 2 APPII	0435.9	1631N	1.1,11.3	31.5	131.25	82.10	2	KS
STT 86	0436.6	1945N	8.2,8.2	40.6	0.46	43.11	3	D1
				24.5	0.44	67.09	2	D3
STF 567	0436.7	1929N	8.9,9.4	330.2	2.16	43.11	3	D1
STF 576	0438.1	1302S	6.8,8.1	172.2	12.46	82.14	2	KS

PAIR	RA 2000	DEC	MAGS	PA	SEP	DATE	N	OBS
STF 572	0438.5	2656N	7.3,7.3	196.5	3.90	42.52	6	D1
				193.6	4.24	73.16	2	A1
STF 11 APP	0439.2	1555N	4.8,5.2	193.9	4.24	73.16	2	A1
HJ 3683	0440.3	5857S	7.0,7.2	271.8	2.96	80.25	4	RF
STF 577	0442.3	3730N	8.6,8.6	46.0	1.27	43.13	5	D1
				33.4	1.08	67.21	5,4	D3
A 1013	0443.2	5932N	7.3,7.3	327.2	0.41	42.21	4	D1
BU 883	0451.2	1104N	7.8,7.8	240.	oval	66.0	1	D3
BU 552	0451.8	1339N	6.8,9.8	294.8	0.92	43.13	3	D1
SHJ 48	0456.4	0510S	5.6,9.2	75.8	66.55	82.18	2	KS
STF 616	0459.3	3753N	5.1,8.1	357.5	5.64	42.92	5	D1
				0.7	5.35	73.0	2	A1
STF 623	0500.0	2719N	6.8,8.3	206.1	20.8	73.1	2	A1
STF 627	0500.5	0337N	6.6,7.0	260.3	21.7	73.0	2	A1
				260.2	21.62	82.13	2	KS
STF 630	0502.0	0137N	6.5,7.7	50.8	14.6	73.0	2	A1
STT 95	0505.0	1948N	7.0,7.6	314.7	0.92	44.15	2	D1
				306.8	0.97	66.2	3	D3
				307.8	1.02	67.01	3	D3
				305.6	0.75	73.77	1	D4
STT 98	0507.4	0830N	5.9,6.7	102.9	0.90	42.86	7	D1
				59.4	0.84	64.7	4	D2
				61.1	0.81	65.8	3	D3
				57.6	0.86	67.10	3	D3
				38.7	0.66	75.15	3	D4
STF 635	0507.8	5459N	8.7,8.7	320.4	0.94	66.94	5	D3
STF 645	0509.8	2802N	6.1,8.6	28.9	11.8	73.0	2	A1
STF 654	0513.3	0252N	4.6,8.4	60.	7.00	43.10	1	D1
				64.0	6.73	73.1	3	A1
STT 517	0513.4	0158N	6.9,7.1	49.0	0.44	67.41	4	D3
STF 668	0514.5	0812S	0.1,9.3	203.7	10.1	73.0	3	A1
STF 653	0515.5	3241N	5.2,7.4	225.4	14.4	73.0	1	A1
STF 681	0520.7	4658N	6.7,8.7	181.6	23.2	73.0	2	A1
STF 634	0522.3	7918N	5.2,9.2	123.0	17.55	73.2	3	A1
				124.0	20.00	79.37	3	DG
STF 696	0522.8	0332N	5.0,7.1	29.5	32.0	73.0	2	A1
				30.0	31.1	82.11	2	RW
STF 701	0523.3	0826N	6.0,7.8	140.1	5.96	73.0	3	A1
WNC 2	0523.9	0053S	6.1,7.2	163.2	2.63	67.15	2	D3
A 847	"	"	8.0,8.1	151.	0.35	67.15	2	D3

PAIR	RA 2000 DEC		MAGS	PA	SEP	DATE	N	OBS
DA 5	0524.4	0224S	3.8,4.8	79.1	1.48	43.14	3	D1
				81.8	1.42	67.13	4,3	D3
HJ 3759	0526.0	1942S	5.8,8.6	317.4	26.50	82.13	3	RF
HO 226	0527.1	2736N	8.6,8.6	252.0	0.80	65.8	2	D3
				257.6	0.64	67.10	4	D3
STF 716	0529.2	2509N	5.8,6.6	203.6	4.75	43.13	5	D1
				205.7	4.96	73.2	3	A1
				206.8	4.76	77.00	10	WS
STF 728	0530.7	0556N	4.5,6.0	40.0	0.5	45.19	1	D1
				50.3	0.77	64.8	3	D2
				54.8	0.77	65.8	4	D3
				58.5	0.79	67.8	4	D1
				50.9	0.86	75.15	3	D4
STF 729	0531.2	0317N	5.8,7.1	25.7	1.84	43.11	4	D1
				26.0	1.90	64.7	3,4	D2
STF 14 APP	0532.0	0018S	2.5,6.6	0.0	52.2	73.1	1	A1
STF 730	0532.2	1703N	6.0,6.5	142.7	9.71	78.90	3	GH
STF 718	0532.3	4924N	7.5,7.5	73.5	7.5	73.2	2	A1
BU 1267	0535.1	3056N	8.8,8.8	201.9	0.6	65.76	2	D3
STF 738 AB	0535.1	0956N	3.7,5.6	43.0	4.32	43.13	5	D1
				45.8	4.48	63.1	1,9	D2
				43.3	4.34	77.30	5	WS
				43.8	4.38	81.33	6,3	WS
BC	"	"	5.6,11.2	184.8	28.91	82.11	3	KS
STF 747	0535.2	0601S	4.7,5.6	228.	35.4	82.12	1	RW
STF 748 CA	0535.3	0523S	5.4,6.8	311.4	13.2	73.1	2	A1
CB	"	"	,7.9	343.2	16.9	73.1	2	A1
CD	"	"	,6.8	61.1	13.4	73.1	2	A1
STF 752	0535.4	0555S	2.9,7.0	141.1	11.8	73.1	2	A1
STF 742	0536.4	2200N	7.2,7.8	267.1	3.75	42.20	5	D1
STF 749	0537.2	2656N	6.4,6.5	151.3	1.12	64.6	1	D2
HU 1240	0538.6	3030N	6.1,6.5	round		65.8	1	D3
STF 753	"	"	,8.0	268.3	12.2	73.0	1	A1
STT 112	0539.8	3758N	7.8,8.5	61.4	0.65	43.15	3	D1
				57.5	0.80	65.8	3	D3
				56.9	0.84	67.07	3	D3
STF 766	0540.3	1521N	7.0,8.2	274.2	10.1	73.1	2	A1
STF 774	0540.7	0157S	2.0,4.2	163.2	2.30	44.23	1	D1
				161.7	2.51	73.1	3	A1
				162.8	2.39	77.37	6,4	WS

PAIR		RA	2000	DEC	MAGS	PA	SEP	DATE	N	OBS
BU 1007		0541.1		1632N	5.6,5.8	round		65.8	3	D3
STF 764		0541.4		2929N	6.8,7.4	13.3	26.0	73.0	2	A1
STT 115		0544.5		1503N	7.5,8.3	115.1	0.58	43.16	3	D1
						120.7	0.55	65.82	1	D3
BU 560		0547.4		2929N	8.0,8.0	141.4	1.28	43.10	1	D1
						131.8	0.41	65.76	1	D3
STF 795		0548.0		0627N	6.1,6.1	209.5	1.31	43.14	5	D1
						214.3	1.55	73.19	3	A1
STT 118		0548.4		2052N	6.1,7.6	311.2	0.4	65.8	2	D3
STF 3115		0549.1		6248N	6.5,7.6	358.7	0.86	67.08	3	D3
STF 780		0551.1		6545N	6.9,8.1	104.1	3.82	82.28	4	DG
STF 802		0552.5		4008N	9.0,9.6	108.2	2.82	42.19	2	D1
A 1570		0557.6		4238N	9.9,10.4	350.3	1.20	67.29	2	D3
STT 545		0559.7		3714N	2.7,7.2	323.6	3.15	43.11	5	D1
						321.7	3.19	44.15	1	D1
						312.8	3.60	73.19	3	A1
DUN 23		0604.8		4828S	7.0,7.4	110.8	2.57	82.13	3	RF
STT 121		0605.3		7400N	7.6,8.8	round		67.2	1	D3
STT 855	AB	0609.0		0230N	6.0,7.0	114.5	29.6	73.0	2	A1
						113.	28.9	82.18	1	RW
	AC	"		"	,8.9	106.6	88.5	73.0	1	A1
STT 134		0609.3		2426N	8.5,9.8	189.0	30.6	73.1	2	A1
STF 845		0611.7		4843N	6.1,6.8	356.4	7.7	73.1	2	A1
KUI 24		0614.4		1754N	6.5,6.5	138.3	0.57	65.80	5,6	D3
						138.	0.55	66.78	2	D3
						133.0	0.32	73.80	1	D4
STF 877		0614.7		1435N	7.3,7.8	263.9	5.80	43.17	5	D1
BU 1008		0614.9		2230N	var,8.8	264.5	1.51	64.8	3	D2
						260.5	1.41	65.16	3	D3
STF 872		0615.6		3609N	6.8,7.8	216.2	12.0	73.1	2	A1
						216.2	12.07	77.26	3	CP
						216.4	11.22	82.95	2	KS
STF 881		0622.1		5923N	6.2,7.7	128.3	0.71	65.7	3	D3
SHJ 70		0627.7		2048N	6.6,8.0	203.2	26.55	81.91	2	KS
STF 919	BC	0628.9		0703S	5.7,6.2	286.9	2.80	42.20	1	D1
	AC	"		"	4.7,6.2	123.2	10.12	42.20	1	D1
	AB	"		"	4.7,5.7	131.1	7.01	42.20	1	D1
STF 924		0632.4		1747N	7.1,8.0	211.4	20.7	73.0	2	A1
STF 918		0634.0		5229N	7.2,8.2	337.3	4.46	79.37	3	DG
						333.9	4.82	77.10	5	WS

PAIR	RA 2000 DEC	MAGS	PA	SEP	DATE	N	OBS
STF 932	0634.3 1444N	8.1,8.2	319.5	2.00	43.17	3	D1
STF 928	0634.7 3832N	7.6,8.2	133.8	3.49	43.17	3	D1
STT 149	0636.5 2717N	7.0,9.5	round		65.8	1	D3
STF 943	0637.3 2311N	9.7,11.0	136.4	28.47	82.15	3	KS
STT 152	0639.5 2816N	6.0,7.8	32.6	0.80	43.15	4	D1
STF 945	0640.4 4059N	7.3,8.2	295.2	0.55	66.0	5,3	D3
			114.7	0.60	66.97	4	D3
S 533	0643.9 2508N	3.2,9.2	94.2	111.23	82.18	2	KS
STF 946	0644.9 5927N	8.3,10.1	131.0	4.18	42.84	3	D1
AGC 1	0645.2 1641S	-1.4,8.5	72.	10.44	65.76	3,2	D3
STF 948 AB	0646.3 5927N	5.3,6.2	97.7	1.65	43.15	7	D1
			95.4	1.68	45.19	1	D1
			89.8	1.76	65.70	3	D3
AC	" "	5.3,7.2	305.1	8.63	43.15	7	D1
BC	" "	6.2,7.2	303.1	10.22	43.15	7	D1
STT 78 APP	0646.7 4335N	5.4,8.4	33.8	34.4	73.2	2	A1
STT 156	0647.4 1812N	6.7,7.2	274.7	0.61	43.52	4	D1
			78.8	0.58	65.79	2,3	D3
			78.0	0.52	67.15	4	D3
STF 958	0648.3 5543N	6.3,6.3	258.8	4.73	42.89	6	D1
			256.9	5.18	77.03	4	GH
STF 963	0653.2 5928N	5.7,6.9	233.0	0.37	65.60	6	D3
STF 982	0654.6 1310N	4.8,7.1	149.2	6.80	73.07	3	A1
STF 981	0655.5 3010N	8.9,8.9	322.5	2.53	42.19	4	D1
			137.3	2.47	66.92	5	D3
STT 159	0657.3 5825N	4.8,5.9	38.4	0.91	65.64	4	D3
A 1575	0703.0 5403N	8.2,9.2	283.3	0.64	42.26	2	D1
DUN 39	0703.3 5911N	6.0,7.1	85.2	1.58	82.28	4	RF
STT 81 APP	0704.1 2034N	var,8.0	348.4	98.7	73.0	2	A1
STF 1009	0705.6 5245N	6.9,7.0	149.5	3.71	67.55	1,2	D3
STF 1033	0714.8 5233N	7.7,8.3	275.7	1.53	66.0	2,3	D3
			277.9	1.44	67.14	3	D3
HJ 3945	0716.6 2319S	4.8,6.8	53.4	26.77	82.28	4	RF
STT 170	0717.2 0919N	7.6,7.9	100.4	1.69	43.87	3	D1
			91.8	1.50	64.8	2	D2
			91.3	1.24	67.37	3	D3
STF 1066	0720.2 2159N	3.5,8.5	220.0	6.06	73.15	3	A1
STF 1083	0725.6 2030N	7.2,8.3	44.4	6.45	73.0	2	A1
STF 1093	0730.3 4959N	8.8,8.8	178.4	0.8	65.8	3,2	D3
STF 1108	0732.8 2253N	6.6,8.4	178.3	11.7	73.0	2	A1

PAIR	RA 2000 DEC	MAGS	PA	SEP	DATE	N	OBS
STF 1110	0734.6 3153N	2.0,2.9	198.6	3.55	42.22	11,13	D1
			198.3	3.41	43.19	7	D1
			196.6	3.30	44.25	10	D1
			196.2	3.25	45.26	7	D1
			156.0	1.95	63.14	11	D2
			153.5	1.97	64.76	8,7	D2
			150.8	1.93	65.76	10	D3
			144.2	1.89	67.29	6	D3
			119.8	2.07	73.11	3	A1
			117.5	2.0	73.77	2	D4
			120.2	2.01	75.15	3	D4
			106.6	2.36	77.43	14,11	WS
			90.7	2.82	82.30	6	WS
AB - C		1.7,8.8	163.3	71.8	73.1	2	A1
STT 175	0735.2 3058N	5.8,6.4	329.0	0.3	65.6	8,3	D3
STT 174	0735.9 4302N	6.5,8.1	86.9	2.23	73.1	3	A1
STF 1126	0740.1 0515N	6.4,6.7	154.7	1.10	43.88	3	D1
			159.0	1.08	65.82	3	D3
STT 177	0741.7 3726N	8.0,9.0	round		66.2	1	D3
HJ 3997	0743.5 7417S	7.2,7.3	121.7	1.93	82.28	3	RF
STT 179	0744.5 2424N	3.7,8.2	240.4	6.99	73.1	3	A1
STF 1138	0745.5 1441S	6.1,6.8	340.1	16.6	73.1	2	A1
			341.	17.4	82.29	1	RW
STF 1140	0748.5 1821N	7.9,9.6	275.4	6.3	73.0	2	A1
STT 186	0803.3 2616N	7.5,8.2	77.0	0.87	66.2	2	D3
BU 581	0804.3 1218N	8.7,8.7	284.1	0.51	43.16	3	D1
			178.6	0.37	66.2	4,3	D3
			186.1	0.34	67.25	4	D3
			193.6	0.37	68.2	3	D3
STF 1177	0805.6 2732N	6.6,7.5	350.5	3.44	42.97	8	D1
			168.7	3.50	65.8	3,2	D3
			351.0	3.37	78.15	3	GH
STF 1187	0809.5 3214N	7.1,8.0	32.5	2.48	44.20	3	D1
			27.9	2.78	65.81	2	D3
STF 1196AB	0812.2 1740N	5.6,6.0	76.4	0.86	42.55	5	D1
			68.8	0.81	43.17	7	D1
			64.2	0.89	44.23	4	D1
			56.3	0.92	45.29	4	D1
			176.6	1.06	63.10	4,2	D2
			344.8	1.14	65.81	7	D3

PAIR	RA 2000	DEC	MAGS	PA	SEP	DATE	N	OBS
STF 1196AB	0812.2	1740N	5.6,6.0	342.3	1.02	67.20	3	D3
				340.2	1.11	67.84	3	D3
				335.7	1.09	68.23	4	D3
				329.1	1.1	70.94	4	D4
				316.9	1.00	73.22	4	D4
				313.4	1.00	73.79	4	D4
				308.2	0.92	75.15	2	D4
				264.0	0.74	82.15	3	KS
AB – C	"	"	5.0,6.3	93.5	5.51	63.10	4	D2
				84.8	5.69	73.79	4	D4
				80.0	5.27	82.17	5	WS
				80.7	6.13	78.69	6,3	WS
AC	"	"	5.6,6.3	95.2	6.38	42.22	4	D1
				95.9	6.28	43.37	4	D1
				95.9	6.20	44.23	4	D1
BC	"	"	6.0,6.3	98.7	5.41	42.22	4	D1
				100.5	5.43	43.57	4	D1
				100.6	5.43	44.23	4	D1
HU 1123	0814.8	3630N	8.9,9.2	156.2	0.44	43.19	2	D1
STF 1216	0821.4	0136S	6.9,7.6	242.5	0.42	65.8	1	D3
				264.6	0.48	67.19	2	D3
STT 93 APP	0824.6	4200N	6.2,8.7	174.0	82.6	73.1	2	A1
STF 1224	0826.7	2433N	7.1,7.6	48.2	5.67	42.24	4	D1
				48.8	5.80	73.2	3	A1
				47.9	5.59	77.30	4	DG
				48.1	5.51	82.28	5	DG
STF 1223	0826.8	2656N	6.3,6.3	217.3	4.98	42.24	5	D1
				217.0	5.39	73.1	3	A1
				217.2	4.91	77.82	9,7	WS
STF 1245	0835.8	0637N	6.0,7.2	26.0	10.6	73.0	2	A1
				24.1	9.81	78.13	3	GH
				27.	10.3	82.23	1	RW
STF 1263	0844.2	4141N	8.7,9.3	23.2	85.30	82.19	2	KS
STF 1266	0844.4	2827N	8.8,10.0	62.8	23.80	82.29	1	KS
STF 1268	0846.7	2846N	4.2,6.6	307.4	30.6	73.0	2	A1
				307.0	30.03	82.27	2	WS
STF 1273	0846.8	0625N	3.6,7.8	260.8	3.01	43.25	6	D1
				277.5	3.25	73.05	3	A1
STF 1275	0851.5	5732N	8.4,8.4	198.5	2.05	43.28	2	D1
A 1584	0853.1	5458N	8.2,8.2	91.0	0.72	42.28	2	D1

PAIR	RA 2000	DEC	MAGS	PA	SEP	DATE	N	OBS
STF 1291	0854.2	3034N	6.1,6.6	318.7	1.48	43.25	5	D1
HJ 460 AB	0855.2	2816N	6.4,9.9	333.4	46.30	82.29	1	KS
AC	"	"	6.4,	200.7	280.87	82.29	1	KS
KUI 37	0900.8	4148N	4.3,6.3	319.1	0.54	42.36	7	D1
				302.7	0.52	43.33	11	D1
				139.	0.4	73.77	1	D4
STF 1300	0901.3	1516N	9.3,9.4	192.4	5.12	43.30	2	D1
STF 1298	0901.4	3215N	5.9,8.0	136.7	4.43	73.1	2	A1
STF 1311	0907.5	2259N	6.9,7.3	199.5	7.75	73.1	2	A1
				198.6	7.52	78.24	2	GH
STF 1306	0910.4	6708N	5.0,8.2	45.4	1.77	43.26	5	D1
STF 1321	0914.9	5242N	8.1,8.1	84.7	17.68	73.19	3	A1
				85.9	17.44	76.85	12,10	WS
STF 1332	0917.4	2336N	7.8,8.1	27.3	6.90	82.22	2	KS
				88.1	17.84	82.15	4	WS
STF 3121	0918.0	2835N	8.1,8.1	55.5	0.3	43.21	3	D1
				29.0	0.62	73.22	2	D4
STF 1333	0918.5	3522N	6.4,6.7	49.1	1.77	43.27	4	D1
				49.0	1.77	63.0	4	D2
				48.4	1.82	73.37	5	D4
STF 1334	0918.9	3649N	3.9,6.6	228.5	2.44	63.5	2,4	D2
				231.0	2.56	67.02	2,5	D3
STF 1338	0921.0	3812N	6.6,6.8	243.0	1.18	73.39	4	D4
STF 1348	0924.4	0621N	7.5,7.6	139.4	1.98	43.30	3	D1
STF 1356	0928.5	0904N	5.9,6.7	151.0	0.84	43.62	7	D1
				358.5	0.53	73.23	4	D4
				1.8	0.5	75.32	2	D4
STF 1360	0930.5	1035N	8.3,8.6	242.9	13.8	73.1	2	A1
STF 1351	0931.5	6304N	3.8,9.0	269.3	22.5	73.2	2	A1
STT 101APP	0931.9	0942N	5.4,8.4	76.3	36.6	73.0	2	A1
STF 1350	0934.2	6747N	8.1,8.2	248.8	10.20	82.38	5	DG
H 58	0935.9	1423N	6.2,10.0	83.	41.3	82.32	1	RW
STF 1362	0938.1	7306N	7.2,7.2	126.4	5.19	82.38	5	DG
STF 1374	0941.4	3856N	7.3,8.6	295.9	3.22	42.68	5	D1
				303.3	3.15	78.32	9,7	WS
A C 5	0952.5	0806S	5.8,6.2	35.	0.53	42.28	5	D1
				97.	0.5	73.30	1	D4
STF 1399	0957.1	1946N	7.7,9.6	175.2	30.7	73.1	2	A1
STF 1402	1004.9	5529N	8.1,9.6	102.4	30.79	78.41	6	DG
STT 215	1016.3	1744N	7.3,7.5	187.1	1.23	67.14	5	D3

PAIR	RA 2000 DEC		MAGS	PA	SEP	DATE	N	OBS
STF 215	1016.3	1744N	7.3,7.5	184.7	1.07	71.08	3	D4
				188.8	1.37	73.31	2	D4
				187.5	1.2	75.33	2	D4
STF 1415	1017.9	7104N	6.7,7.3	166.7	16.8	73.2	2	A1
				166.6	16.63	82.35	4	DG
STF 1424	1020.0	1951N	2.6,3.8	120.9	4.33	65.81	3,4	D3
				123.7	4.42	70.40	2	A2
				124.8	4.29	72.34	3	D4
				123.1	4.78	81.80	6	WS
STF 1426	1020.5	0626N	8.4,8.9	296.2	0.97	43.30	3	D1
STF 1428	1026.0	5238N	7.9,8.4	86.8	3.16	67.31	5	D3
HU 879	1027.9	3643N	4.5,7.0	233.2	0.48	42.66	6	D1
STF 1439	1029.4	2049N	8.9,9.4	282.6	1.77	43.29	2	D1
STF 1450	1035.1	0839N	5.8,8.5	156.1	2.41	73.2	3	A1
STF 1457	1038.7	0544N	8.0,9.0	323.3	1.65	42.33	2	D1
STT 228	1047.4	2235N	8.6,9.5	175.7	0.59	67.29	4	D3
STT 229	1048.1	4107N	7.4,7.8	287.6	0.75	65.93	1	D3
				289.3	0.89	67.29	3	D3
STF 1487	1055.6	2445N	4.5,6.3	109.7	6.51	43.85	2	D1
				113.2	6.80	73.37	1	D4
				109.8	6.29	82.38	5	WS
BU 1077	1103.7	6145N	2.0,4.8	290.	0.73	42.40	6	D1
				284.0	0.73	43.36	9	D1
HO 378	1105.0	3825N	8.3,8.5	237.4	0.64	67.30	3	D3
STF 1510	1108.0	5250N	7.6,8.9	332.6	4.89	78.40	5	DG
STF 1517	1113.7	2008N	7.7,7.7	not seen		72.39	1	D4
				332.8	0.40	73.32	2	D4
STT 232	1115.1	3734N	8.6,9.1	241.2	0.57	67.30	2	D3
STF 1516	1115.5	7328N	7.7,8.2	103.2	49.6	73.2	3	A1
STF 1523	1118.2	3133N	4.4,4.9	256.4	1.82	43.34	12	D1
				251.0	1.78	44.38	8	D1
				245.6	1.76	45.29	3	D1
				144.0	2.42	63.30	5,6	D2
				137.3	2.55	64.01	13,14	D2
				137.0	2.59	64.85	5,6	D2
				136.7	2.60	65.36	7	D3
				134.0	2.64	66.05	10	D3
				131.4	2.71	66.95	5,8	D3
				132.6	2.76	68.25	8,6	D3
				123.7	2.91	70.35	1	A2

PAIR	RA 2000 DEC	MAGS	PA	SEP	DATE	N	OBS
STF 1523	1118.2 3133N	4.4,4.9	120.1	3.09	72.33	4	D4
			118.7	3.02	73.23	3	D4
			116.6	3.10	74.35	3	D4
			116.9	3.02	75.31	3	D4
			111.9	2.96	75.90	14	DG
			108.7	2.99	77.66	17,15	WS
			104.4	3.00	79.37	6	DG
			100.9	2.80	81.35	5	DG
			97.6	2.97	82.33	4	WS
STF 1524	1118.5 3305N	3.7,10.1	147.3	7.51	73.2	3	A1
STF 1527	1119.1 1416N	6.9,8.1	23.2	2.50	43.39	3	D1
			32.1	2.00	73.11	3	A1
STF 1536	1123.8 1032N	4.1,7.3	299.7	0.66	43.36	9	D1
			297.9	0.62	44.39	3	D1
BSO 5	1124.9 6139S	8.2,9.2	237.6	5.83	81.41	5	RF
STI 725	1125.5 5841N	10.1,11.6	15.5	14.78	76.44	2	DG
STF 1540 AB	1126.9 0300N	6.2,7.9	150.	27.8	82.38	1	RW
STF 1543	1129.1 3920N	5.4,8.4	358.9	5.51	43.35	1	D1
			358.6	5.33	73.2	3	A1
			357.0	5.23	77.49	2	CP
STT 234	1130.8 4117N	7.6,8.0	225.	0.3	43.39	3	D1
STF 1547	1131.8 1422N	6.4,8.4	329.2	15.2	73.2	3	A1
			326.7	15.52	80.31	1	CP
STT 235	1132.4 6105N	5.8,7.1	39.0	0.84	43.35	5	D1
			88.0	0.79	65.57	5	D3
			98.	0.89	67.02	3	D3
STF 1552	1134.7 1648N	6.1,7.4	207.3	3.48	67.32	5	D3
			207.3	3.21	79.35	1	CP
STF 1555	1136.3 2747N	6.4,6.8	131.1	0.5e	64.0	4,1	D2
			142.	0.43	65.67	4	D3
			139.0	0.48	67.06	8	D3
			149.	0.5	70.94	1	D4
			143.0	0.61	73.32	4	D4
STF 1559	1138.8 6421N	6.8,7.8	323.1	1.67	73.37	2	D4
STF 1561	1138.9 4507N	6.4,8.5	255.8	9.76	43.37	2	D1
			252.3	9.64	73.2	3	A1
			252.8	9.79	77.41	2	CP
STT 237	1139.0 4109N	8.4,10.0	256.7	1.59	42.85	2	D1
BU 794	1153.7 7346N	7.1,8.4	73.8	0.50	43.42	2	D1
			126.0	0.47	66.0	2	D3

PAIR	RA	2000	DEC	MAGS	PA	SEP	DATE	N	OBS
A 1088	1200.5		6912N	7.8,8.5	round		66.0	1	D3
STF 1596	1204.3		2128N	6.0,7.5	238.5	3.51	43.37	1	D1
					235.1	3.90	82.42	2	DG
STF 3123	1206.1		6842N	7.9,7.9	129.9	0.41	43.41	3	D1
STF 1604	AB1208.4		1151S	6.9,9.4	89.0	9.15	73.1	2	A1
					59.1	14.21	79.33	3	DG
AC	"		"	,9.3	66.6	15.55	73.1	2	A1
STF 1606	1210.8		3954N	7.3,8.0	311.7	0.76	42.40	4	D1
					313.8	0.77	43.39	4	D1
					292.0	0.62	66.0	4	D3
					289.3	0.41	70.41	1	A2
					280.4	0.66	73.36	2	D4
SHJ 136	1211.0		8143N	6.5,8.5	74.6	69.84	72.38	4	DG
S 634	1211.4		1647S	7.2,8.4	292.9	5.47	81.35	3	RF
STF 1608	1211.5		5326N	8.2,8.4	221.4	13.02	79.48	4	DG
					221.6	12.44	77.45	6	DG
STF 1619	1215.1		0715S	8.0,8.3	272.9	6.46	77.43	5	DG
STF 1622	1216.1		4040N	5.9,8.2	260.6	11.6	73.2	2	A1
STF 1625	1216.2		8008N	7.3,7.8	217.9	13.83	72.69	26	DG
STF 1627	1218.1		0356S	6.6,6.9	196.2	20.2	73.1	2	A1
STF 1633	1220.6		2704N	7.0,7.1	245.1	9.01	73.1	2	A1
STT 249	1223.8		5410N	8.1,8.9	289.7	0.42	43.38	2	D1
					278.0	0.31	67.33	3	D3
					268.5	0.4	73.33	1	D4
STF 1639	1224.4		2535N	6.6,7.8	329.2	1.31	67.04	5	D3
					327.0	1.32	73.32	2	D4
STT 250	1224.4		4306N	8.4,8.7	346.4	0.43	43.38	1	D1
					340.	0.34	67.33	4	D3
STF 1643	1227.2		2702N	9.2,9.5	195.6	2.64	64.4	3	D2
STF 1717	1228.4		8840N	9.4,10.8	326.1	7.80	76.63	3	DG
STF 1647	1230.6		0943N	8.5,8.8	232.5	1.41	43.36	2	D1
					238.8	1.31	67.12	4	D3
					241.5	1.50	81.43	2	DG
STF 1657	1235.1		1823N	5.2,6.7	270.7	20.3	73.2	2	A1
					274.5	19.09	78.29	2	GH
					271.4	20.18	82.18	5	RW
STF 1661	1236.1		1124N	9.1,9.1	245.4	2.52	43.38	1	D1
					244.7	2.64	77.43	2	DG
STF 1669	1241.3		1301S	6.0,6.1	312.3	5.56	81.35	3	RF
HJ 4539	1241.5		4858S	3.1,3.1	357.3	1.65	80.33	2	RF

PAIR	RA 2000 DEC	MAGS	PA	SEP	DATE	N	OBS
STF 1670	1241.7 0127S	3.6,3.7	307.5	4.97	63.11	7,6	D2
			303.	4.87	64.93	1,2	D2
			305.8	4.65	65.4	3,1	D3
			304.9	4.74	65.9	3,4	D3
			305.1	4.73	66.98	4,6	D3
			303.5	4.59	68.36	1,2	D3
			304.3	4.43	70.40	1	A2
			301.4	4.32	73.41	3	D4
			301.2	4.52	74.40	3,1	D4
			299.1	4.03	77.52	21,18	WS
			295.7	3.83	80.40	6	WS
STF 1678	1245.4 1422N	6.8,8.5	178.0	34.8	73.1	2	A1
HJ 4547	1245.6 6059N	4.7,9.5	11.1	27.54	81.44	5	RF
STF 1694	1249.3 8324N	5.3,5.8	325.6	21.42	74.58	16	DG
STF 1687	1253.3 2115N	5.2,8.0	120.2	0.94	42.68	7	D1
			117.3	1.00	44.42	1	D1
STF 1689	1255.5 1130N	7.1,9.4	217.4	29.2	73.1	3	A1
STF 1692	1256.1 3818N	2.9,5.4	228.4	19.3	73.1	2	A1
			227.1	18.67	78.31	5,3	WS
			227.6	19.59	81.48	2	RW
STF 1695	1256.3 5405N	6.0,7.9	279.9	3.55	67.40	2	D3
STT 256	1256.4 0057S	7.2,7.6	89.2	0.73	42.39	3	D1
			94.1	0.72	74.37	3,2	D4
STF 1699	1258.7 2728N	8.6,8.6	7.3	1.62	67.31	4	D3
BU 1082	1300.6 5622N	4.9,8.5	317.2	0.93	43.38	7	D1
BU 929	1303.9 0340S	7.1,7.4	206.9	0.57	43.39	3	D1
			198.4	0.65	73.41	4	D4
STF 1728	1310.0 1731N	5.2,5.2	194.6	0.45	43.45	3	D1
			197.	0.33	44.43	4	D1
			15.3	0.47	65.35	6	D3
			11.3	0.60	66.0	6,4	D3
			17.	0.64	67.02	2	D3
			189.8	0.36	70.38	1	A2
			15.0	0.25	71.04	4	D4
STT 261	1312.0 3205N	7.2,7.7	340.7	2.19	67.09	3	D3
			341.9	2.19	70.38	1	A2
STF 1734	1320.7 0257N	6.7,7.4	180.0	1.12	67.42	1	D3
			181.5	1.07	70.40	1	A2
			180.6	1.18	73.40	2	D4
			151.2	14.4	73.2	2	A1

PAIR	RA 2000 DEC		MAGS	PA	SEP	DATE	N	OBS
STF 1744	1323.9	5456N	2.4,4.0	152.8	15.53	77.35	2	GH
				151.6	14.43	81.61	7	WS
STF 1742	1324.3	0124N	7.6,8.1	0.	1.38	73.40	2	D4
STT 269	1332.8	3454N	7.3,7.8	221.8	0.33	65.24	3,2	D3
				232.2	0.36	67.24	2	D3
				236.	0.3	70.98	2	D4
				235.	0.3	73.36	1	D4
				231.7	0.3	74.40	1	D4
STF 1757	1334.3	0009S	7.7,7.8	108.0	2.45	67.42	4	D3
				109.8	2.56	77.81	8	DG
				111.8	2.38	81.44	4	RF
STF 1768	1337.5	3617N	5.1,7.0	109.0	1.69	65.95	4	D3
				110.7	1.64	67.26	4	D3
				103.2	1.52	70.43	1	A2
				110.4	1.70	72.46	3	D4
STF 1770	1337.8	5042N	6.8,8.3	121.3	1.61	67.22	5	D3
				119.0	1.31	70.42	1	A2
BU 612	1339.6	1044N	6.3,6.3	218.	0.38	65.98	1	D3
				227.1	0.32	67.30	4	D3
				240.	0.25	71.08	1	D4
HJ 4608	1342.3	3359S	7.5,7.6	183.0	4.42	81.60	3	RF
STF 1781	1346.1	0507N	7.8,8.2	7.0	0.55	67.31	3	D3
STF 1785	1349.2	2659N	7.9,8.2	118.0	1.99	42.42	7	D1
				119.7	2.05	43.46	7	D1
				124.2	2.13	44.54	5	D1
				146.6	3.12	63.14	6,5	D2
				147.4	3.14	66.1	3	D3
				147.8	3.14	67.15	5	D3
				151.9	3.30	70.42	1	A2
				155.0	3.27	72.41	3	D4
				153.6	3.27	73.21	3	D4
				155.8	3.31	74.28	3	D4
				157.3	3.30	78.56	4	DG
STF 1788	1355.0	0803S	6.5,7.7	92.2	3.38	77.43	5	DG
STF 1795	1358.9	5307N	6.8,10.0	3.5	8.12	82.35	2	KS
STT 276	1408.2	3644N	8.6,9.4	203.7	0.39	67.36	3	D3
STT 278	1412.0	4411N	8.4,8.6	333.8	0.32	67.28	3	D3
STT 277	1412.4	2843N	8.3,8.5	41.7	0.41	73.44	2	D4
STF 1820	1413.1	5520N	8.8,9.1	95.8	2.39	43.54	1	D1
				102.1	2.32	74.40	4,3	D4

PAIR	RA 2000 DEC		MAGS	PA	SEP	DATE	N	OBS
STF 1820	1413.1	5520N	8.8,9.1	95.8	2.39	43.54	1	D1
STF 1821	1413.5	5147N	4.6,6.6	236.3	13.5	73.2	1	A1
				235.7	13.60	81.61	6	WS
STF 1816	1413.9	2906N	7.5,7.6	84.3	0.94	66.1	6,3	D3
				91.0	0.83	67.10	3	D3
				86.1	0.86	70.40	1	A2
STF 1817	1414.2	2642N	8.9,9.5	1.5	0.50	67.14	6	D3
STF 1834	1420.3	4831N	7.9,8.0	97.0	0.68	44.07	4	D1
				102.2	1.09	67.09	4	D3
STF 1835	1423.4	0827N	5.1,6.6	191.8	6.30	78.52	7	WS
STF 1835	1423.4	0827N	5.1,6.6	190.3	6.32	81.57	1	RW
STF 1838	1424.1	1115N	7.4,7.5	334.2	8.71	78.49	8	WS
STF 1843AB	1424.7	4750N	7.6,9.1	186.2	20.08	82.42	2	KS
AC	"	"	7.6,	64.5	97.83	82.42	2	KS
STF 1850	1428.6	2817N	7.0,7.4	262.0	25.87	82.38	2	KS
A 570	1432.3	2641N	6.6,6.8	318.5	0.25	70.41	1	A2
STF 1863	1438.1	5135N	7.4,7.7	77.8	0.58	44.07	4	D1
				69.2	0.65	74.35	2	D4
Alpha Cen	1439.6	6050S	0.0,1.7	210.5	21.71	80.40	2	RF
STF 1864	1440.7	1626N	4.9,5.8	107.5	5.77	43.02	6	D1
				104.8	5.77	66.0	2	D3
				108.9	5.58	67.01	6,8	D3
				108.7	5.78	82.01	11	WS
STF 1872	1441.0	5757N	7.5,8.5	47.5	7.63	79.49	5	DG
STF 1865	1441.1	1344N	4.4,4.8	132.2	1.08	44.57	5	D1
				129.5	1.35	70.48	5	D4
				126.8	1.07	70.41	3	A2
				126.5	1.27	73.44	2	D4
				125.4	1.32	79.56	4	DG
STF 1871	1441.4	5124N	8.0,8.0	304.5	1.86	67.28	3	D3
				304.3	1.84	73.42	2	D4
				301.2	2.27	81.63	5	DG
STF 1877	1445.0	2704N	2.7,5.1	338.5	2.78	65.6	3,6	D3
				337.0	2.77	67.09	2	D3
				332.4	2.70	73.43	4	D4
				339.0	3.24	80.66	8	WS
STT 285	1445.5	4222N	7.7,8.2	55.4	0.41	43.49	5	D1
				57.2	0.49	44.54	3	D1
				326.	0.3	67.16	5	D3
STF 1884	1448.5	2422N	6.2,7.8	58.3	1.93	70.42	1	A2

PAIR	RA	2000	DEC	MAGS	PA	SEP	DATE	N	OBS
BU 106	1449.3		1409S	5.8,6.7	0.3	1.71	73.43	3	D4
STF 1890	1449.6		4843N	6.1,6.8	44.1	2.90	66.1	6,3	D3
					42.4	2.95	67.45	5	D3
STT 287	1451.4		4455N	8.5,8.6	157.4	1.03	42.68	5	D1
					164.2	1.12	67.16	3	D3
STF 1888	1451.4		1907N	4.8,6.7	4.7	5.61	43.47	11	D1
					3.2	5.68	44.52	7	D1
					347.0	6.87	64.40	2	D2
					347.2	7.06	64.5	1,2	D2
					342.4	7.00	66.1	3,4	D3
					342.2	6.92	67.22	4	D3
					341.8	7.04	70.38	1	A2
					339.2	7.30	70.51	3	D4
					339.4	6.93	72.30	25	DG
					336.2	7.10	73.33	3	D4
					336.3	7.36	74.42	2	D4
					336.7	6.95	75.48	22	DG
					334.7	6.79	78.08	33	WS
					332.9	7.22	81.47	20	WS
STT 288	1453.4		1543N	6.9,7.6	176.0	1.55	67.16	3	D3
					178.4	1.63	70.37	1	A2
STI 2317	1459.4		5510N	9.7,10.7	123.6	24.38	73.57	4	DG
SHJ 191	1459.6		5352N	6.8,7.4	342.1	39.82	73.60	6	DG
BU 348	1501.8		0008S	6.0,8.3	107.3	0.39	70.51	1	A2
STF 1909	1503.9		4739N	5.3,6.2	251.8	2.13	43.45	16	D1
					252.4	2.05	44.48	12	D1
					253.5	2.00	45.74	5	D1
					279.5	0.83	63.30	9	D2
					283.0	0.64	65.3	13,12	D3
					291.8	0.64	66.1	5,4	D3
					301.0	0.56	67.22	5	D3
					313.1	0.53	68.49	5	D3
					334.2	0.50	70.48	4	D4
					335.9	0.47	70.44	3	A2
					347.	0.5	71.52	1	D4
					356.4	0.48	72.43	5	D4
					1.5	0.60	73.35	6	D4
					6.8	0.53	74.36	3	D4
STF 1910	1507.5		0914N	7.5,7.5	109.9	4.02	79.54	5	DG
A 1116	1511.6		1008N	8.5,8.5	40.4	0.47	42.52	1	D1

PAIR	RA	2000	DEC	MAGS	PA	SEP	DATE	N	OBS
STF 1919	1512.8		1917N	6.8,7.7	9.6	23.74	80.96	6	WS
STF 1934	1517.4		4348N	9.4,9.4	17.6	8.56	77.54	6	DG
STF 1932	1518.3		2649N	7.1,7.6	240.4	1.04	64.4	2	D2
					241.6	1.14	65.8	1	D3
					243.5	1.07	67.16	3	D3
					244.5	1.0	71.06	2	D4
					247.1	1.16	73.50	3	D4
BU 32	1521.1		0044N	5.5,10.1	22.3	2.98	70.41	1	A2
STF 1937	1523.2		3018N	5.6,6.1	11.3	0.87	44.50	7	D1
					119.6	0.53	64.38	2	D2
					124.2	0.6e	64.52	2	D2
					132.2	0.54	65.27	10	D3
					144.8	0.55	66.15	5	D3
					152.9	0.57	67.17	5	D3
					165.7	0.59	68.40	6	D3
					183.2	0.62	70.39	2	A2
					183.3	0.63	70.48	5	D4
					190.5	0.65	71.45	3	D4
					200.0	0.59	72.38	4	D4
					208.6	0.62	74.25	3	D4
					213.2	0.68	74.25	3	D4
STF 1938	1524.5		3721N	7.2,7.8	23.6	2.03	63.04	6,4	D2
					20.6	2.08	70.38	2	A2
					19.4	2.07	72.50	4	D4
					17.6	2.29	72.98	23	DG
					20.6	2.01	73.42	4	D4
					15.7	2.28	76.85	25	DG
					14.2	2.41	81.21	15	DG
HU 149	1524.6		5413N	7.5,7.6	276.1	0.44	70.51	1	A2
STT 296	1526.5		4400N	7.6,9.2	283.5	1.69	70.50	1	A2
STF 1956	1533.2		4149N	8.5,10.0	not seen		73.46	5	D4
STF 1954	1534.8		1032N	4.2,5.2	181.0	3.76	43.0	12	D1
					179.2	3.95	67.47	5	D3
					183.1	4.04	70.42	1	A2
					175.9	4.05	80.71	9	WS
STT 298	1536.1		3948N	7.4,7.7	121.	0.3	42.50	4	D1
					146.7	0.36	43.48	4	D1
					156.6	0.58	44.54	5	D1
					162.5	0.55	45.73	3	D1
					189.2	1.28	66.1	3	D3

PAIR	RA 2000	DEC	MAGS	PA	SEP	DATE	N	OBS
STT 298	1536.1	3948N	7.4,7.7	192.9	1.13	67.45	4	D3
				195.9	0.91	70.41	3	A2
				194.6	1.12	70.51	4	D4
				205.3	1.04	73.42	6	D4
STF 1963	1537.9	3006N	8.8,9.2	296.3	5.14	67.12	3	D3
				295.5	4.97	77.97	4,2	WS
STF 1962	1538.7	0848S	6.5,6.6	189.2	12.08	82.55	5	DG
STF 1965	1539.4	3638N	5.1,6.0	306.0	6.20	67.59	5,8	D3
				306.6	6.41	77.53	6	WS
				304.7	6.27	79.83	7	WS
STF 1989	1539.7	7958N	7.3,8.3	30.0	0.65	67.28	5	D3
STF 1969	1541.4	5959N	8.9,9.6	round		66.2	1	D3
HU 580	1541.6	1941N	5.3,5.3	257.0	0.20	70.41	1	A2
STF 1967	1542.8	2618N	4.0,7.0	291.0	0.60	43.57	4	D1
BU 619	1543.1	1340N	6.9,7.4	1.6	0.60	67.28	3	D3
				3.6	0.53	70.41	1	A2
				8.5	0.57	73.52	3	D4
STF 1988	1556.8	1228N	7.4,8.1	255.9	2.48	78.20	7,5	WS
STT 303	1600.9	1315N	7.5,8.0	167.2	1.37	73.52	3	D4
STF 1998 AB	1604.4	1122S	4.8,5.1	40.8	0.70	44.05	1	D1
				0.3	1.18	67.53	3	D3
				7.5	1.34	72.52	2	D4
				11.0	1.17	73.49	3	D4
AC	"	"	4.8,7.2	44.7	7.50	73.54	2	D4
BC	"	"	5.1,7.2	51.0	6.75	73.54	2	D4
STF 1999	1604.4	1126S	7.4,8.1	100.4	10.92	73.53	2	D4
BU 812	1607.1	1654N	9.2,9.3	112.5	0.70	43.54	1	D1
STF 2010	1608.1	1703N	5.3,6.5	11.9	27.99	78.20	7,5	WS
				12.2	27.46	82.53	3	RW
BU 120 AB	1612.1	1927S	4.4,6.9	357.8	1.03	73.51	3	D4
BU 120 CD	"	"	6.9,7.9	49.0	1.4	73.51	3	D4
STF 2021	1613.3	1333N	7.5,7.7	348.8	4.88	70.43	1	A2
				349.6	4.26	78.55	5	DF
STF 2032	1614.7	3352N	5.8,6.7	225.6	5.75	43.04	13	D1
				229.6	6.32	63.3	7,4	D2
				229.0	6.24	66.1	4,1	D3
				230.7	6.22	67.95	10	D3
				230.8	6.35	70.50	3	A2
				232.2	6.53	77.21	9	WS
				233.8	6.70	82.19	3	RW

PAIR	RA 2000 DEC	MAGS	PA	SEP	DATE	N	OBS
STT 309	1619.2 4140N	8.6,8.8	284.	0.33	67.28	4	D3
STF 2054	1623.8 6141N	5.9,7.1	354.1	0.98	67.53	3	D3
			355.6	1.02	70.41	1	A2
			351.7	1.12	73.51	3	D4
STF 2049	1628.0 2559N	7.1,8.1	202.4	0.97	73.40	2	D4
STF 2052	1628.9 1825N	7.8,7.8	209.2	0.62	43.55	5	D1
			162.8	0.93	63.15	2,3	D2
			147.2	1.06	67.20	2	D3
			147.8	0.93	70.46	3	A2
			140.5	1.20	72.52	3	D4
			141.6	1.0	73.47	3	D4
STF 2055	1631.0 0159N	3.9,6.0	239.1	0.43	42.59	4	D1
			176.6	0.99	67.15	2	D3
			4.1	0.87	70.38	1	A2
			5.2	1.23	73.34	5	D4
STT 313	1632.6 4006N	7.7,8.3	137.3	0.88	65.3	5,4	D3
			135.6	0.92	67.44	3	D3
			136.9	0.72	73.44	3	D4
STF 2078	1636.3 5255N	5.6,6.6	106.6	3.22	65.3	1	D3
			107.9	3.33	67.98	4,5	D3
			105.3	3.51	78.59	5	DG
STF 2084	1641.1 3136N	3.0,6.5	33.7	0.99	64.4	1	D2
			20.3	0.70	65.3	2	D3
			5.5	0.65	65.60	5,4	D3
			356.	0.56	66.2	1	D3
			309.2	0.48	67.22	6,2	D3
			206.7	1.2	72.47	6,1	D4
			195.3	1.15	73.52	5	D4
STF 2091	1642.1 4112N	8.3,8.8	311.8	0.65	67.56	2	D3
STF 2085	1642.5 2136N	7.3,8.8	312.5	5.88	81.60	5	DG
HU 664	1643.7 5132N	8.4,8.4	306.2	0.38	72.56	3	D4
D 15	1643.9 4329N	9.1,9.1	152.3	1.21	67.56	2	D3
			144.0	1.17	73.57	2	D4
STF 2094	1644.2 2331N	7.4,7.7	72.7	1.23	67.16	2	D3
STF 2098AB	1645.7 3000N	9.1,10.1	145.8	14.88	82.51	3	KS
AC	" "	,10.4	129.5	65.78	82.51	3	KS
AD	" "	,15.7	17.5	65.24	82.51	3	KS
STF 2106	1651.1 0925N	7.0,8.7	189.7	0.53	73.56	2	D4
STT 315	1651.5 0113N	5.7,7.6	not seen		73.55	4	D4
STF 2107	1651.9 2840N	6.7,8.2	79.6	1.20	65.9	4	D3

PAIR	RA 2000 DEC	MAGS	PA	SEP	DATE	N	OBS
STF 2107	1651.9 2840N	6.7,8.2	83.7	1.08	70.57	2	A2
			85.4	1.44	73.45	2	D4
STF 2118	1656.3 6502N	6.9,7.4	74.0	1.02	65.6	2	D3
			71.6	1.07	67.39	6	D3
			71.5	1.12	73.56	2	D4
STT 340	1657.2 8651N	8.5,9.0	225.2	31.37	72.62	8	DG
STF 2114	1701.9 0827N	6.5,7.7	183.0	1.16	70.54	2	A2
			187.	1.5	73.56	2	D4
STF 2120	1704.8 2805N	7.3,10.1	232.9	18.90	77.68	6	DG
STF 2130	1705.4 5427N	5.8,5.8	96.0	2.20	43.55	12	D1
			95.1	2.16	44.61	5	D1
			69.9	2.15	63.1	2	D2
			67.6	2.01	65.3	3	D3
			67.5	2.01	65.6	3	D3
			63.4	2.10	67.20	5	D3
			63.9	2.14	68.43	5	D3
			55.6	2.10	72.32	4	D4
			56.0	2.15	73.57	4,1	D4
			47.9	2.50	78.59	5	DG
STF 2122	1706.9 0139S	6.3,8.5	277.8	21.13	80.75	1	RW
STF 2135	1712.0 2114N	7.5,8.8	189.7	7.44	77.65	6	DG
KUI 79	1712.1 4544N	10.1,10.6	272.8	0.76	67.34	4	D3
			231.2	1.0	73.55	3	D4
STF 2140	1714.6 1423N	3.5,5.4	111.7	4.66	43.63	2	D1
			106.9	4.61	70.6	3	A2
			107.1	4.96	77.48	4,2	WS
			105.8	4.72	80.83	9	WS
STF 3127	1715.0 2450N	3.2,8.3	265.2	9.07	81.70	1	RW
			262.8	8.58	77.81	7	WS
SHJ 243	1715.3 2736S	5.3,5.3	155.2	4.56	80.75	2	RF
BSO 13	1719.0 4638S	5.6,8.8	245.3	8.02	80.60	2	RF
MLB 4	1719.0 3459S	6.1,7.6	306.8	1.83	82.56	3	RF
STF 2161	1723.7 3708N	4.5,5.5	316.0	4.00	67.68	4,6	D3
			318.1	4.19	80.62	9	WS
STF 2164	1723.7 4716N	8.8,9.8	12.4	9.18	77.64	6	DG
BU 1201	1726.3 6746N	8.8,8.8	356.	0.35	72.57	2	D4
STF 2180	1729.0 5053N	7.7,7.9	259.6	2.97	81.63	5	DG
HO 417	1729.3 3758N	9.3,9.3	147.7	0.37	42.66	4	D1
KUI 82 AB-C	1729.4 2924N	9.3,9.3	302.3	49.05	82.48	2	KS
STF 2173	1730.3 0103S	5.9,6.2	334.5	1.03	42.64	14	D1

PAIR	RA 2000 DEC	MAGS	PA	SEP	DATE	N	OBS
STF 2173	1730.3 0103S	5.9,6.2	164.2	0.82	63.12	3,2	D2
			131.4	0.32	73.39	5	D4
STF 35 APP	1732.2 5511N	5.0,5.0	312.5	62.03	82.86	2	KS
STF 34 APP	1734.6 0935N	5.8,8.5	189.2	42.22	82.70	2	RW
STF 2186	1735.9 0100N	8.4,8.4	81.8	3.07	80.69	5	DG
STF 2207	1737.0 6707N	8.3,8.8	119.1	0.44	67.30	2	D3
			105.5	0.52	73.60	3	D4
STF 2199	1738.6 5546N	7.8,8.4	75.9	1.70	42.15	9	D1
			70.5	1.83	72.56	3	D4
STF 2218	1740.3 6340N	7.1,8.3	326.7	1.53	65.6	2	D3
			326.9	1.63	67.28	6	D3
			327.4	1.86	72.56	3	D4
STF 2203	1741.2 4140N	7.6,6.9	302.9	0.85	67.35	3	D3
			301.4	0.86	72.56	2	D4
STF 2241	1742.0 7210N	4.9,6.1	15.9	30.42	80.74	3	DG
STF 2202	1744.6 0235N	6.2,6.6	93.5	20.54	82.64	3	RW
STF 2213	1744.8 3108N	8.0,8.5	331.8	4.43	80.67	4	DG
A.C.7	1746.5 2745N	10.2,10.7	53.6	1.39	42.62	3	D1
			250.0	1.13	67.36	4,1	D3
			310.	0.56	73.52	5	D4
STF 2215	1747.2 1742N	5.8,7.8	272.9	0.64	67.24	3	D3
STT 337	1750.5 0715N	8.2,8.7	round		43.65	1	D1
			181.9	0.27	73.59	2	D4
STF 2242	1751.2 4455N	8.0,8.0	326.8	3.48	67.33	3	D3
STT 338	1752.0 1520N	6.8,7.1	5.2	0.80	43.65	1	D1
			358.	0.84	65.33	1	D3
			355.6	0.83	67.59	2	D3
			357.	1.10	73.34	2	D4
STF 2245	1756.2 1820N	7.4,7.4	110.9	2.63	80.64	5	DG
RMK 22	1757.2 5522S	7.0,8.0	92.8	2.44	82.71	2	RF
STF 2259	1759.0 3003N	7.4,8.4	278.4	19.86	81.59	5	DG
STF 2273	1759.3 6409N	7.5,7.8	283.0	21.06	81.70	5	DG
STF 2308	1800.1 8000N	5.8,6.2	230.3	19.02	80.58	2	DG
STF 2264	1801.5 2136N	5.1,5.2	258.	6.33	68.58	2,4	D3
			256.0	6.09	77.66	7	WS
			257.4	6.41	81.65	1	RW
STF 2267	1801.6 4011N	8.6,8.6	254.0	0.73	67.29	3	D3
STF 2278	1802.9 5625N	7.1,8.1	184.1	14.54	81.93	5	RW
STF 2262	1803.0 0811S	5.3,6.0	273.7	1.93	72.60	2	D4
			269.5	1.92	73.53	3	D4

PAIR	RA 2000 DEC	MAGS	PA	SEP	DATE	N	OBS
STF 2262	1803.0 0811S	5.3,6.0	272.2	2.08	82.27	5	RF
STF 2272	1805.4 0232N	4.3,6.3	110.7	6.60	43.68	6	D1
			110.7	6.37	44.60	2	D1
			87.8	3.84	63.12	9,10	D2
			82.	3.76	64.38	1	D2
			80.9	3.56	64.53	2,4	D2
			78.3	3.28	65.57	5,6	D3
			78.0	3.13	66.1	3	D3
			72.0	2.87	67.34	6	D3
			70.0	2.65	68.31	10	D3
			44.4	2.59	71.58	9	DG
			40.0	2.03	72.24	4	D4
			35.8	2.19	72.58	6	DG
			24.9	1.96	73.23	4	D4
			25.4	2.18	73.60	5	DG
			14.7	2.26	74.66	7	DG
			12.4	1.90	75.27	3	D4
			5.5	2.30	75.64	6	DG
			356.9	2.38	76.55	5	DG
			347.0	2.02	77.60	10	WS
			339.5	2.16	78.55	13	WS
			328.1	2.37	79.65	6	WS
			321.4	2.51	80.64	6	WS
			313.8	2.61	81.59	5	DG
			307.7	2.57	82.63	9	WS
STF 2276	1805.7 1200N	7.0,7.4	256.3	6.63	77.76	3	GH
			258.6	6.80	81.94	7	WS
STT 341	1805.9 2126N	7.2,8.5	91.2	0.35	43.70	2	D1
			87.	0.41	66.5	3,2	D3
			96.	0.39	67.38	3,2	D3
			91.3	0.38	72.59	3	D4
			95.1	0.37	73.60	3	D4
HU 1186	1806.3 3824N	8.7,8.8	96.1	0.39	72.59	2	D4
STF 2280	1807.8 2605N	5.9,6.0	182.6	14.37	78.31	7	WS
			182.	14.99	81.87	1	RW
STF 2281	1809.5 0401N	5.9,7.4	358.9	0.42	67.37	4	D3
			349.6	0.32	73.60	3	D4
HU 674	1809.7 5024N	7.5,8.0	232.7	0.72	72.60	2	D4
STF 2289	1810.2 1628N	6.4,7.5	224.2	1.15	67.59	3	D3
			224.8	1.14	70.58	3	A2

PAIR	RA 2000 DEC		MAGS	PA	SEP	DATE	N	OBS
STF 2289	1810.2	1628N	6.4,7.5	222.9	1.10	73.60	3	D4
STF 2294	1814.5	0010N	8.5,8.8	98.3	0.94	67.37	3	D3
				97.3	0.83	73.62	3	D4
STT 353	1820.7	7120N	4.4,6.1	round		65.6	1	D3
STF 2323	1824.1	5848N	4.9,7.9	352.3	3.94	81.72	3	DG
A.C.11	1824.9	0135S	6.8,7.0	358.6	0.75	67.63	2	D2
				0.7	1.0	73.60	2	D4
STF 2315	1825.0	2723N	6.6,7.6	150.4	0.42	43.67	3	D1
				136.7	0.47	66.1	5	D3
				136.3	0.54	67.41	4	D3
				133.2	0.63	72.61	3	D4
				137.1	0.52	73.50	3	D4
HU 66	1825.3	4845N	7.9,8.1	274.0	0.38	43.78	1	D1
				265.0	0.25	73.53	2	D4
STT 351	1825.3	4845N	7.7,8.2	22.0	0.7	43.78	1	D1
				22.0	0.70	73.53	2	D4
STF 2316	1827.2	0011N	5.4,7.7	320.4	3.81	79.73	7	DG
STF 2330	1831.2	1311N	8.1,9.8	168.6	16.86	77.68	4	DG
STF 2339	1833.8	1744N	7.1,8.0	272.7	1.98	70.57	3	A2
A 1377 AB	1834.0	5221N	6.2,6.2	82.1	0.29	73.63	3	D4
AB-C	"	"	5.4,8.8	269.6	26.01	73.63	3	D4
STT 359	1835.5	2336N	6.4,6.7	185.7	0.53	65.8	2	D3
				195.1	0.51	67.50	4	D3
				193.7	0.56	70.57	3	A2
				197.0	0.60	72.60	1	D4
				191.7	0.53	73.45	3	D4
STT 358	1835.9	1659N	6.8,7.2	167.6	1.73	70.57	3	A2
				168.0	1.47	73.63	1	D4
				162.4	1.88	78.70	5	DG
				162.0	1.94	82.72	3	RF
STT 357	1835.9	1144N	8.1,8.2	104.	0.27	73.59	2	D4
STF 2351	1836.2	4115N	7.7,7.7	340.9	5.22	43.63	8	D1
STF 2384	1838.6	6708N	8.6,9.1	307.8	0.71	67.62	3	D3
STF 2368	1838.9	5221N	7.6,7.8	323.6	1.85	73.46	2	D4
HO 437	1840.6	3138N	8.4,8.6	119.	0.45	43.78	1	D1
STF 2367	1841.3	3018N	7.4,7.9	56.	0.36	67.52	4	D3
				round		73.36	1	D4
STF 2372	1842.1	3445N	6.2,8.4	82.8	24.41	82.87	2	KS
STF 2398	1843.3	5933N	9.3,9.8	160.8	16.40	45.80	1	D1
				166.7	14.84	73.68	3	D4

PAIR	RA 2000	DEC	MAGS	PA	SEP	DATE	N	OBS
STF 2398	1843.3	5933N	9.3,9.8	165.0	13.68	74.34	8	DG
STF 2382	1844.3	3940N	5.1,6.1	0.4	2.69	65.7	4	D3
				358.7	2.71	67.38	4	D3
				355.7	2.60	73.60	4	D4
				357.0	2.67	78.37	9	WS
STF 2383	1844.3	3940N	5.1,5.4	98.5	2.28	65.7	2,5	D3
				96.0	2.31	67.38	4	D3
				97.6	2.31	70.48	3	A2
				91.5	2.36	73.60	4	D4
				90.7	2.59	78.47	8	WS
STF 38 APP	1844.7	3736N	4.3,5.9	148.7	43.65	82.71	3	RW
STF 2375	1845.5	0530N	6.2,6.6	116.3	2.55	78.70	6	DG
STF 2379	1846.4	0058S	6.1,7.9	121.	12.87	81.88	1	RW
STF 39 APP	1850.1	3322N	var,8.6	148.8	46.02	82.73	3	RW
STF 2420	1851.2	5922N	4.9,7.9	322.2	36.18	79.74	5	DG
STF 2415	1854.5	2037N	7.0,8.9	292.9	1.63	73.59	3	D4
STF 2417	1856.1	0412N	4.5,5.4	103.0	22.34	82.51	4	WS
STF 2421	1856.1	3346N	8.8,9.6	58.8	23.81	78.65	6	DG
BU 648	1857.1	3253N	5.3,7.5	288.5	0.79	42.65	5	D1
				287.8	0.75	43.74	2	D1
				274.9	0.73	44.60	4	D1
				273.3	1.02	45.70	3	D1
STF 2422	1857.2	2605N	8.0,8.1	80.7	0.80	73.42	4	D4
STF 2438	1857.5	5814N	6.8,7.4	3.5	0.87	73.43	3	D4
STF 2437	1901.8	1911N	8.2,8.4	42.0	0.65	43.76	2	D1
				not	seen	73.59	3	D4
STF 2434	1902.7	0042S	8.5,8.5	98.3	25.15	79.65	4	DG
SHJ 286	1904.9	0402S	5.5,7.2	209.6	39.07	73.71	3	D4
				210.6	38.26	82.77	2	RW
STF 2456	1905.7	3831N	8.6,9.2	170.6	19.17	76.72	7	DG
STF 2446	1905.8	0633N	7.1,9.1	154.3	9.66	81.76	2	KS
STF 2449	1906.3	0709N	7.2,7.9	289.5	7.57	81.71	2,1	KS
HJ 5084	1906.4	3704S	5.0,5.1	155.8	1.70	82.56	3	RF
STF 2455	1906.8	2210N	7.4,8.5	31.7	7.02	78.77	5	WS
STF 2457	1907.1	2235N	7.4,8.9	201.4	9.91	78.61	3	DG
STF 2461	1907.4	3230N	5.0,9.1	299.0	3.75	81.69	3	DG
STF 2474	1909.1	3436N	6.5,8.6	263.	15.80	81.80	1	RW
A 863	1909.8	0018S	9.4,10.7	round		66.0	1	D3
STF 2481	1911.1	3847N	8.3,8.3	210.5	4.40	73.65	1	D4

PAIR	RA 2000 DEC	MAGS	PA	SEP	DATE	N	OBS
STF 2481	1911.1 3847N	8.3,8.3	205.4	4.27	77.10	10	DG
SE 2	" "	8.3,9.3	69.	0.35	42.76	2	D1
			round		66.0	1	D3
			102.	0.38	73.65	2	D4
STF 2486	1912.1 4950N	6.6,6.8	213.5	8.57	45.18	3	D1
			211.0	8.17	66.4	2,1	D3
			209.7	8.05	67.78	6	D3
			208.1	8.29	73.70	2	D4
			209.3	7.14	78.73	5	DG
			209.8	7.60	82.21	8	WS
BU 139	1912.6 1651N	6.7,8.0	313.3	0.70	73.62	3	D4
STT 371	1915.9 2727N	7.0,7.1	338.0	0.93	65.9	6	D3
			156.2	0.67	73.61	2	D4
STF 2491	1916.2 2816N	8.4,9.7	50.	1.20	73.60	3,1	D4
STF 2509	1916.9 6313N	7.2,8.3	328.5	1.54	67.63	3	D3
BU 1129	1921.6 5223N	7.7,7.7	round		65.79	1	D3
STF 2525	1926.5 2719N	8.5,8.7	295.1	1.60	67.59	4	D3
STF 43 APP	1930.7 2758N	3.2,5.4	54.7	34.32	76.15	10	DG
			54.	34.3	82.76	3	RW
STF 2549	AC1931.2 6319N	7.4,9.3	285.5	29.33	79.71	4	DG
	AD " "	,8.0	271.0	55.00	79.71	4	DG
STT 377	1936.2 3539N	9.3,9.4	215.9	1.0	43.78	1	D1
H 26	1937.3 1627N	5.7,8.0	81.8	90.32	81.69	1	KS
STF 2556	1939.4 2216N	7.7,8.2	89.4	0.32	43.67	6	D1
			51.	0.36	65.8	5	D3
H 84	1939.5 1634N	6.6,9.0	301.2	28.22	81.67	2,1	KS
STF 2574	1940.5 6240N	8.1,8.1	248.1	0.34	73.69	3	D4
STF 46 APP	1941.9 5031N	6.3,6.4	314.1	39.84	82.68	3	WS
STT 380	1942.6 1149N	5.6,6.8	82.5	0.51	44.76	4	D1
STT 383	1943.0 4043N	6.9,8.4	20.8	0.82	43.44	4	D1
STT 384	1943.7 3819N	7.6,7.9	194.9	1.12	65.8	1	D3
STF 2579	1945.0 4507N	3.0,7.9	246.7	2.20	65.78	3,4	D3
			240.3	2.19	70.62	3	A2
STF 2576	1945.6 3336N	9.3,9.3	178.8	0.48	43.70	7	D1
			159.4	0.47	44.62	5	D1
			133.5	0.47	45.74	4	D1
			12.4	1.48	67.74	3	D3
			183.7	2.25	73.09	26	DG
			6.6	1.67	73.43	3	D4
			178.5	2.13	76.99	22	DG

PAIR	RA 2000	DEC	MAGS	PA	SEP	DATE	N	OBS
STF 2576	1945.6	3336N	9.3,9.3	177.0	1.97	79.77	2	DG
STF 2578	1945.7	3605N	6.4,7.2	125.	15.60	81.87	1	RW
STT 386	1948.2	3710N	8.2,8.5	74.1	0.94	67.27	3	D3
STF 2603	1948.2	7016N	4.0,7.6	10.9	3.02	44.11	3	D1
				10.4	3.08	65.82	3,2	D3
STF 2583	1948.7	1148N	6.1,6.9	108.3	1.43	70.64	3	A2
STT 387	1948.7	3519N	6.9,7.9	257.5	0.43	43.21	10	D1
				188.5	0.6	65.8	2	D3
				189.2	0.53	67.06	4	D3
A.G.C. 11	1948.9	1908N	5.4,6.4	147.8	0.20	70.63	1	A2
HO 581	1954.9	4152N	7.9,8.4	231.2	0.3	42.71	2	D1
STF 2597	1955.3	0644N	6.7,7.8	single		82.	1	KS
STF 2605	1955.6	5226N	4.9,7.4	179.9	3.11	67.44	4	D3
STF 2606	1958.6	3316N	7.6,8.3	139.4	0.92	67.73	4	D3
STT 395	2001.8	2456N	5.9,6.3	111.4	0.77	42.70	4	D1
				120.1	0.86	64.8	2	D2
				117.4	0.87	65.8	3	D3
				117.0	0.85	67.27	4,3	D3
				116.0	0.75	70.60	3	A2
				118.7	0.87	73.43	2	D4
STF 2624	2003.5	3602N	7.2,7.8	175.2	1.90	43.77	4	D1
				174.0	2.07	67.20	3	D3
STF 2626	2004.2	3031N	8.9,9.1	125.5	0.98	67.35	4	D3
STF 2642	2005.5	6342N	9.6,9.6	359.8	2.20	44.05	4	D1
STF 2652	2009.0	6205N	7.2,7.5	226.5	0.33	66.80	5,3	D3
STT 400	2010.2	4357N	7.5,8.5	319.1	0.62	43.76	4	D1
				not seen		73.5	1	D4
S 735	2011.3	0007S	7.1,8.5	208.5	55.35	82.73	2	KS
STF 2644	2012.6	0052N	6.8,7.1	206.5	3.37	82.73	4	KS
STT 403	2014.3	4206N	7.1,7.3	173.1	0.82	44.28	6	D1
				173.	0.6	73.42	1	D4
BUP AB	2014.6	3648N	5.0,6.6	155.5	215.42	82.77	3	KS
AC	"	"	5.0,10.0	22.0	215.73	82.77	2	KS
BD	"	"	6.6,10.2	119.9	218.4	82.77	1	KS
STF 2671	2018.4	5524N	6.0,7.4	336.2	3.50	65.8	2	D3
				338.0	3.38	67.72	3	D3
				341.1	3.35	77.78	3	GH
STT 406	2019.9	4522N	7.4,8.3	123.0	0.66	65.72	1	D3
				122.	0.55	67.50	4	D3
				113.0	0.53	73.66	4	D4

PAIR	RA 2000 DEC	MAGS	PA	SEP	DATE	N	OBS
D 22	2025.5 4005N	8.0,9.1	151.1	2.92	42.78	1	D1
HO 130	2026.2 3712N	9.2,9.4	286.7	1.57	67.53	4	D3
S 755	2030.9 4914N	6.6,9.2	278.0	59.98	82.59	2	KS
S 756	2031.3 4914N	5.6,10.3	326.4	59.68	82.59	2	KS
BU 151	2037.5 1416N	4.1,5.1	331.	0.55	44.72	5	D1
			336.6	0.55	45.75	5	D1
			318.3	0.39	70.72	1	A2
			343.7	0.56	73.40	2	D4
STF 2705	2037.7 3322N	7.4,8.4	264.7	3.02	43.77	3	D1
STT 533	2039.1 1005N	5.2,11.8	282.2	34.7	70.72	1	A2
STT 410	2039.6 4036N	6.5,6.8	185.0	0.84	64.8	2	D2
			6.3	0.84	65.8	2	D3
			9.1	0.81	67.61	3	D3
			9.7	0.70	70.63	3	A2
STF 2716	2041.1 3219N	5.9,8.0	45.1	2.59	43.80	3	D1
STF 2723	2045.0 1219N	6.9,8.7	110.7	1.17	44.00	4	D1
STF 2726	2045.6 3043N	4.3,9.5	61.4	6.25	44.77	3	D1
BU 676	2046.2 3358N	2.6,11.6	268.9	47.3	70.72	1	A2
STF 2725	2046.3 1554N	7.5,8.2	5.4	5.42	43.74	1	D1
STF 2727	2046.7 1608N	4.5,5.5	269.	10.05	64.6	1,4	D2
			270.0	9.75	65.8	2,4	D3
			269.1	9.68	67.90	2	D3
			268.0	9.10	78.71	12	WS
			267.5	9.59	81.70	8	RW
STT 413	2047.4 3629N	4.8,6.1	34.1	0.74	45.82	3	D1
			29.5	0.75	64.8	2	D1
			24.1	0.77	70.70	4	A2
			26.2	0.73	73.73	3	D4
BU 268	2047.6 4204N	7.7,8.6	213.4	0.45	42.78	1	D1
BU 155	2051.1 5125N	7.3,8.0	38.6	0.79	65.76	2	D3
			37.2	0.91	67.20	4	D3
HO 144	2052.3 2008N	8.0,8.0	166.9	0.3	67.36	4	D3
HO 146	2053.6 3514N	8.7,8.7	50.2	0.28	67.55	6	D3
STT 418	2054.8 3242N	8.1,8.2	107.4	1.18	65.78	2	D3
			286.3	1.05	67.48	3	D3
STF 2741	2058.6 5028N	5.8,7.1	27.6	2.07	42.92	3	D1
			24.3	1.85	67.22	4,6	D3
STF 2737	2059.1 0418N	5.8,6.3	284.1	0.98	65.8	1,2	D3
			287.0	1.04	70.60	3	A2
			285.0	1.00	73.43	2	D4

PAIR	RA 2000	DEC	MAGS	PA	SEP	DATE	N	OBS
STF 2737BC	2059.1	0418N	5.3,7.1	68.5	10.06	81.89	2	RW
STF 2742	2102.2	0711N	7.4,7.4	220.9	2.67	43.72	1	D1
				216.3	2.73	67.27	3	D3
STF 2751	2102.2	5640N	6.1,7.1	171.8	1.87	65.8	3	D3
				350.9	1.60	67.25	3	D3
STF 2744	2103.1	0132N	7.0,7.5	129.5	1.38	70.67	4	A2
STF 2758	2106.3	3839N	5.6,6.3	138.6	26.69	45.77	3	D1
				144.2	28.58	72.96	34	DG
				145.0	28.67	73.72	4	D4
				145.3	28.65	77.52	22,19	WS
STF 2760	2106.8	3408N	8.0,8.8	239.0	2.01	43.85	2	D1
				239.7	1.86	44.71	5	D1
				240.7	1.77	45.78	5	D1
				322.8	0.65e	64.68	3,2	D2
				332.5	0.64	65.70	11	D3
				343.5	0.74	66.81	2	D3
				345.7	0.58	67.56	9	D3
				350.8	0.58	68.57	3,1	D3
				17.6	0.71	73.62	5	D4
STF 2769	2110.5	2228N	6.9,7.7	300.5	18.12	81.90	1	RW
STF 2780	2111.8	6000N	6.0,7.0	215.7	1.23	70.68	3	A2
H I 48	2113.7	6425N	7.1,7.3	250.6	0.79	67.44	2	D3
STT 432	2114.4	4109N	7.8,8.2	112.9	1.35	65.76	2	D3
				116.2	1.27	67.60	3	D3
				117.9	1.33	70.67	3	A2
STT 535	2114.5	1001N	5.3,5.4	21.5	0.34	67.13	8,4	D3
				22.	0.3	73.41	2	D4
HO 286	2119.4	3815N	6.6,6.6	round		65.8	2	D3
STT 437	2120.8	3228N	6.9,7.6	208.9	2.06	64.8	1,3	D2
				28.0	2.41	65.72	3,2	D3
				27.2	2.26	70.67	3	A2
STT 435	2121.4	0254N	8.1,8.6	229.8	0.51	67.70	3	D3
HO 157	2123.0	3202N	9.2,9.2	24.2	3.41	45.81	1	D1
				24.0	3.94	65.76	2	D3
STF 2799	2128.9	1105N	7.5,7.5	272.3	1.66	70.59	3	A2
				271.5	1.90	78.78	6	DG
STF 2804	2133.0	2043N	7.6,8.3	347.2	3.13	67.52	2,3	D3
				349.9	3.12	78.82	4	DG
STT 443	2137.6	0643N	9.5,9.8	348.5	8.93	82.87	3	KS
STF 56 APP	2137.8	0637N	6.3,8.6	348.8	39.31	82.88	5	WS

PAIR	RA	2000	DEC	MAGS	PA	SEP	DATE	N	OBS
STT 445	2139.3		2043N	9.2,9.7	114.	0.74	67.72	2	D3
BU 1212	2139.5		0003S	7.3,7.8	275.	0.45	65.8	3,1	D3
					306.	0.35	67.68	5	D3
HO 166	2143.9		2751N	8.8,8.8	130.	0.36	65.8	5,3	D3
					124.8	0.35	66.86	3	D3
					108.	0.3	72.58	1	D4
					107.	0.37	73.63	5	D4
STF 2822	2144.1		2845N	4.7,6.1	253.9	0.62	43.74	3	D1
					256.2	0.71	44.65	5	D1
					264.2	0.78	45.79	4	D1
					285.2	1.68	64.77	2,1	D2
					285.5	1.75	65.75	7,5	D3
					290.1	1.84	67.47	4	D3
					288.4	1.86	70.63	3	A2
					293.5	1.95	73.57	4	D4
					295.8	2.13	77.68	5	WS
S 798 BC	2144.2		0953N	2.5,8.5	313.8	144.52	81.77	2	KS
STF 2828	2149.5		0324N	9.0,10.4	138.2	32.98	81.83	2	KS
BC	"		"	10.3,10.5	39.7	4.58	81.83	2	KS
COU 14	2150.2		1718N	5.5,7.5	214.	0.3	67.55	6,2	D3
STF 2843	2151.6		6545N	7.1,7.3	145.4	1.64	67.73	3	D3
STF 2840	2152.0		5547N	5.5,7.3	195.7	18.39	82.90	3	RW
STT 458	2156.4		5946N	7.0,8.5	348.2	0.83	67.83	3	D3
BU 275	2157.3		6117N	7.7,7.7	351.6	0.38	67.74	4	D3
STF 2848	2158.0		0556N	7.2,7.5	55.2	11.04	81.90	2	KS
STF 2863	2203.7		6437N	4.6,6.5	274.8	7.54	73.75	3	D4
					275.9	7.70	77.70	2	GH
STF 2881	2214.5		2935N	7.6,8.1	91.3	1.37	42.90	1	D1
HO 180	2215.7		4354N	8.2,8.2	236.3	0.66	67.56	4	D3
BU 1216	2220.2		2931N	9.3,9.6	288.0	0.61	67.55	4	D3
BU 172	2224.1		0451S	6.6,6.6	312.9	0.47	67.61	4	D3
					301.8	0.33	73.80	3	D4
KR 60 AB	2228.1		5742N	9.4,10.9	58.	3.10	65.82	1	D3
					195.3	1.17	66.72	3,1	D3
					238.8	1.6	73.80	3	D4
" AC	"		"	,10.1	62.2	102.22	73.80	3	D4
" AE	"		"	,12.5	127.7	221.60	73.80	2	D4
STF 2909	2228.8		0002S	4.4,4.6	284.4	2.50	43.82	1	D1
					283.0	2.33	44.86	2	D1
					281.9	2.40	45.79	5	D1

PAIR	RA 2000 DEC	MAGS	PA	SEP	DATE	N	OBS
STF 2909	2228.8 0002S	4.4,4.6	251.8	1.93	64.71	7,12	D2
			248.2	1.92	65.82	5,7	D3
			252.0	1.97	66.92	1,6	D3
			248.1	1.91	67.47	6,4	D3
			248.0	1.93	68.56	3,4	D3
			236.8	1.79	73.62	7	D4
			232.9	1.96	78.14	11,6	WS
STF 58 APP	2229.2 5825N	var,7.5	191.9	40.72	82.87	3	KS
STF 2912	2229.9 0425N	5.8,7.2	115.9	0.73	73.78	3	D4
STF 2920	2234.5 0413N	8.1,9.2	142.3	14.0	72.9	1	A1
			144.1	13.84	82.81	2	KS
STF 2922	2235.8 3938N	6.8,6.6	184.4	22.57	78.72	3	GH
			186.8	22.71	82.73	1	RW
HO 296	2240.8 1432N	6.6,6.6	round		42.78	1	D1
			71.0	0.36	67.11	6	D3
			70.9	0.44	68.04	2	D3
			59.6	0.42	70.64	3	A2
			53.6	0.65	72.58	1	D4
			50.3	0.45	73.59	5	D4
STF 2932	2241.4 3002N	9.4,9.9	282.0	21.45	81.86	3	KS
STF 2934	2241.8 2125N	8.7,9.7	284.0	0.85	45.30	4	D1
S 816	2243.0 3013N	3.0,9.3	338.6	92.97	81.88	2	KS
STT 480	2246.1 5804N	8.0,9.0	116.9	30.97	82.86	2	KS
STF 2943	2247.7 1404S	5.8,9.0	122.4	22.65	73.79	2	D4
STF 2950	2251.3 6141N	6.1,7.4	288.9	1.71	67.82	4,6	D3
			291.1	1.8	73.53	2	D4
A 632	2252.1 5744N	8.2,9.0	191.6	0.68	42.84	3	D1
COU 240	2256.4 2257N	7.4,7.8	289.6	0.65	67.35	10	D3
			287.0	0.62	72.64	2	D4
STT 483	2259.2 1144N	6.0,7.5	257.8	0.72	42.86	3	D1
HLD 56	2259.7 4149N	9.3,9.4	108.3	0.91	43.82	2	D1
STF 2974	2305.0 3322N	8.1,8.1	164.4	2.65	42.87	8	D1
STF 2978	2307.5 3249N	6.3,7.5	146.6	8.00	78.72	3	GH
BU 385	2310.3 3228N	7.3,8.1	100.	0.67	65.81	1	D3
STF 2993	2314.0 0856S	8.3,9.4	176.7	25.7	72.9	1	A1
AC "	"	,11.4	123.2	95.6	72.9	1	A1
STF 3001	2318.5 6807N	5.0,7.6	212.6	2.88	65.84	5,4	D3
			215.2	3.08	67.88	3	D3
			218.8	2.76	73.61	3	D4
BU 80	2318.9 0525N	9.0,10.0	281.5	1.05	42.90	2	D1

PAIR	RA 2000	DEC	MAGS	PA	SEP	DATE	N	OBS
STF 2998	2319.1	1327S	5.5,7.5	351.3	13.1	72.9	1	A1
				350.0	12.68	82.79	1	RW
STT 494	2320.8	2157N	8.3,9.0	83.6	3.39	41.90	2	D1
STF 3007	2322.8	2034N	6.7,9.7	90.5	6.0	72.9	1	A1
STF 3008	2323.8	0827S	7.2,8.2	163.0	4.18	78.83	4	DG
STF 3012	2327.6	1638N	8.2,9.3	192.0	2.89	81.93	2	KS
STF 3013 BC	"	"	9.3,9.3	64.4	52.86	81.93	2	KS
STT 496	2330.0	5833N	4.9,9.3	218.9	0.89	42.85	2	D1
BU 720	2334.0	3120N	6.0,6.0	62.9	0.5e	64.60	3	D2
				242.8	0.47	65.6	3	D3
				251.6	0.67	67.75	4	D3
				250.1	0.50	70.71	3	A2
				72.0	0.4	70.96	2	D4
				256.2	0.5	72.58	1	D4
				250.6	0.45	73.52	5	D4
				252.6	0.6	73.83	1	D4
STT 500	2337.5	4426N	6.3,7.2	345.5	0.50	43.82	1	D1
				167.2	0.56	65.60	4	D3
				349.8	0.53	67.9	2	D3
				353.4	0.45	70.66	4	A2
BU 858	2341.3	3234N	7.4,8.9	240.0	0.62	42.93	3	D1
ES 700	2350.6	5412N	7.2,11.2	35.3	14.68	82.83	3	KS
STT 510	2351.6	4205N	7.7,8.0	135.7	0.49	65.6	2	D3
STF 3042	2351.9	3753N	7.8,7.8	83.3	5.65	77.86	3	GH
STF 3050	2359.5	3343N	6.6,6.6	289.5	1.53	65.82	1	D1
				114.0	1.49	70.64	3	A2
				300.5	1.63	73.60	4	D4

(ii) Notes

PAIR   NOTES

STT 547   ADS 48. P=362 years (1985.0 = 5".94) o,o
STF 3062*   ADS 61. P=106.8 years (1985.0 = 1".44).
BU 255   ADS 147. Very slowly widening. 1875, 99°,0".4.
BU 1026   ADS 148. P=72 years (1985.0 = 0".17)
STF 12   ADS 191. 35 Psc. Fixed. y,Pb.

STF 4   ADS 221. P=112.5 years (1985.0 = 0".53)
STF 23   ADS 241. Optical pair. 1836, 360°,12".7. Comes 11.8 at 103".
STF 24   ADS 252. Fixed. w,Pb.
STT 12   ADS 434. P=640 years (1985.0 = 0".57). Circular orbit. Py,Py.
STF 39   ADS 475. Fixed. AB = D2 (Distance = 0".5).

STF 40   ADS 486. Fixed. Comes 12.8 at 25". y,Pb.
HJ 323   ADS - . 1879, 290°, 65".2.
STT 4 App   ADS 513. Pi And. (=H V 7AB). w,b. Comes 11.4 at 55".
STF 1 App   ADS 639. Change in PA and sep. 1834, 55°,46".4. wsh,ry?
STF 60*   ADS 671. Eta Cas. P=480 years (1985.0 = 12".23). Widening
             for some years yet. y,p.

STF 61   ADS 683. 65 Psc. Fixed, cpm. Py,Pb.
BU 232   ADS 684. P=218.6 years (1985.0 = 0".85). Comes 10.2 at 27".
STT 20   ADS 746. 66 Psc. P=360 years (1985.0 = 0".49). b,w. Comes
             12.8 at 151".

STF 73*   ADS 755. 36 And. P=164.7 years (1985.0 = 0".67). y,y. Comes
             11 at 160".
BU 500   ADS 768. Closing since discovery. 1878, 289°, 1".0.
BU 1099   ADS 784. P=83.4 years (1985.0 = 0".24).
BU 302   ADS 805. 1876, 92°, 0".8.

STF 79   ADS 824. Fixed. Pb,Pb.
STT 21   ADS 862. P=450 years (1985.0 = 0".92). Highly inclined orbit
             now widening.
STF 88   ADS 899. Psi Psc. Fixed. y,Pb. Comes to A, 11.2 at 94".
STT 515   ADS 940. Phi And. P=372 years (1985.0 = 0".46). y,y.
             Slowly widening.

BU 303   ADS 955. Little motion. 1876, 284°, 0".6.
BU 235   ADS 963. Binary? 1875, 74 , 0".5. C (9.0 at 59") forms
             STT 12 App. Comes to C, (11.3 at 8") forms STT 24. Comes
             to A, 10.4 at 43".

A 655   ADS 974. P=197.6 years (1985.0 = 0".31).
STF 98   ADS 988. Fixed.
STF 100   ADS 996. Zeta Psc. Fixed. y,Pb. B has comes 12.2 which forms
             BU 1129 and is probably binary. Single at times.
BU 1100   ADS 999. P=75 years (uncertain). (1985.0 = 0".48).

PAIR	NOTES

STF 102 ADS 1040. 1833, 309^c, 0".6. Four comites within 100", mags 8.5,10.6,11.2 and 13.1.

BU 4 ADS 1097. P=180 years (1985.0 = 0".42). Comes 13.4 at 23".

STF 117 CD ADS 1129. Psi Cas is mag 5.0 star at 283°, 25". Distance distance decreasing. Comes 14.0 at 3" to Psi is BU 1101.

STF 121 ADS 1144. 1831, 279°, 13".8.

STF 131 ADS 1209. Fixed. Comes 10.9 at 28".

A 816 ADS 1226. Little motion. 1904, 313^c, 0".4.

STF 138 ADS 1254. Binary of long period. w,w.

HU 1030 ADS 1264. Fixed.

DUN 5 ADS - . P=483.7 years (1985.0 = 11".20).

HJ 3461 ADS 1394. 1836 , 70^c, 4".7. Comes 11.5 at 142".

STF 162 ADS 1438. Probable long period binary. 1836, 224 , 1".9. w,w. Comites 8.4 at 19", 10.2 at 137".

STT 34 ADS 1411. P=165.4 years (Baize, 1985.0 = 0".52) or 390 years (Heintz, 1985.0 = 0".47).

STF 174 ADS 1457. 1 Ari. 1830, 170^c, 2".57. Py,Pb.

HO 311 ADS 1473. Direct motion. 1890, 174^c, 0".4.

STF 163 ADS 1459. Fixed. Comes 10.4 at 115".

STF 180 ADS 1507. Gamma Ari. 1830, 360°, 8".63. Comes 9.6 at 18", distance decreasing.

STF 183 ADS 1522. P=192.9 years (Walker, 1985.0 = 0".15) or 368 years (Couteau, 1985.0 = 0".30).

STF 186* ADS 1538. P=155 years (Palacios, 1985.0 = 1".13) or 170.3 year (Freitas-Mourao, 1985.0 = 1".33).

STF 4 App ADS 1534. 56 And. Comes 11.2 at 18" to A, and comes 9.4 at 204" to B.

STF 182 ADS 1531. Fixed. Comes 13.3 at 30". w,Pb.

STT 21 App ADS 1563. Lambda Ari. (= H V 12 AB). Fixed. y,b.

HJ 1100 ADS 1571. 1901, 310°, 38".8.

BU 513* ADS 1598. 48 Cas. P=60.44 years (1985.0 = 0".79). Widening. Comites 13.2 at 24" and 12.6 at 51".

STF 202* ADS 1615. Alpha Psc. P=720 years (1985.0 = 1".66). b,g.

STF 205& ADS 1630. Gamma And. A - BC closing, 1830, 62, 10".3.

STT 38 BC, P=61.1 years (1985.0 = 0".55), a very eccentric orbit.y,b,▮

STF 222 ADS 1689. 59 And. Fixed. o,Pb.

STF 227 ADS 1697. Iota Tri. 1836, 80^v, 3".8. y,Pb.

STF 231 ADS 1703. Fixed. Comes 11.5 at 173".

STF 228* ADS 1709. P=144.7 years (1985.0 = 1".07).

STF 234 ADS 1737. P=150 years (1985.0 = 0".88) now near widest separation. Comes 10.9 at 83".

PAIR   NOTES

STF 239   ADS 1752. Fixed.
STF 249   ADS 1795. Fixed. bsh,b.
STF 257   ADS 1833. P=209.3 years (1985.0 = 0".23).
STF 271   ADS 1904. Fixed. o,Pb.

STF 274   ADS 1924. Fixed.
STF 93   ADS 1477. Alpha UMi. Multiple system. Visual companion is
             physical, 1834, 210^c, 18".3. oy,bsh. Primary is a Cepheid,
             spectroscopic binary and has an invisible companion, P=30.5
             years. Comites 12.1 at 83" and 13.1 at 45".

STT 42   ADS 1938. Binary, but no orbit available as yet.
STF 5 App.   ADS 1982. 30 Ari. Fixed. y,Pb.
STF 285   ADS 2004. 1832, 178^c, 1".8. oy,b.
STT 43   ADS 2034. P=475 years (1985.0 = 1".01).
STF 299   ADS 2080. Gamma Cet. 1832, 287^c, 2".6.

STF 296   ADS 2081. Theta Per. P=2720 years? (1985.0 = 19".73). w,b.
STF 305   ADS 2122. P=720 years (Rabe, 1985.0 = 3".66) or 1543 years
             (Hopmann, 1985.0 = 3".65). y,Pb. Comes 12.6 at 88".
STF 307   ADS 2157. Eta Per. Fixed. a,b. Comes 9.9 at 66".
STF 314   ADS 2185. Binary. 1830, 295^c, 1".5. bw,bw. Primary is itself
             a very close pair (= A 2906) and probably binary.

BU 524   ADS 2200. 20 Per. P=31.6 years (van den Bos, 1985.0 = 0".18)
             or 62.3 years (Da Silva-Pinheiro, 1985.0 = 0".18). Comes 10
             at 15" forms STF 318.
BU 525   ADS 2253. P=433.5 years (Baize, 1985.0 = 0".42) or 241.9
             years (Costa-Morales, 1985.0 = 0".49). Slowly opening.

STF 333   ADS 2257. Epsilon Ari. Binary, 1831, 190^c, 0".58. w,w.
             Comes 12.7 at 146".
STF 331   ADS 2270. Fixed. bw,b.
STF 346   ADS 2336. 52 Ari. Binary? 1832, 264^c, 0".7. Comites 10.8 at
             5", 10.8 at 102" and 12.3 at 133".

STF 320   ADS 2294. Fixed? 1831 , 229^c, 4".6.
STF 6 App   ADS   - . Fixed.
HJ 3555   ADS 2402. Alpha For. P=314 years (1985.0 = 4".20).
STF 360   ADS 2390. P=617 years (1985.0 = 2".54). 1831, 146, 1".3.

STT 50   ADS 2377. P=344.9 years (1985.0 = 1".04). Now widening.
             Comes 13.2 at 27" = HJ 2172.
STF 367   ADS 2416. P=790 years (1985.0 = 1".03).
STT 52   ADS 2436. P=330 years (1985.0 = 0".43). Comes 12.7 at 80".
STT 53   ADS 2446. P=118.2 years (1985.0 = 0".85)

PAIR	NOTES

STF 401   ADS 2582. Fixed. w,w.
STF 396   ADS 2592. Fixed. y,b. Comes 10.8 at 165".
STF 412   ADS 2616. 7 Tau. P=568 years (1985.0 = 0".63). w,w. Comes
          10.0 at 22".
STF 400* ADS 2612. P=287.7 years (Baize, 1985.0 = 1".35) or 221 years
          (van Biesbroeck, 1985.0 = 1".36).

BU 533   ADS 2628. Binary? 1878, 66°, 0".4.
A 1535   ADS 2630. P=153 years (Morel, 1985.0 = 0".61) or 220.5 years
          (Heintz, 1985.0 = 0".68).
STF 422   ADS 2644. P=2101 years? (1985.0 = 6".63). 1832, 232 , 6".2.
          oy, bsh.

STT 37 App ADS   - . 1823, 95°, 41".1.
STF 430   ADS 2681. Fixed. y,Pb,Pb.
STF 427   ADS 2679. Fixed. ysh,bsh.
P III 97 ADS 2691. (=WEB AD). Fixed. ay,b. Comites 13.8 at 21" (dist.
          increasing, 13 at 35" and 10.8 at 168".

STF 452   ADS 2778. 30 Tau. Fixed. Pb,Pb.
STT 65   ADS 2799. P=62.28 years (1985.0 = 0".52).
KUI 15   ADS   - . Slow retrograde motion, 1937, 215°, 0".3.
STT 66   ADS 2815. Binary? 1846, 136 , 0".5.

STF 470   ADS 2850. 32 Eri. y,b. Comes 11.6 at 166".
STT 67   ADS 2867. 1847, 44ᶜ, 1".9.
STF 471   ADS 2888. Epsilon Per. Fixed. Comes 13.9 at 78".
STF 479   ADS 2926. Fixed.
STT 531* ADS 2995. P=706 years (1985.0 = 1".55).

STF 495   ADS 2999. Fixed. Y,Bsh.
STF 460   ADS 2963. 49 Cep. P=415 years (1985.0 = 0".74).
STT 77   ADS 3082. P=200 years (1985.0 = 0".75). Comites 9.0 at
          56" (forms STT 43 App) and 8.5 at 129".
STT 44 App ADS   - . Fixed.

STF 511   ADS 3098. P=254 years (1985.0 = 0".39).
STT 48 App ADS 3137. Phi Tau. (=SHJ 40). 1821, 240°, 56".8. oy,b.
STF 528   ADS 3161. Chi Tau. Fixed. Pb,g.
STT 82   ADS 3169. P=255.5 years (1985.0 = 1".40). p,b.
HU 304   ADS 3182. 66 Tau. P=51.6 years (1985.0 = 0".12).

STF 534   ADS 3179. 62 Tau. Fixed. ysh,b. Comes 12.0 at 111".
STF 548   ADS 3243. Fixed. y,b. Comes 10.6 at 121".
STF 552   ADS 3273. Fixed.
STF 550   ADS 3274. 1 Cam. Fixed. Py,Pb. Comes 11.1 at 150".
STF 559   ADS 3297. Fixed.

PAIR	NOTES

STF 2 App IIADS 3321. Alpha Tau. 1832 , 75°, 109". Other comites.
STT 86   ADS 3329. Probably binary. 1845, 79 , 0".6.
STF 567   ADS 3330. 1831, 303 , 1".4. w,w.
STF 576   ADS 3355. Fixed.
STF 572   ADS 3353. 1830, 210 , 3".2. y,b.

STF 11 App ADS —   Sigma Tau. 1836, 193°, 431".2.
HJ 3683   ADS — . P=552.3 years (1985.0 = 3".02).
STF 577   ADS 3390. P=654.6 years (1985.0 = 1".09). Slowly closing. y,y.
A 1013   ADS 3391. 1905, 311 , 0".5.
BU 883   ADS 3475. P=16.3 years (1985.0 = 0".21). Never wider than
            0".3. Comes mag. 14 at 17".

BU 552   ADS 3483. P=100.9 years (1985.0 = 0".23). Just past minimum
            distance. Comes mag. 12.7 at 45".
SHJ 48   ADS — . 1821, 75 , 65".9.
STF 616   ADS 3572. Omega Aur. 1828, 352°, 6".5. w,Pb.

STF 623   ADS 3587. Fixed. w,Pb.
STF 627   ADS 3597. Fixed. y,g.
STF 630   ADS 3623. Fixed. y,Pb. B is A 2630 (fixed). Mag 9.5 at 130".
STT 95   ADS 3672. Binary? 1845, 344°, 0".6. w,w.
STT 98   ADS 3711. 14 Ori. P=198.9 years (1985.0 = 0".68). y,b.

STF 635   ADS 3689. Opening since discovery. 1830, 281°, 0".4.
STF 645   ADS 3730. Fixed. Py,Pb. B is BU 1047 (binary).
STF 654   ADS 3797. Rho Ori. Fixed. o,b. Comes 11.8 at 182".
STT 517   ADS 3799. P=312 years (1985.0 = 0".47). Comes 13 at 7".
STF 668   ADS 3823. Beta Ori. Fixed. b,w. Comes often suspected to be
            a very close and difficult binary (BU 555).

STF 653   ADS 3824. 14 Aur. Fixed. w,? Comites 11.1 at 11" and 10.4
            at 184".
STF 681   ADS 3903. Fixed. y,b.
STF 634   ADS 3864. 19 Cam. 1834, 349°, 34". Due to pm of A.

STF 696   ADS 3962. 23 Ori. Fixed. Py,b.
STF 701   ADS 3978. Fixed. w,Pb.
WNC 2&   ADS 3991. A — BC is WNC 2. Binary, 1866, 171°, 1".4. w,y.
A 847   BC is also binary, P=48.0 years (1985.0 = 0".12), orbit
            highly inclined to the line of sight.

DA 5   ADS 4002. Eta Ori. Little motion. 1849, 87°, 1".0. w,b.
            Primary is also a spectroscopic pair, P=9 years, resolved
            by speckle, dist = 0".044. Comes 9.4 at 115".
HJ 3759   ADS 4034. 1837, 315°, 28".7.
HO 226   ADS 4032. Widening. 1887, 230°, 0".5. Comes 10.5 at 25".

PAIR	NOTES
STF 716	ADS 4068. 118 Tau. 1829, 197°, 4".9. ysh,bsh. Comes 11.6 at 141".
STF 728	ADS 4115. 32 Ori. P=586 years (1985.0 = 0".96) but van den Bos (1956) and Cester (1964) think motion in linear. w,w.
STF 729	ADS 4123. 33 Ori. Fixed. Pb,b. Comes 13.4 at 95".
STF 14 App.	ADS 4134. Delta Ori. Fixed. w,w. Comes 14.0 to A at 35" forms BU 558. A is also a close visual pair, discovered by Heintz in 1978 (=Hz 42). Mags 3.2,3.3, separation =0".15. A is also a spectroscopic binary, P=5.7 days.
STF 730	ADS 4131. Fixed.
STF 718	ADS 4119. Fixed. Pb,w. Comes 9.2 at 119".
BU 1267	ADS 4166. 1892, 218°, 0".8.
STF 738	ADS 4179. Lambda Ori. Fixed. w,b. Comites 11.1 at 29",78".
STF 747	ADS 4182. Fixed.
STF 748	ADS 4186. Theta Ori. The Trapezium. Fixed.
STF 752	ADS 4193. Iota Ori. Fixed. bw,b. Enmeshed in nebulosity.
STF 742	ADS 4200. P=2959 years? (1985.0 = 4".03). 1837, 251°, 3".3. colours o,o.
STF 749	ADS 4208. Probable binary, 1829, 23°, 0".7. w,w. Pair nearby, 10.4, 10.9, 290°, 4".4.
STF 753&	ADS 4229. 26 Aur. AB - C is STF 753. Fixed. w,b. AB is
BU 1240	BU 1240, P=53.2 years (1985.0 = 0".12). Comes to A, 11.5 at 33".
STT 112	ADS 4243. Probably binary. 1848, 85°, 0".6.
STF 766	ADS 4256. Fixed. Py,b.
STF 774	ADS 4263. Zeta Ori. P=1508 years? (1985.0 = 2".35). 1836, 151 , 2".6. Comes to A, 10.0 at 58".
BU 1007	ADS 4265. 126 Tau. P=78.45 years (1985.0 = 0".12).
STF 764	ADS 4262. Fixed. w,b.
STT 115	ADS 4323. 1847, 123°, 0".8. Comes 11.0 at 93".
BU 560	ADS 4371. 1877, 208°, 0".9.
STF 795	ADS 4390. Likely long period binary. o,o.
STT 118	ADS 4392. Fixed. Comes 8.6 at 76" forms STT 67 App.
STF 3115	ADS 4376. Closing since discovery. 1831, 36°, 1".7.
STF 780	ADS 4405. Fixed. Comites 10.0 at 13" and 13.4 at 20" (distances increasing).
STF 802	ADS 4456. Fixed. w,w. Comes 10.6 at 192".
A 1570	ADS 4531. Fixed.
STT 545	ADS 4566. Theta Aur. Long period binary. 1871, 6°, 2".2. Comites 10.7 at 50", 9.2 at 131", distances increasing.

PAIR   NOTES

DUN 23   ADS   - . P=463.5 years (1985.0 = 2".51).
STT 121   ADS 4603. P=163 years (1985.0 = 0".23). Closing since
            discovery. 1843, 191°, 0".4.
STT 855   ADS 4749. Fixed. w,b,w.
STT 134   ADS 4744. Fixed. o,b. On n.f. edge of M35.

STF 845   ADS 4773. 41 Aur. 1830, 353 , 8".0. w,Pb.
KUI 24   ADS   - 1934, 137°, 0".3.
STF 877   ADS 4840. Fixed.
BU 1008   ADS 4841. Eta Gem. P=473.7 years (1985.0 = 1".55). Primary
            is an M3 variable. 1882, 301ᶜ, 1".0.

STF 872   ADS 4849. 1828, 217°, 11".3. w,Pb. Comites 11.4 at 202" and
            11.5 at 174".
STF 881   ADS 4950. 4 Lyn. Binary. 1830, 90ᶜ, 0".8. Py,b. Comites
            12.9 at 26" and 11,12.9 at 100".
SHJ 70   ADS 5080. 1822, 205ᶜ, 32".7. Comes 12.4 at 78".

STF 919   ADS 5107. Beta Mon. Fixed. w,w,w. Comes to A, 12.2 at 25"
            forms BU 570.
STF 924   ADS 5166. 20 Gem. Fixed. Py,Pb.
STF 918   ADS 5178. 1829, 322°, 4".4. Comes 10 at 137".
STF 932   ADS 5197. P=2360 years? (1985.0 = 1".75). 1830 ,
            342 , 2".4).

STF 928   ADS 5191. Fixed. ysh,bsh. Comes 11.0 at 129".
STT 149   ADS 5234. P=114.8 years (1985.0 = 0".62).
STF 943   ADS   - . 1829, 155ᶜ, 15".5. Comes 14.4 at 13".
STT 152   ADS 5289. 54 Aur. Fixed. y,b.

STF 945   ADS 5296. Closing since discovery. 1830, 249 , 1".1.
S 533   ADS 5381. Fixed.
STF 946   ADS 5368. Fixed.
AGC 1*   ADS 5423. Alpha CMa. P=50.09 years (1985.0 = 8".18). Comes
            is the brightest known white dwarf. Occasionally thought
            double. bw,w. Comes 14.0 at 32".

STF 948   ADS 5400. 12 Lyn. P=699 years (1985.0 = 1".69) for AB. AC,
            1831, 308 , 8".7 - little change. y,Pb,b. Comes 10.5 at 170".
STT 78 App ADS 5425. Psi Aur. (=SHJ 75). 1823, 17 , 55".4. o,b.
STT 156   ADS 5447. P=1057 years? (1985.0 = 0".54).

STF 958   ADS 5436. Fixed. y,rsh. Comes 11.2 at 164".
STF 963   ADS 5514. 14 Lyn. P=480 years (1985.0 = 0".44). Comes 11.1
            at 112".
STF 982   ADS 5559. 38 Gem. P=3190 years? (1985.0 = 7".04). ysh,bsh.
            Comes 10.3 at 112".

PAIR	NOTES
STF 981	ADS 5570. P=5343 years? (1985.0 = 1".62). Closing since discovery. 1831, 149°, 3".7.
STT 159	ADS 5586. 15 Lyn. 1844, 323°, 0".5. y,b. Comites 12.4 at 29" and 12.9 at 27".
A 1575	ADS 5704. Fixed.
DUN 39	ADS - . 1826, 76°, 2".5.
STT 81 App	ADS 5742. Zeta Gem (=SHJ 77 AC). Primary is a Cepheid variable. y,b. Comites 10.5 at 87", 12.0 at 80", 12.9 at 27".
STF 1009	ADS 5746. Widening, 1830, 159°, 2".9. Pb,Pb. Comes to B, mag 11.0 at 179".
STF 1033	ADS 5896. Fixed. y,b.
HJ 3945	ADS 5951. 1837, 65°, 27".2.
STT 170	ADS 5958. Widening since discovery. 1844, 133°, 1".0. Py,Py.
STF 1066	ADS 5983. Delta Gem. P=1200 years? (1985.0 = 6".02). y,Pb.
STF 1083	ADS 6060. No change. y,g.
STF 1093	ADS 6117. P=381.4 years (1985.0 = 0".76). Widening.
STF 1108	ADS 6160. Fixed. y,b.
STF 1110*	ADS 6175. Alpha Gem. P=511.3 years (Muller, 1985.0 = 2".67) or 420.1 years (Rabe, 1985.0 = 2".59). Castor C , 8.8 at 73" is part of the system. All three stars are spectroscopic binaries.
STT 175	ADS 6185. 1847, 334°, 0".5. Distance decreasing. or,or. Comes 9.3 at 81".
STT 174	ADS 6191. 1851, 85°, 2".0. Distance increasing? y,b.
STF 1126	ADS 6263. Probably binary. 1829, 132°, 1".5. bsh,bsh. Comes 10.6 at 44".
STT 177	ADS 6276. P=200 years (Couteau-Laques, 1985.0 = 0".51) or 180 years (Muller, 1985.0 = 0".44).
HJ 3997	ADS - . 1836 , 100°, 2".0.
STT 179	ADS 6321. Kappa Gem. Probable long period binary. 1853, 233°, 6".2. Py,Pb.
STF 1138	ADS 6348. 2 Pup. Fixed. y,l. Comes 10.4 at 101".
STF 1140	ADS 6376. Fixed. y,Pb.
STT 186	ADS 6538. Fixed. w,w.
BU 581	ADS 6554. P=44.8 years (1985.0 = 0".51). Comes 10.5 at 4".8 is a member of the system.
STF 1177	ADS 6569. Fixed. w,b.
STF 1187	ADS 6623. P=4390 years? 1985.0 = 2".77. 1829, 71°, 1".6.
STF 1196	ADS 6650. Zeta Cnc. AB has P=59.7 years (1985.0 = 0".66).

PAIR	NOTES

BC, P=1150 years? (1985.0 = 5".92). y,y,Pb. Irregularities in the motion of C reveal a dark component C. Period of Cc = 17.5 years.

HU 1123   ADS 6681. Fixed.

STF 1216   ADS 6762. P=435 years (1985.0 = 0".63). Widening slowly.

STT 93 App   ADS - . 41 Lyn (=S 565). 1824, 165°, 73". y,Pb.

STF 1224   ADS 6811. 24 Cnc. (Not Upsilon Cnc as given in ADS and Webb. 1830, 37°, 5".8). w,bsh. B is A 1746 (P=21.82 years 1985.0 = 0".17).

STF 1223   ADS 6815. Phi Cnc. 1829, 212°, 4".6. w,w.

STF 1245   ADS 6886. Fixed. y,l. Comites 10.7 at 93", 12.0 at 117" and 8.8 at 122".

STF 1263   ADS - . 1829 , 4°, 5".4. Due to proper motion of A.

STF 1266   ADS - . Fixed.

STF 1268   ADS 6988. Iota Cnc. Fixed. o,Pb.

STF 1273*   ADS 6993. Epsilon Hya. AC is STF 1273, P=890 Years (1985.0 = 2".73). y,g. AB is rapid binary, P=15.03 years (1985.0 = 0".23). A and B are also spectroscopic binaries. A comes mag 12.5 is also attached to the system.

STF 1275   ADS 7033. Fixed. Comes 12.6 at 40" forms HJ 2466 AC.

A 1584   ADS 7054. P=74.1 years (1985.0 = 0".16). Closing.

STF 1291   ADS 7071. 57 (Iota Cnc). 1829, 333°, 1".5. Mag 9.2 at 56".

HJ 460   ADS - . Fixed.

KUI 37   ADS   10 UMa. P=21.85 years (1985.0 = 0".56). Comites 10.8 at 142", 9.8 at 127" and 10.5 at 225". Distances increasing due to large pm of AB.

STF 1300   ADS 7139. 1830, 210°, 4".1. Widening.

STF 1298   ADS 7137. 66 Cnc. Fixed. w,Pb. Comes 10.8 at 187".

STF 1311   ADS 7187. Fixed. ysh,w. Comes 12.6 at 28" forms HO 644 AC.

STF 1306*   ADS 7203. Sigma UMa. P=1067 years (1985.0 = 3".38).

STF 1321   ADS 7251. P=975 years (1985.0 = 17".54). o,o.

STF 1332   ADS 7281. 1829, 16°, 5".6.

STF 3121   ADS 7284. P=34.2 years (1985.0 = 0".48). Now at its widest.

STF 1333   ADS 7286. 1828, 39°, 1".4. ysh,bsh.

STF 1334   ADS 7292. 38 Lyn. 1829, 240°, 2".7. Retrograde motion. w,b. Comites 10.8 at 88", 10.7 at 178".

STF 1338   ADS 7307. P=219.7 years (1985.0 = 0".80). w,w. Comes 11.4 at 143".

STF 1348   ADS 7352. 1831, 334°, 1".1. Pb,Pb.

STF 1356   ADS 7390. Omega Leo. P=116.8 years (1985.0 = 0".46).

PAIR	NOTES

STF 1360   ADS 7406. Fixed. Pb,g. Comites 12.3 at 85" and 11.2 at 158".
STF 1351   ADS 7402. 23 UMa. Fixed. y,bsh. Comes 10.5 at 100".
STT 101 App ADS 7416. 6 Leo (=SHJ 107). Fixed. o,Pb.
STF 1350   ADS 7425. Fixed. Comes 9.0 at 30".
H 58   ADS 7448. Fixed.

STF 1362   ADS 7446. Fixed.
STF 1374   ADS 7477. 1838, 275°, 3".3.
A.C.5   ADS 7555. Gamma Sex. P=75.6 years (1985.0 = 0".56). Comes
           12.1 at 36" forms HJ 4256 AC.
STF 1399   ADS 7589. Fixed. Py,g.

STF 1402   ADS   - . 1831 , 96°, 21".1.
STT 215*   ADS 7704. P=552 years (Wierzbinski, 1985.0 = 1".41) or
           444 years (Zaera, 1985.0 = 1".39). w,w.
STF 1415   ADS 7705. Fixed. Comes 10.6 at 150".
STF 1424   ADS 7724. Gamma Leo. P=619 years (1985.0 = 4".32). o,o.
           Distant comites 9.6 and 10.0.

STF 1426   ADS 7730. 1832, 257°, 0".6. Direct motion. Comes 9.3 at 8".
STF 1428   ADS 7762. 1831, 84°, 3".8.
HU 879   ADS 7780 Beta LMi. P=37.9 years (Baize (1950), 1985.0 =
           0".46) or 37.2 years (Baize (1976), 1985.0 = 0".39).

STF 1439   ADS 7802. 1829, 131ᵛ, 2".0.
STF 1450   ADS 7837. 49 Leo. Fixed. w,Pb.
STF 1457   ADS 7864. 1829, 288ᶜ, 0".7.
STT 228   ADS 7926. 1851, 196ᶜ, 0".5.
STT 229   ADS 7929. Long period binary. 1846, 347 , 0".7.

STF 1487   ADS 7979. 54 Leo. 1830, 103ᶜ, 6".2.
BU 1077   ADS 8035. Alpha Uma. P=44.66 years (1985.0 = 0".79).
HO 378   ADS 8047. 1891, 219°, 0".4. Widening since discovery.
STF 1510   ADS 8065. 1832, 341ᵛ, 3".9.
STF 1517   ADS 8094. P= 4050 years? (1985.0 = 0".42). Widening?

STT 232   ADS 8102. Fixed.
STF 1516   ADS 8100. Optical pair due to large pm of A. 1832, 299 ,
           9".75. Comes to A, 11.2 at 7" forms STT 539 and is
           probably a physical component.
STF 1523* ADS 8119. Xi UMa. P=59.84 years (1985.0 = 2".32). Py,Py.
           Both stars are spectroscopic binaries.

STF 1524   ADS 8123. Nu UMa. Fixed. y,b.
STF 1527* ADS 8128. P=148 years? (1985.0 = 1".37). ysh,g.
STF 1536* ADS 8148. Iota Leo. P=192 years (1985.0 = 1".32).
BSO 5   ADS   - . P=421 years (1985.0 = 5".76).

PAIR   NOTES

STI 725   ADS - . 1910, 2°, 10".5. Increase in angle and distance.
STF 1543   ADS 8175. 57 UMa. 1831, 11^{c}, 5".4. w,r? Comites 11.6
            at 217", 7.8 at 346" and two to 7.8, 10.2 at 98" and
            10.3 at 129".
STT 234   ADS 8189. P=86.44 years (1985.0 = 0".37).

STF 1547   ADS 8196. 88 Leo. 1782, 318^{b}, 14".6. w,Pb.
STT 235   ADS 8197. P=72.9 years (1985.0 = 0".52). Widening.
STF 1552   ADS 8220. 90 Leo. Fixed. w,w. Comes 8.8 at 63".
STF 1555   ADS 8231. Highly inclined orbit. 1829, 339°, 1".2.
            Comes 10.2 at 21" forms HJ 503 AC.

STF 1559   ADS 8249. Fixed.
STF 1561   ADS 8250. 1831, 266°, 10".5. A has a pm of 0".6
            annuallly. Comites 8.6 at 90", 9.5 at 121" and
            12.4 at 91".
STT 237   ADS 8252. 1845, 287°, 0".7.

BU 794   ADS 8337. P=77.15 years (1985.0 = 0".21). Closing.
            Comites 14.0 at 5".6 and 13.3 at 27".
A 1088   ADS 8387. Direct motion. 1905 , 223°, 0".3.
STF 1596   ADS 8406. 2 Com. Fixed. Py,Pb.
STF 3123   ADS 8419. P=115.5 years (1985.0 = 0".18). Opening.
            Comes 15.6 at 3" is probably physical. Comes 8.0 at
            26" is double (0".2).

STF 1604   ADS 8440. 1831, 93^{c}, 12".0 (AB). 1831, 97 , 58".0 (AC).
STF 1606   ADS 8446. P=326.8 years (1985.0 = 0".32).
SHJ 136   ADS - . 1876, 76^{c}, 66".7.

S 634   ADS 8444. 1877, 280°, 6".8.
STF 1608   ADS 8450. 1832 , 224°, 10".6.
STF 1619   ADS 8477. 1829, 288^{c}, 7".8.
STF 1622   ADS 8489. 2 CVn. Fixed. o,b.
STF 1625   ADS 8494. Fixed.

STF 1627   ADS 8505. Fixed. w,w.
STF 1633   ADS 8519. Fixed. bw,bw.
STT 249   ADS 8535. Closing since discovery, 1853, 315°, 0".5.
            Comes 11.2 at 13".
STF 1639   ADS 8539. P=678 years (1985.0 = 1".54).

STT 250   ADS 8540. 1845, 331^{c}, 0".4. Little motion.
STF 1643   ADS 8553. P=2200 years? (1985.0 = 1".89).
STF 1717   ADS 8604. 1832, 341°, 7".8.
STF 1647   ADS 8575. P=4273 years? (1985.0 = 1".32).
STF 1657   ADS 8600. 24 Com. Fixed. Py,bsh.

PAIR	NOTES
STF 1661	ADS 8606. 1828, 226°, 2".6.
STF 1669	ADS 8627. 1828 , 299°, 5".4. Comes 10.5 at 59".
HJ 4539	ADS - . Gamma Cen. P=84.5 years (van den Bos, 1985.0 = 1".52) or P=84.6 years (Wierzbinski, 1985.0 = 1".51).
STF 1670*	ADS 8630. Gamma Vir. P=171.4 years (1985.0 = 3".49). Highly eccentric orbit, closing to 0".4 in AD 2008. w,w. Comes 12.2 at 124".
STF 1678	ADS 8659. 1832, 212°, 32".6. Pb,oy.
HJ 4547	ADS - . Iota Cru. 1882, 40°, 27".1.
STF 1694	ADS 8682. Fixed.
STF 1687	ADS 8695. 35 Com. P=510 years (1985.0 = 1".08). y,y. Comes 9.1 at 29", b.
STF 1689	ADS 8704. 1827, 198°, 28".7. Dy,g.
STF 1692	ADS 8706. Alpha CVn. Fixed. w,w.
STF 1695	ADS 8710. 1832, 289°, 3".3. Comes 10.4 at 124".
STT 256	ADS 8708. 1848, 57°, 0".7.
STF 1699	ADS 8721. 1830, 1°, 1".5. Small change in angle.
BU 1082*	ADS 8739. 78 UMa. P=115.7 years (1985.0 = 1".41).
BU 929	ADS 8759. 48 Vir. 1879, 229°, 0".5. Widening.
STF 1728	ADS 8804. 42 Com. P=25.8 years (1985.0 = 0".61). Beginning to close. Orbit almost edge-on to the line of sight. Comes 10.2 at 90", closing due to pm of AB.
STT 261	ADS 8814. 1843, 359°, 0".6. y,Pb.
STF 1734	ADS 8864. 1830, 198°, 0".7. Widening. w,w.
STF 1744	ADS 8891. Zeta UMa. Long period binary, 1830, 148°, 14".4. C (Alcor) has the same pm as AB. A and B are also spectroscopic binaries. w,w.
STF 1742	ADS 8890. Fixed. bw,bw.
STT 269	ADS 8939. P=54.8 years (1985.0 = 0".09).
STF 1757*	ADS 8949. P=334 years (1985.0 = 2".06). Mag 11.6 at 45".
STF 1768	ADS 8974. 25 CVn. P=240 years (1985.0 = 1".83). Eccentric orbit. Comes 8.7 at 217". Py,w.
STF 1770	ADS 8979. Fixed. o,b.
BU 612	ADS 8987. P=22.35 years (1985.0 = 0".31). Near maximum distance. Comes 11.0 at 125", approaching.
HJ 4608	ADS - . 1848, 174 , 4".4.
STF 1781	ADS 9019. P=312.5 years (1985.0 = 0".41).
STF 1785	ADS 9031. P=155 years (1985.0 = 3".41). Py,bw.
STF 1788	ADS 9053. 1831, 54 , 2".2. Comites mags 10.3 at 128" and 10.9 at 157".

PAIR   NOTES

STF 1795   ADS 9077. Fixed.
STT 276   ADS 9121. 1845, 196°, 0".6. Comes at 9".7. IDS gives
            magnitude as 10.0 and 10.8.
STT 278   ADS 9159. P=215 years (1985.0 = 0".27).

STT 277   ADS 9158. 1845, 334°, 0".4. Comes 9.3 at 14".2 forms
            STF 1812. Further comes 11.8 at 73".
STF 1820   ADS 9167. P=810 years? (1985.0 = 2".27). Circular orbit?
            1831, 47 , 2".4.
STF 1821   ADS 9173. Kappa Boo. 1832, 238°, 12".6. w,bsh.

STF 1816   ADS 9174. Closing. 1831, 80°, 1".9.
STF 1817   ADS 9177. Closing. 1832, 7°, 1".6.
STF 1834   ADS 9229. P=321 years (1985.0 = 1".28). w,w. Orbit of
            high eccentricity and inclination.
STF 1835   ADS 9247. 1832, 186°, 6".1. BC is BU 1111 (P=39.5
            years (1985.0 = 0".25).

STF 1838   ADS 9251. Fixed.
STF 1843   ADS 9259. Fixed. Star C at 97" not in the IDS.
STF 1850   ADS 9277. Fixed.
A 570   ADS 9301. P=30.0 years (1985.0 = 0".15).

STF 1863   ADS 9329. 1830, 110°, 0".6.
Alpha Cen* ADS   - . P=79.92 years (Heintz, 1985.0 = 21".32) or
            P=79.91 years (Wielen, 1985.0 = 21".20). Star C
            (Proxima Centauri) is 2ᵛ 11' away and is the nearest
            star to the Sun.

STF 1864   ADS 9338. Pi Boo. 1830, 99°, 5".8. w,w. Mag 10.0 at 128".
STF 1872   ADS 9346. 1830, 38 , 7".5. Comes 11.3 at 76".
STF 1865   ADS 9343. Zeta Boo. P=123.4 years (1985.0 = 1".02).
            Beginning to close. Very eccentric orbit. Comes 10.9
            at 99" is H VI 104.

STF 1871   ADS 9350. 1829, 283°, 1".8. Widening. w,w.
STF 1877   ADS 9372. Epsilon Boo. 1829, 321°, 2".6. y,b. Comes
            12.0 at 177"
STT 285   ADS 9378. P=88.4 years (1985.0 = 0".29). Widening.
STF 1884   ADS 9389. 1829, 55°, 1".7.

BU 106   ADS 9396. Mu Lib. Opening. 1875, 335°, 1".4. Comites
            13.9 at 25", 12.5 at 27".
STF 1890   ADS 9406. 39 Boo. 1830, 44°, 3".7. w,w.
STT 287   ADS 9418. P=400 years (1985.0 = 1".08).
STF 1888*   ADS 9413. Xi Boo. P=151.5 years (1985.0 = 7".15). Now
            beginning to close. or, b. Comites 12.6 at 67" and
            9.6 at 149".

PAIR   NOTES

STT 288*   ADS 9425. P=215.4 years (1985.0 = 1".14). Beginning to
             close. Pb,Pb.
STI 2317   ADS   - . 1910, 139°, 13".4.

SHJ 191   ADS 9474. Fixed.
BU 348   ADS 9480. 2 Ser. 1875, 115°, 0".5.
STF 1909*   ADS 9494. 44 Boo. P=225.0 years (1985.0 = 1".31).
             Opening. Very highly inclined orbit. B is a W UMa star.
STF 1910   ADS 9507. Fixed.

A 1116   ADS 9530. 1905, 21°, 0".4.
STF 1919   ADS 9535. 1832, 10°, 24".8.
STF 1934   ADS 9573. AB 1830, 45°, 5".3.
STF 1932   ADS 9578. P=203 years (1985.0 = 1".46). B has a dark
             companion, period = 50 years.

BU 32   ADS 9596. 6 Ser. 1875, 13°, 2".3.
STF 1937   ADS 9617. Eta CrB. P=41.56 years (1985.0 = 0".80). Now
             opening. y,y. Comites 1.0 at 215" and 12.6 at 58".
STF 1938*   ADS 9626. Mu Boo. P=260.1 years (1985.0 = 2".07). Now
             closing slowly. w,w. Mu is 108" distant, magnitude 4.5
             and forms STF 28 App.

HU 149   ADS 9628. 1900, 296°, 0".2.
STT 296   ADS 9639. 1845, 328°, 1".5. Comes 12.5 at 67.
STF 1956   ADS 9694. 1831, 41°, 2".7. Closing with little change in PA.
STF 1954   ADS 9701. Delta Ser. P=3168 years? (1985.0 = 4".30). ysh,bsh.

STT 298   ADS 9716. P=55.88 years (1985.0 = 0".55). Now closing
             rapidly. w,w. Comes 7.9 at 121" is apparently physical.
STF 1963   ADS 9727. 1829, 291°, 4".2. w,w. Comes 13.4 at 31".
STF 1962   ADS 9728. Fixed.
STF 1965   ADS 9737. Zeta CrB. 1822, 299°, 6".2. Binary. bsh,Pb.

STF 1989   ADS 9769. Pi UMi. P=150.7 years (1985.0 = 0".60).
             Highly eccentric orbit. Distance fixed for some years.
STF 1969   ADS 9756. P=325 years (1985.0 = 0".51). Now opening.
             1831, 43 , 1".5.
HU 580   ADS 9744. Iota Ser. P=11.07 years (van den Bos, 1985.0
             = 0".09) or 22.14 years (van den Bos, 1985.0 = 0".08).
             Components are equally bright making determination of
             quadrant difficult. Comites 13.4 at 143", 12.6 at 151".

STF 1967   ADS 9757. Gamma CrB. P=91.0 years (1985.0 = 0".53).
             Widening. Highly inclined orbit.

PAIR	NOTES

STF 2207   ADS 10690. 1832, 128°, 1".1. Probable binary.
STF 2199   ADS 10699. 1830, 116°, 1".7. Retrograde motion.
STF 2218   ADS 10728. 1836, 355°, 2".5. Angle decreasing.
STF 2203   ADS 10722. 1830, 334°, 0".7. Retrograde motion.
STF 2241   ADS 10759. Fixed. Comites 11.4 at 190", 12.4 at 101".

STF 2202   ADS 10750. Fixed. Comes 12.5 at 96".
STF 2213   ADS 10765. Fixed.
A.C.7   ADS 10786. BC is A.C.7. P=43.2 years (1985.0 = 1".53). Nearing maximum separation. (Mu Her). Mu Her is 3.5 at 35" and forms STF 2220 with BC. It has a comes mag 11.2 at 256".

STF 2215   ADS 10795. 1831, 311°, 0".8. Retrograde motion.
STT 337   ADS 10828. P=500 years (1985.0 = 0".30).
STF 2242   ADS 10849. Fixed.
STT 338   ADS 10850. 1845, 44°, 0".7. Slow binary. w,w. Comites 12.9 at 28" and 9.9 at 95".

STF 2245   ADS 10905. Fixed.
RMK 22   ADS   - . 1880, 88°, 2".5.
STF 2259   ADS 10955. Fixed.
STF 2273   ADS 10985. Fixed. Comes 12.7 at 24" and 14.7 at 19".

STF 2308   ADS
STF 2264   ADS 10993. 95 Her. 1829, 262°, 6".1. Colours w,w but both stars suspected of varying in colour.
STF 2267   ADS 11001. 1830, 234°, 1".4. Closing.
STF 2278   ADS 11035. 1831, 22°, 39". Comites 8.5 at 38", 9.7 at 201" and 14.1 at 5" to the 9.7.

STF 2262   ADS 11005. Tau Oph. P=280 years (1985.0 = 1".81). y,y. Comes 9.3 at 100".
STF 2272*   ADS 11046. 70 Oph. P=88.1 years (1985.0 = 2".12). y,p. Many comites.

STF 2276   ADS 11056. Fixed. Comes 12.0 at 61".
STT 341   ADS 11060. P=20.0 years (1985.0 = 0".46). Orbit of very high eccentricity and inclination. Comites 9.6 at 28", 38", 63" and 108". Also 8.6 at 136".
HU 1186   ADS 11071. P=101.5 years (1985.0 = 0".33). Starting to close.

STF 2280   ADS 11089. 100 Her. Fixed.
STF 2281   ADS 11111. 73 Oph. P=270 years (1985.0 = 0".38). Slowly widening. Comes 12.6 at 68".
HU 674   ADS 11128. 1904, 279°, 0".5. Retrograde motion.

PAIR	NOTES

STT 340   ADS 10437. 1847, 237°, 31".5.

STF 2114   ADS 10312. 1830, 136°, 1".3. Probable binary. y,l.

STF 2120   ADS 10332. 1829, 11°, 7".3.

STF 2130*   ADS 10345. Mu Dra. P=482 years (1985.0 = 1".89). Now closing slowly. Comes 13.8 at 13" forms BU 1088 and appears physical.

STF 2122   ADS 10347. 1831, 280°, 20".4. Fixed?

STF 2135   ADS 10394. AB 1829, 166°, 6".7.

KUI 79   ADS   - . P=12.98 years (Baize, 1985.0 = 1".12) of P=12.98 years (Eggen, 1985.0 = 1".10). Near maximum separation. Rare opportunity to see such a short period pair.

STF 2140   ADS 10418. Alpha Her. P=8230 years? (Hopmann, 1985.0 = 4".63) or P=3600 years (Baize, 1985.0 = 4".65). o,g. Comes 11.1 at 80".

STF 3127   ADS 10424. Delta Her. 1830, 174°, 25".8. Two faint comites at 51" and 91".

SHJ 243   ADS 10417. 36 Oph. P=548.7 years (1985.0 = 4".67). Star 6.7 at 700" has common proper motion. Other comites mags 8.2 and 13.5.

BSO 13   ADS   - . P=693.2 years (Wieth-Knudsen, 1985.0 = 8".14) or P=2204 years? (Wielen, 1985.0 = 8".37). Comites 12.5 at 42" and 14 at 47".

MLB 4   ADS   - . P=42.18 years (1985.0 = 1".92). Closing. Comes 9.9 at 31" forms HJ 4935. See added a mag 12.8 at 14". Distances changing due to large pm of AB.

STF 2161   ADS 10526. Rho Her. 1830, 307°, 4".5. A is a speckle pair, distance = 0".29. Comes 13.3 at 119".

STF 2164   ADS 10530. 1829, 17°, 8".8.

BU 1201   ADS 10573. Fixed.

STF 2180   ADS 10597. Fixed.

HO 417   ADS 10589. 1892, 151°, 0".4.

KUI 82 AB-C   ADS 10585. Mags 8,8.2 (est). AB = A 351 (P=60 years), 1985.0 = 0".58. 1933, 286°, 33".

STF 2173*   ADS 10598. P=46.08 years (Duncombe-Ashbrook, 1985.0 = 1".00) or P=46.40 years (Wilson, 1985.0 = 0".97). Orbit of high inclination.

STF 35 App   ADS 10628. Nu Dra. Fixed.

STF 34 App   ADS 10635. Fixed. Comites 10.8 at 94", 91".

STF 2186   ADS 10650. Fixed.

PAIR	NOTES

STF 2289   ADS 11123. P=3040 years? (1985.0 = 1".23). w,c.
STF 2294*   ADS 11186. P=278 years (Luyten, 1985.0 = 1".12) or
P=200 years (Wilson, 1985.0 = 1".01). Orbit of high
eccentricity.
STT 353   ADS 11311. Phi Dra. 1856, 64°, 0".6.

STF 2323   ADS 11336. 1833, 6°, 3".1. Five other comites.
A.C.11   ADS 11324. P=240 years (1985.0 = 0".79).
STF 2315   ADS 11334. P=775 years (1985.0 = 0".71). Mag 13.5 at 45".
STT 351&   ADS 11344. AC is STT 351, 1846, 25°, 0".5, widening
HU 66   slowly. AB is HU 66, 1898, 310°, 0".3 – retrograde
motion. One of the closest triples known.

STF 2316   ADS 11353. 1828, 314°, 4".0.
STF 2330   ADS 11418. 1829, 177°, 20".2.
STF 2339   ADS 11454. 1830, 272°, 2".3. Primary is HU 322, a
close pair in orbital motion.

A 1377   ADS 11468. P=184.6 years (Wilson, 1985.0 = 0".32),
P=338.0 years (Baize, 1985.0 = 0".32) or P=169.5
years (Baize, 1985.0 = 0".25). Comes 8.8 at 26"
forms STF 2348.
STT 359   ADS 11479. P=210.9 years (1985.0 = 0".63). w,w.

STT 358   ADS 11483. P=296.2 years (Starikova, 1985.0 = 1".49)
or 3083 years? (Hopmann, 1985.0 = 1".53).
STT 357   ADS 11484. P=256 years (1985.0 = 0".34).
STF 2351   ADS 11500. 1830, 340°, 5".2. Fixed.
STF 2384   ADS 11568. P=137 years (1985.0 = 0".50). Mag 12.5 at 113".

STF 2368   ADS 11558. 1831, 331°, 2".0). Comes 10.7 at 37".
HO 437   ADS 11566. 1892, 116°, 0".4. Comites 10.7 at 40",
13.9 at 23" and 11.2 at 4" to 10.7 (increasing).
STF 2367   ADS 11579. P=90 years (1985.0 = 0".14). Very
eccentric orbit. Comites 8.6 at 14", 11.9 at 23"
and 10.9 at 149".

STF 2372   ADS 11593. Comes 11.4 at 90".
STF 2398*   ADS 11632. P=453 years (Heintz, 1985.0 = 13".82)
or P=294.7 years (Baize, 1985.0 = 13".19). Comes
12.8 at 200" (increasing due to pm of AB).

STF 2382*   ADS 11635 AB. Epsilon^1 Lyr. P=1165 years? (1985.0 =
2".65). w,w. Linked with STF 2383.
STF 2383*   ADS 11635 CD. Epsilon^2 Lyr. P=565 years? (1985.0 =
2".36). Several comites to each pair.
STF 38 App ADS 11639. Zeta Lyr. Fixed. Comes 15.8 at 25"
(distance decreasing) forms BU 968. A further 13.3
at 47" (increasing) and a 11.5 at 62".

PAIR   NOTES

STF 2375   ADS 11640. 1829, 177 , 2".2. Each component is a very
              close pair discovered by Finsen and nicknamed by him
              "Tweedledum and Tweedledee". They have similar
              position angles and separations (~0".15). Both are
              showing orbital motion.

STF 2379   ADS 11667. Fixed. Comes 11.3 at 26".
STF 39 App   ADS 11745. Beta Lyr. Fixed.
STF 2420   ADS 11779. 1833, 346°, 30".3. Comes 11 at 150".

STF 2415   ADS 11816. 1831, 299°, 2".0.
STF 2417   ADS 11853. Theta Ser. 1830, 104 , 21".6. Mag 7.9 at 214".
STF 2421   ADS 11858. 1829, 69°, 21".2.
BU 648*   ADS 11871. P=61.2 years (Schrutka-Rechtenstamm, 1985.0
              =1".15) or P=60.8 years (Vlaicu, 1985.0 = 1".16). Now
              at its greatest separation. Comites 12.1 at 55" and
              12.2 at 91".

STF 2422   ADS 11869. 1832, 106°, 0".9. Long period binary.
STF 2438   ADS 11897. P=259.1 years (1985.0 = 0".90).
STF 2437   ADS 11956. 1830, 81°, 1".1. Closing since discovery.

STF 2434   ADS 11971. 1831, 147°, 25".6. Comes 10.6 at 0".9
              to B has closed in from 1".9 in 1831.
SHJ 286   ADS 12007. 15 Aql. 1823, 207°, 35".6. o,1.
STF 2456   ADS   - . AB 1829, 14°, 29".1. Quadrant change.
STF 2446   ADS 12029. 1831, 154°, 10".1. Mag 10.2 at 35".

STF 2449   ADS 12037. Fixed.
HJ 5084*   ADS   - . P=120.4 years (1985.0 = 1".35).
STF 2455   ADS 12050. 1828, 144°, 4".9. Comes 11.9 at 94".
STF 2457   ADS 12053. Fixed.
STF 2461   ADS 12061. 17 Lyr. 1830, 331°, 3".7. Many comites.

STF 2474   ADS 12101. 1830, 259°, 17".3.
A 863   ADS 12108. 1904 , 123°, 0".4.
STF 2481&   ADS 12145. A-BC is STF 2481, 1830, 234°, 3".8. BC is
SE 2   SE 2, P=63.1 years (1985.0 = 0".54).
STF 2486   ADS 12169. 1832, 225°, 10".5. ysh,ysh. Comites 13.3
              at 25" (decreasing) and 11.4 at 180" (increasing).

BU 139   ADS 12160. Fixed. Comes 7.9 at 113" forms STT 177 App
              Also comites 9.5 at 29" and 12.7 at 28".
STT 371   ADS 12239. 1846, 154°, 0".8. w,w. Comes 8.6 at 48" (b).
STF 2491   ADS 12246. 1828, 207°, 1".1.

PAIR	NOTES

STF 2509   ADS 12296. 1832, 353ᶜ, 0".5. Becoming wider.
BU 1129   ADS 12366. 1889, 344°, 0".3.
STF 2525   ADS 12447. P=990 years (1985.0 = 1".90). Eccentric orbit.
STF 43 App ADS 12540. Beta Cyg. Fixed. A double (0".4). found
by speckle interferometry. Composite spectrum.

STF 2549   ADS 12586. 1832 , 291ᶜ, 21".1. Comes mag 12.2
at 2" to A forms BU 655. Comites 9.3 at 26" and 8.0
at 51" (distances increasing).
STT 377   ADS 12667. 1842, 51ᵛ, 0".9. Comes 10.1 at 25".
H 26   ADS 12693. 1782 , 82ᵛ, 91".9.

STF 2556   ADS 12752. P=342.5 years (1985.0 = 0".39).
H 84   ADS 12750. Fixed.
STF 2574   ADS 12803. 1832, 129ᶜ, 1".0.
STF 46 App ADS 12815. 1832, 136ˀ, 37".3.
STT 380   ADS 12808. Chi Aql. Fixed. Comes 12.3 at 82". Also
10.3 at 140" forms J 1858. Nearby pair, 11.0, 11.5,
317°, 9".4. is HLM 26.

STT 383   ADS 12831. 1845, 27ᵛ, 0".9.
STT 384   ADS 12851. Fixed. w,w.
STF 2579   ADS 12880. Delta Cyg. P=827 years (1985.0 = 2".38).
bw,Pb. Comes 12.0 at 66".

STF 2576*   ADS 12889. P=224.7 years (1985.0 = 2".19). w,w.
STF 2578   ADS 12893. Fixed. Four comites.
STT 386   ADS 12965. 1846, 78ᵛ, 1".0.
STF 2603   ADS 13007. Epsilon Dra. 1832, 354ᶜ, 2".8. Py,bsh.

STF 2583   ADS 12962. Pi Aql. 1829, 121ᵛ, 1".5. Pb,c. Comes
12.2 at 34".
STT 387   ADS 12972. P=156.5 years (1985.0 = 0".60).
A.G.C.11   ADS 12973. Zeta Sge. AB is A.G.C.11, P=22.8 years
(1985.0 = 0".22). C (8.8 at 9") forms STF 2585.

HO 581   ADS 13125. P=25.69 years (1985.0 = 0".22). Now
closing rapidly.
STF 2597   ADS 13104. 1826 , 92°, 1".9. Closing.
STF 2605   ADS 13148. Psi Cyg. 1831, 185ᵛ, 3".3. Py,Pb. Comites
13.6 at 21" and 10.2 at 165".

STF 2606   ADS 13196. 1832, 131ᵛ, 1".2.
STT 395   ADS 13277. 16 Vul. 1844, 79 , 0".6.
STF 2624   ADS 13312. 1830 ,179ᵛ, 2".0. w,w. Comites 9.1 at 43"
and 11.0 at 29".
STF 2626   ADS 13329. Fixed.

PAIR	NOTES

STF 2642   ADS 13392. 1832, 165°, 2".4. Comes 12.5 at 73".
(Distance decreasing).

STF 2652   ADS 13449. 1832, 280°, 0".3. Long period binary.

STT 400   ADS 13461. P=86.16 years (1985.0 = 0".20).

S 735   ADS   - . Fixed.

STF 2644   ADS 13506. Fixed.

STT 403   ADS 13572. 1848, 173°, 0".8. Star C, 9.0 at 11".6
forms STF 2657.

BUP   ADS   - . 29 Cyg. AB fixed, AC 1887 , 23°, 225".2,
AD 1894 , 120°, 216".5.

STF 2671   ADS 13692. 1831, 341°, 3".0. w,w. Comes 12.5 at 84".

STT 406   ADS 13723. P=113.5 years (1985.0 = 0".58).

D 22   ADS 13847. 1875, 140°, 2".8. Comes 13.8 at 19"
whose distance is decreasing.

HO 130   ADS 13856. Fixed.

S 755   ADS   - . Fixed. Comes 13.5 at 21".

S 756   ADS   - . Fixed.

BU 151   ADS 14073. Beta Del. P=26.65 years (1985.0 = 0".25)
near minimum separation. Comes 11.0 at 39" forms
STF 2704. Also 13.1 at 23".

STF 2705   ADS 14078. Fixed. py,pb. Comites 11.2 at 183", 12.9 at 5".4.

STT 533   ADS 14101. Kappa Del. 1852, 11 , 10".4. Rectilinear motion.

STT 410   ADS 14126. 1850, 23°, 0".6. bw,bw. Comes 8.6 at 69".

STF 2716   ADS 14158. 49 Cyg. Fixed. Py,Pb. Comes 11.8 at 68".

STF 2723   ADS 14233. 1831, 86°, 1".5. Round in 1958.

STF 2726   ADS 14259. 1830, 57°, 6".6.

BU 676   ADS 14274. Gamma Cyg. 1878, 321°, 37".7. Optical.

STF 2725   ADS 14270. 1829, 358°, 4".2. w,w.

STF 2727   ADS 14279. Gamma Del. 1830, 274 , 11".9. y,g.

STT 413   ADS 14296. Lambda Cyg. P=391.3 years (1985.0 = 0".85).
w,Pb. Comes 9.9 at 85" forms S 765.

BU 268   ADS 14306. 1875, 221°, 0".4.

BU 155   ADS 14370. 1876, 25°, 0".6. w,b. Comites 12.0 at 14",
10.9 at 195".

HO 144   ADS 14379. 1886, 168°, 0".4. Rapid change.

HO 146   ADS 14404. 1886, 56°, 0".4.

STT 418   ADS 14421. 1842, 302°,0".6. w,w.

STF 2741   ADS 14504. 1831, 36°, 1".9. Py,Pb. Comes 10.5 at 140".

STF 2737   ADS 14499. Epsilon Equ. P=101.4 years (1985.0 = 1".03).
Orbit very highly inclined. Star C is physical, mag 7.1,
(1833, 78 , 10".8) - orbit hyperbolic?. Mag 12.4 at 89".

PAIR   NOTES

STF 2742   ADS 14556. 2 Equ. 1831, 225°, 2".6. Py,Pb.
STF 2751   ADS 14575. 1831, 344°, 1".9.
STF 2744   ADS 14573. 1830, 190°, 1".5. w,w. Comes 12.8 at 89".
STF 2758*   ADS 14636. 61 Cyg. P=653 years? (1985.0 = 29".37). y,y.

STF 2760   ADS 14645. 1829, 223°, 13".7. Change due to pm. Comes
            9.8 at 60".
STF 2769   ADS 14710. Fixed.
STF 2780   ADS 14749. 1831, 229°, 1".1. w,w. Comes 8.7 at 121".
H I 48   ADS 14783. P=84.4 years (1985.0 = 0".57). Closing.

STT 432   ADS 14778. 1847, 130°,1".2. y,b.
STT 535   ADS 14773. Delta Equ. P=5.70 years (1985.0 = 0".32).
            Closing rapidly. A highly inclined orbit. Comes 9.5
            at 60" forms STF 2777 - separating due to pm of AB.
HO 286   ADS 14859. Rapid binary, often single. Period uncertain.

STT 437   ADS 14889. 1845, 68°, 1".4. y,Pb. Comes 11.2 at 86".
STT 435   ADS 14894. 1848, 203°, 0".6.
HO 157   ADS 14928. Fixed.
STF 2799   ADS 15007. 1831, 333°, 1".4. Retrograde motion. bw,bw.
            Comes 9.3 at 130".

STF 2804   ADS 15076. 1828, 314°, 2".9. The PA in Webb is a
            misprint. Burnham's measure should be 335.7°. y,y.
            Comes 11.6 at 97".
STT 443   ADS 15144. Fixed.
STF 56 App ADS 15147. Fixed. Comes 13.5 at 88".

STT 445   ADS 15177. Fixed.
BU 1212   ADS 15176. 24 Aqr. P=48.70 years (1985.0 = 0".40).
            Orbit of high eccentricity. Comes 10.9 at 36",
            distance decreasing due to pm of AB.
HO 166   ADS 15267. P=80.5 years (1985.0 = 0".37). Beginning
            to close.

STF 2822*   ADS 15270. Mu^2 Cyg. P=507.5 years (1985.0 = 1".68).
            ysh,bw. Highly inclined orbit. Mu^1 (mag 6.9) is at 196"
            distance is decreasing. Comes 13.3 to Mu forms ES 521
S 798   ADS 15268. Epsilon Peg. Fixed. Comes 11.3 at 82".

STF 2828   ADS 15348. 1829 , 142° , 23".8. Comes 10.4 at 28"
            and 14.9 at 10".
COU 14   ADS   - . 13 Peg. P=31.0 years (1985.0 = 0".31).
STF 2843   ADS 15407. 1831 , 134°, 2".4.
STF 2840   ADS 15405. 1832 , 194°, 20".0. Mag 13.2 at 55".

PAIR	NOTES
STT 458	ADS 15481. Fixed. Comes 12.2 at 23".
BU 275	ADS 15499. 1876, 183°, 0".3.
STF 2848	ADS 15493. Fixed.
STF 2863	ADS 15600. Xi Cep. P=3800 years? (1985.0 = 8".04. w,b. Comes 12.7 at 97".
STF 2881	ADS 15769. 1830, 111°, 1".8.
HO 180	ADS 15794. 1886, 222°, 0".5.
BU 1216	ADS 15843. 1890, 318°, 0".6.
BU 172	ADS 15902. 51 Aqr. P=190 years (1985.0 = 0".23). Comites 10.1 at 54", 10.0 at 116" and 8.5 at 132".
KR 60	ADS 15972. P=44.60 years (Lippincott, 1985.0 = 3".11) or P=44.36 years (Wielen, 1985.0 = 3".09). Fainter star is DO Cep, a flare star. Suspected dark comes to A. Many other comites in the IDS.
STF 2909*	ADS 15971. Zeta Aqr. P=856 years? (1985.0 = 1".60). Perturbation of B with period 25.5 years. ysh,bsh.
STF 58 App	ADS 15987. Delta Cep. Primary variable. Fixed. Comes 13 at 20".
STF 2912	ADS 15988. 37 Peg. P=140 years (1985.0 = 0".98). Orbit of high inclination, now closing slowly.
STF 2920	ADS 16069. Fixed. Py,Pb.
STF 2922	ADS 16095. 8 Lac. Fixed. Many comites.
HO 296	ADS 16173. P=20.93 years. (1985.0 = 0".13). Now opening quickly. y,y, Third body suspected from period variation.
STF 2932	ADS - . Fixed. Mag 11.3 at 30".
STF 2934	ADS 16185. P=520 years (1985.0 = 0".95). A has a dark companion with a period of 81 years.
S 816	ADS 16211. Eta Peg. Fixed? BC is BU 1144 BC (0".2). Comes 14 at 63" to BC and 16 at 5".7 to 14.
STT 480	ADS 16260. Fixed.
STF 2943	ADS 16268. Tau¹ Aqr. 1783, 110°, 35".6.
STF 2950	ADS 16317. 1832, 319°, 2".0. y,b. Comes 10.7 at 39".
A 632	ADS 16326. P=98.25 years (1985.0 = 0".74).
COU 240	ADS - . Discovered in 1968.
STT 483	ADS 16428. 52 Peg. P=286 years (1985.0 = 0".67).
HLD 56	ADS 16435. 1881, 125°, 0".9.
STF 2974	ADS 16496. Fixed.
STF 2978	ADS 16519. Fixed.
BU 385	ADS 16561. 1876, 136°, 0".4. Comes 9.0 at 58" forms HJ 5532.

STF 2993   ADS 16611. AB fixed. Py,p. AC, 1824, 109°, 158"
            forms S 826 – distance decreasing due to pm of AB.
STF 3001   ADS 16666. Omicron Cep. P=796 years? (1985.0 = 2".87).
            Py,Pb. Comes 12.8 at 46".

BU 80   ADS 16665. P=91.8 years (1985.0 = 0".71). Eccentric
            orbit. Comites 10 at 106", 9.4 at 210", 9.8 at 206".
STF 2998   ADS 16672. 94 Aqr. 1830, 345°, 13".4. Py,Pb. A is a
            speckle pair, dist. = 0".14. This is the 6.4 year
            period spectroscopic binary, previously known.

STT 494   ADS 16686. Fixed.
STF 3007   ADS 16713. 1829, 79°, 5".7. y,b. Comes 9.0 at 91",
            distance increasing.
STF 3008   ADS 16725. 1830, 273ᵘ, 7".5.
STF 3012   ADS 16766. Fixed

STF 3013   ADS 16766. Fixed. STF 3013A = STF 3012B.
STT 496   ADS 16795. 1 Cas. 1851 , 337ᵘ, 1".5 (AB). Multiple
            star with six other components.
BU 720   ADS 16836. 72 Peg. P=241.2 years (1985.0 = 0".51). y,y.
STT 500   ADS 16877. 1845, 299ᵘ, 0".4. g,g. Comes 10.5 at 116".

BU 858   ADS 16928. 1881, 277°, 0".5. Comes 12.3 at 23" is BU 389.
ES 700   ADS 17038. Fixed.
STT 510   ADS 17050. 1848, 348ᵘ, 0".4. Comes 9.0 at 121" is HJ 1911.
STF 3042   ADS 17054. 1832, 89ᵘ, 4".2.
STF 3050   ADS 17149. P=813.6 years (Franz, 1985.0 = 1".82) or
            P=355.0 years (Heintz, 1985.0 = 1".59). bw,bw. Comes
            12.9 at 181".

* Denotes pairs which are worth following in small or medium-sized
  apertures because of pronounced orbital motion.

Pairs of known separation for calibrating micrometers.

The list of wide pairs given below has been prepared from photographic measures made at the United States Naval Observatory, and
published in several different volumes of the Publications of the
United States Naval Observatory, (Franz et al.,1963; Josties et al.,
1978). In each case the published values for separation and P.A.
(corrected for precession to the epoch 2000·0) have been fitted with
a linear relationship, and the coefficients found were used to inter-
polate the positions for the epochs 1985, 1990, 1995 and 2000. The
position angles thus found have then been 'de-corrected' for precession
to give the true value for the given epoch. In nearly all cases the
error of fit has resulted in residuals of 0·01 arc-sec in separation
and 0·1 degrees in position angle.

	STF 60		STF 296	
Date	PA	SEP	PA	SEP
1985	310·6	12·30	304·1	19·98
1990	313·6	12·59	304·3	20·14
1995	316·7	12.88	304·5	20·30
2000	319·7	13·18	304·8	20·45

	STF 1561		STF 1744	
	PA	SEP	PA	SEP
1985	250·3	9·26	151·0	14·42
1990	249·7	9·21	151·0	14·42
1995	249·1	9·15	151·0	14·42
2000	248·5	9·09	152·0	14·41

	STF 2032		STF 2727	
	PA	SEP	PA	SEP
1985	233·8	6·73	267·1	9·51
1990	234·7	6·83	266·9	9·42
1995	235·7	6·94	266·6	9·34
2000	236·6	7·05	266·4	9·25

	STF 27 App		STF 39 App	
	PA	SEP	PA	SEP
1985	78·0	104·92	133·5	39·38
1990	78·0	104·92	133·4	39·45
1995	78·0	104.92	133·3	39·52
2000	78.0	104·92	133·2	39·59

APPENDIX 2

A list of useful addresses.

The Webb Society.

President: Kenneth Glyn Jones, Wild Rose, Church Road, Winkfield,
Windsor, Berks, SL4 4SF, England.

Director,Double Star Section: R.W.Argyle, c/o RGO (Private mail)
Apartado 368, Santa Cruz de la Palma, Tenerife,
Canary Islands.

Secretary: S.J.Hynes, 8 Cormorant Close, Sydney, Crewe, Cheshire,
CW1 1LN, England.

Secretary, N. America: R.J.Morales, 1440 S. Marmora, Tucson,
Arizona 85713, USA.

Publications Officer: C.M.Pither, 12 Southill Road, Charminster,
Bournemouth, BH12 5DJ, England.

British Astronomical Association. (Deep-Sky Section)

Director, John Lewis, 13 Mill Close, Denmead, Portsmouth,
Hants PO7 6PE, England.

Societe Astronomique de France. (Double Star Section)

Secretary: Pierre Durand, 34 Avenue Marcel Sembat, 18000
Bourges, France.

Lunar Occultations.

United Kingdom: G.W.Amery, (BAA Lunar Section) 183 Church Road,
Earley, Reading, RG6 1HN, England.

Europe: IOTA/ES, c/o H-J. Bode, Bartold-Knaust Str.8, 3000
Hanover 91, German Federal Republic.

United States of America: IOTA, P.O. Box 3392, Columbus, Ohio
43210, USA.

Suppliers of Filar Micrometers.

United Kingdom: L.D.Reynolds, 54 Woolsbridge Road, St. Leonards,
Ringwood, Hants., England.

United States of America: Ron Darbinian, Route 3, Box 335-D,
Arroyo Grande, California, 93420, USA.

A New Catalogue of Visual Double Star Orbits.

This catalogue, which supersedes that of Finsen and Worley (1970),
has been compiled by Dr. W.D. Heinz of Swarthmore College
and Dr. C.E. Worley of the U.S. Naval Observatory, and
contains orbits published to 1982·5. Copies can be
obtained by writing to:

The Director, U.S. Naval Observatory,
34th and Massachusetts Ave, N.W.
Washington, DC 20390, U.S.A.

REFERENCES AND BIBLIOGRAPHY

Aitken, R.G. : 1932, New General Catalogue of Double Stars within 120°
    of the North Pole, Carnegie Institute of Washington
    Publication, No. 417.

Aitken, R.G. : 1935, The Binary Stars, (3rd Edn. Dover Pub.)

Airy, G.B. : 1846, Mem. R. astr. Soc. 15, 199.

Alden, H.L. : 1947, Astron. J. 52, 138.

Anderson, J.A. : 1920, Astrophys. J. 51, 257.

Batten, A.H. : 1973, Binary and Multiple Systems of Stars, Pergamon.

Bigourdan, H. : 1895, Ann. Obs. Paris(Memoirs), 21, E 1.

Binnendijk, A. : 1960, The Properties of Double Stars, University of
    Pennsylvania Press.

Burnham, S.W. : 1906, A General Catalogue of Double Stars within 121°
    of the North Pole, Carnegie Institute of Washington
    Publication, No. 5.

Candy, M.P. : 1963, in Practical Amateur Astronomy, (ed. P.Moore),
    Lutterworth Press.

Camichel, H. : 1956, J. Obs., 39, 138.

Code, A.D., Davis, J., Bless, R.C. and Hanbury Brown : 1976,
    Astrophys. J. , 203, 417.

Couteau, P. : 1978, Observing Visual Double Stars, M.I.T Press.

Crossley, E., Gledhill, J. and Wilson J.H. : 1879, A Handbook of
    Double Stars, Macmillan.

Darius, J. and Thomas, P.K. : 1981, J.Phys. E. Sci. Instrum., 14, 761.

Davidson, C.R. and Symms, L.S.T. : 1938, Mon. Not. R. astr. Soc.,
    98, 176.

Dembowski, E. : 1883, Misure Micrometriche di Stelle Doppie e
    Multiple, Rome.

Duruy. M.V. : 1938, J. Obs., 21, 97.

Duruy. M.V. : 1972, Webb Soc. Quarterly J., 5, No.1, 14.

Finsen, W.S. and Worley, C.E. : 1969, Rep. Obs. Circ.7, No. 129.

Finsen, W.S. : 1951, Mon. Not. R. astr. Soc., 111, 391.

Finsen, W.S. : 1951, Popular Astronomy, 59, 399.

Finsen, W.S. : 1954, Un. Obs. Circ., 4, 225.

Finsen, W.S. : 1964, Astron. J., 69, 317.

References and Bibliography

Franz, O.G., Gossner, J.L, Josties, F.J., Lindenblad, I.W., Mikesell, A.H., Mintz, B.F. and Riddle, R.K. : 1963, Publ.U.S.N.O. 18, Part 1.

Gezari, D.Y., Labeyrie, A. and Stachnik, R.V. : 1972, Astrophys. J., 173, L 1.

Hartung, E.J. : 1968, Astronomical Objects for Southern Telecopes, Cambridge University Press.

Hargreaves, F.J. : 1931, Mon. Not. R. astr. Soc., 92, 72.

Hargreaves, F.J. : 1932, Mon. Not. R. astr. Soc., 92, 453.

Heintz, W.D. : 1978, Double Stars, Reidel, (Dortrecht).

Herschel, W. : 1782, Phil. Trans. Royal Soc., 72, 112.

Herschel, W. : 1803, Phil. Trans. Royal Soc., 72, 339.

Hershey, J. : 1973, Astron. J., 73.

Hussey, W.J. : 1901, Pub. Lick Obs. No. 5.

Innes, R.T.A.: 1927, Southern Double Star Catalogue from -19 to -90, Union Observatory.

Jeffers, H.M., van den Bos, W.H. and Greeby, F.M. 1961, Pub. Lick Obs., No 21.

Jonckheere, R. : 1950, Catalogue General de 3,350 étoiles doubles de faible éclat observees de 1906 a 1962, Observertoire de Marseille.

Jonckheere, R. : 1950, J. Obs., 33, 57.

Josties, F.J., Kallakaral, V.V., Douglass, G.G. and Christy, J.W. : 1978, Publ. U.S.N.O., 24, Part 5.

Lewis, T. : 1906, Mem. R. astr. Soc., 56.

Mackie, J. : 1969, J. Brit. astr. Assoc., 80, 48.

Malin, D. and Murdin, P.G.: 1984, The Colours of the Stars, Cambridge University Press.

McAlister, H.A. : 1977, Sky Telesc., 53, No 5, 346.

Meeus, J. : 1971, Sky Telesc., 41, No 1, 21.

Meeus, J. : 1971, Sky Telesc., 41, No 2, 88.

Merton, G. : 1952, J. Brit astr. Assoc., 63, 7.

Michelson, A.A. : 1890, Phil. Mag., 30, 1.

References and Bibliography

Muller, P.   : 1937, Comptes Rendus, 205, 861.

Muller, P.   : 1949, J. Obs., 32, 114.

Muller, P.   : 1962, in Hiltner, W. (ed.), Stars and Stellar Systems,
              2, 440, Chicago University Press.

Muller, P. and Couteau, P. : 1978, Quatrieme Catalogues d'Ephemerides
              d'Etoiles Doubles, Observatoire de Paris.

Phillips, R. : 1980, Webb Soc. Quarterly J., No 39, 8.

Pither, C.M. : 1980, Sky Telesc., 59, No 6, 519.

Polman, J.   : 1977, Sky Telesc., 53, No 5, 391.

Rackham, T.W. : 1959, Astronomical Photography at the Telescope, Faber.

Rakos, K. et al. : 1982, Astron. Astrophys. Suppl., 47, 221.

Richardson, L. : 1924, J. Brit. astr. Assoc., 35, 105.

Richardson, L. : 1925, J. Brit. astr. Assoc., 35, 155.

Richardson, L. : 1927, J. Brit. astr. Assoc., 37, 247.

Richardson, L. : 1927, J. Brit. astr. Assoc., 37, 311.

Richardson, L. : 1928, J. Brit. astr. Assoc., 38, 258.

Rossiter, R.A. : 1955, Catalogue of Southern Double Stars,
              Publ. Univ. Michigan, Vol. 11.

Schwarzchild, K. : 1896, Astron. Nachr., 139, 353.

Sidgwick, J.B. : 1971, Amateur Astronomer's Handbook, Faber.

Sidgwick, J.B. : 1980, Amateur Astronomer's Handbook, 4th Edn., Enslow.

Smyth, W.H.   : 1864, Sidereal Chromatics, London.

Smyth, W.H.   : 1844, A Cycle of Celestial Objects, London.

Stickland, D.J. : 1976, Mon. Not. R. astr. Soc., 176, 477.

Worley, C.E. : 1961, Sky Telesc. , 22, No. 2, 73.

Worley, C.E. : 1961, Sky Telesc. , 22, No. 3, 140.

Worley, C.E. : 1961, Sky Telesc. , 22, No. 5, 261.

NOTES

NOTES